KNEE BABY – 1947

FROM WINTERSVILLE TO BOSTON

In Quiet Defiance

Between 1916 and 1970, more than six million Black Americans left the South, heading to cities in the North and West in search of better opportunities. This period became known as The Great Migration.

The move wasn't about running away. People didn't leave because of signs that said "Whites Only"—Ohio didn't put those up. But Momma understood what others missed. Big letters weren't needed to show that freedom had slipped out of reach. Limits held power, even without making noise. Being safe didn't bring peace. Real change requires more than safety.

The choice to leave had nothing to do with fear. On the surface, everything looked fine. But underneath, each day ran in circles, offering no clear path forward. The roof and meals helped, but that alone didn't build a meaningful life.

Places like Wintersville and Steubenville offered a place to pause—enough to catch a breath and handle the basics. Before the mills came into view, the story was already unfolding.

The mill meant long hours and steady pay. Dad, like many other Black men, took what was available. Wages covered the essentials: rent, groceries, church on Sundays; but that's where it stopped. Life followed the same pattern, week after week. The routine kept everything in place but left no space for anything beyond survival. Folks didn't talk much about the invisible barriers between neighborhoods, but those boundaries shaped where people lived and what they could access.

Staying meant standing still. Momma packed what she could and stepped into the unknown. No map, no promise, only a quiet pull that something better might be out there. Even without a clear path, something in her refused to settle for less. The real shift had already happened within.

Prayer didn't wait for approval; it gave her the courage to act. When the moment came, movement followed. Not out of pressure, but because something deep inside said more could exist beyond what was known.

Leaving meant more than changing location. It offered space to imagine something else. Survival alone wasn't enough. Freedom and the power to choose meant everything.

Each mile toward Boston brought ease. The air felt lighter, and the view didn't stop at the next corner. Strength made no noise; it moved with quiet effort. A wider picture lived in every action. No clear promise lined the path, but the steps kept coming. That vision opened the way for the rest to follow.

CONTENTS

CHAPTER 1

LEAVING LITTLE CHICAGO: A MIGRATION BORN OF QUIET RESOLVE

November 20, 1947 — Steubenville, Ohio

Folks called Steubenville "Little Chicago"—not for its size, but for what stayed hidden behind walls: clubs, bands, fast deals, and trouble-filled nights and stories never printed but well known.

People spoke of connections to Pittsburgh and Youngstown: crime rings, shady dealings, backdoor liquor, and threats sharp enough to keep folks quiet. The danger stayed hushed, but the warning rang loud.

For many Black families, this place never held much promise. It was just one stop on the larger journey north during The Great Migration. Red soil was left behind in search of something better. Steel mills offered hours and pay. Dad, like many others, worked long shifts to put food on the table and keep the lights on. But few believed that was enough—not when something deeper drove the decisions back home.

The Ku Klux Klan operated nearby. Leaders claimed control, and silence let fear spread unchecked. Black families, immigrants, and Catholics paid the price. At night, while publicly preaching "decency," the Klan burned crosses on the lawns of Black homeowners in Steubenville and nearby towns like Wellsburg, East Liverpool, and Mingo Junction.

These cross burnings weren't just symbolic; they were threats meant to keep Black families "in their place, intimidate new migrants, and suppress civil rights organizing.

Rules up north looked different, but the effect was the same. Streets drew boundaries without signs. So did opportunity. No one needed to post "Whites only" to make the message clear.

This area became known for more than factories; it produced people who rose to fame. Dean Martin, born Dino Paul Crocetti, got his start here. Before the spotlight, he dropped out in 10th grade, worked the mill, delivered milk, and ran backroom games, where the rules changed fast and luck outweighed effort.

Another who came up through the streets was Jimmie "The Greek" Snyder. As a teen, he mastered the odds. While others played ball, he took calls, tracked numbers, and read patterns.

Later, he'd sit on national television, calling plays before kickoff. But it all started here, in a tough place where taking risks was the only way to move forward.

Those men made something of themselves, but their lives also reflected the town that shaped them. Steubenville offered just enough to scrape by, never enough for someone with bigger dreams. Some folks settled into the rhythm of steel mills and narrow streets, convinced that was all life had to give. But there were others who quietly longed for more, even if they didn't say it out loud. Momma wasn't content with mere survival. She believed there had to be more than what the town offered. Her vision carried her beyond Steubenville's borders.

Something deeper lived behind her eyes—stretching beyond the mills, the narrow blocks, and the daily limits. Not dreams of fame, but a need for peace, safety, and room to breathe. In her vision Wintersville offered shelter, but not what was needed.

This wasn't running; it was reaching. Dad held on to what felt familiar: church, the job, the rhythm that rarely changed. Movement came not because everything made sense. It came because standing still meant settxling. What guided that decision came from within. Faith and quiet resolve made space for action.

When the time came, no permission was needed. One move set the rest in motion, trusting each mile to bring something worthwhile.

Steubenville carried a big-city feel—loud, rough around the edges, and always buzzing. But life began in a working-class town built on labor and quiet determination. That contrast hit hard. It showed how birth location shapes what feels possible. A rough beginning can still lead to something real, something full of value.

In 2023, Steubenville still carried that "Little Chicago" energy. Trouble never sat far off. Even those keeping to themselves could get pulled in. Still, memories of the city run deep. It still feels like home to many, like Aunt Fannie and Uncle Frank. A job at Wheeling Steel paid the bills.

With faith and discipline, five kids were raised on one paycheck.

CHAPTER 2

DIGNITY UNDER PRESSURE: BLACK FAMILY LIFE IN A DIVIDED AMERICA

Back in 1947, Black families had to tread carefully. The war had ended, and the push north brought new possibilities. The family stood at the center. Making it through meant relying on each other and stretching every resource.

Change began quietly and slowly. A shift from invisibility. A different kind of presence started to emerge in homes built on love and dignity amid racism, poverty, and wounds that still hadn't healed.

Under Jim Crow, in the South Black children were placed in overcrowded, neglected schools. Restaurants, theaters, and other public spaces remained divided. Black folks entered through side doors, used separate restrooms, and sat at the back of trains. When White passengers boarded, standing became the only option, even if a seat had been paid for.

Voting was blocked by poll taxes, literacy tests, and open threats. Ballots were kept out of reach. Housing remained unequal. Black families were pushed into run-down neighborhoods through policies like redlining. On the job, Black workers were given the heaviest loads and the lowest pay. Labor unions often excluded them. The best positions went to others.

Moreover, laws didn't guarantee justice. Crossing racial lines could mean arrest, violence, or worse. Justice didn't always arrive, and harm didn't always come with a warning.

In 1941, labor organizer A. Philip Randolph announced a march demanding fair treatment in the military and defense industry. The pressure forced President Roosevelt to act. Executive Order 8802 followed, banning racial bias in defense contracts.

The first waves of the Civil Rights Movement began to rise. Thurgood Marshall took the NAACP's legal battle to the courts and won key cases. One landmark victory came in 1944, when *Smith v. Allwright* helped dismantle Whites-only voting in Texas.

CHAPTER 3

THE KNEE BABY: IN BETWEEN AND BECOMING

Black families turned inward—sharing stories, preserving traditions, and showing love in quiet, steady ways. One sign of this care can be seen in the role of the *knee baby*.

In Southern Black families, the knee baby is the child born just before the youngest. No longer the baby, but still close enough to rest on a parent's or elder's knee. The name carries meaning, a gentle presence that may go unnoticed. Yet it holds a vital place in the family's rhythm. The knee baby sits between the older children and the youngest, close to both guidance and care. Not fully grown, yet not completely shielded, this child sees the family from a space in between.

Choosing *The Knee Baby* as the name for this memoir speaks to more than birth order. The role shows where a child fits within the family and how they begin to view the world. It marks the shift from being cared for to gradually taking on responsibility.

The knee baby is old enough to remember clearly, and young enough to be shaped by the world unfolding all around. That in-between view offered a full picture, both of struggle and strength.

The name also honors memory. A quiet presence may not lead, but it still matters. These everyday moments pulled the family through, thread by thread.

The title *Knee Baby – 1947* connects a personal journey to a larger moment in time. That year marked the birth and the breaking of baseball's color line by Jackie Robinson, an act that shifted how the nation viewed race and fairness. His calm under pressure left a lasting impact beyond the field.

Like Jackie, the family stood near a turning point. Pressure was real, the path unclear, but something deeper kept them moving. That year wasn't just a number; it marked a change in what Black families believed could be possible.

This path mirrors that same push—the tension between progress and resistance. Life unfolded in that in-between space, like the knee baby. Close enough to feel the weight of struggle, yet close enough to touch the hope of something Dignity showed up not through loud voices, but through steady steps that kept pressing ahead.

Looking back now, a pattern begins to emerge—Momma's strong will, Jackie's quiet strength, and the influence they had on me. No hunger for attention and a yearning for learning how to move through life with purpose when the path wasn't clear.

That thread runs through everything: paying attention to what matters and moving in that direction. My first breath came in Steubenville, but the journey stretched far beyond where it started.

CHAPTER 4

BRILLIANT, OHIO: A FAMILY IN THE FOLD OF THE GREAT MIGRATION

Sports had a pull, encouraging us to watch how it moved—the cheers, the falls, and the shifts in energy. It wasn't just about winning or trophies. The field taught how to make decisions, stay steady, and keep going when pressure rose.

In 1950, the census listed our family in Brilliant, Ohio, a place with a bright name but a simple life. One of the few Black families in rural Appalachia, we got by with the basics.

John, 43, worked at the steel mill and gave sermons on Sundays. That rhythm drained the body but gave life a sense of order. Discipline ruled those days. Emotion stayed hidden. Love showed up through action—hot meals, mended shoes, bills paid. Not much was said, but presence spoke volumes.

Lucille, 36, kept everything moving at home. Mornings began in the dark and stretched late into the night. Cooking, cleaning, laundry—nothing left undone. Every task had a purpose. Fatigue became routine. Smiles came and went, but the effort never stopped. Falling apart wasn't an option, as too many people depended on her. Momma kept pain tucked away. Getting through the day meant rising early, staying busy, and making sure the kids had what they needed.

Ruby Nelle's beginning created a loss. She was born the same day her mother died. Grief wasn't spoken of much, but it hung in the air like a quiet shadow. Responsibility found Ruby Nelle early. Never knowing the woman who brought her into the world, she carried that silence. So, when the chance came to step towards her own future, no one stood in her way. The weight had rested on her long enough. It was time to reach for something that truly belonged to her.

By 17, she was already looking beyond the house. Senior year stirred something inside: thoughts of Boston, college, and life beyond the limits around her. Even before anything was packed, her mind had started to drift. Still, responsibilities filled the home. Meals were made. The younger ones stayed in line. Balance had to be maintained.

Ulysses (Newton) the oldest of the three children Dad had before marrying Momma, was already grown with a family of his own. He didn't live with us, but his presence lingered in family stories. Steady and independent, he had carved out his own path early, carrying the weight of being firstborn with quiet responsibility.

Amos (Bruh) the middle child from Dad's first marriage, was 18 and living on his own by the time I was old enough to remember him. He didn't stay in the house, but he wasn't far from reach. Independent, sharp, and a little more outspoken than Ulysses, Amos still showed up when needed. He had one foot in adulthood and the other still tied to the family.

Melvin, age 12:

Melvin was only with us for a few weeks after the census, but his presence lingered long after he left. He had come up from Georgia to be counted, to be with us for a moment, and then he was gone—back to Grandma and Mr. Holmes. It was a short visit, but in that stretch of time,

something lasting took root. He was 12, full of quiet questions and Southern ways that didn't always match our rhythm up North. Still, his stories stuck with us, especially the ones layered with pride and history from Mr. Holmes.

For me, Melvin's time with us felt like a spark. It lit something inside me that I didn't yet have the words for. After he left, I kept listening for his voice in the sports debates, waiting to hear his laugh from the back room.

Juanita, age 10:

Next to Melvin, Juanita became Momma's helper by default. With Ruby drifting toward adulthood, Juanita stepped in and washed laundry, cleaned dishes, and kept the younger ones in line. She was a child, but responsibility aged her. She rarely complained. Her hands were always busy, her eyes always watching. She looked after me like a second mother, and when danger came, she held her ground. Her scar told a story of bravery far beyond her years.

Johnnie G, age 8:

Johnnie had fire in him. Not the kind that burned wild, but the kind that sparked conversation. He loved a good debate about baseball, boxing, or whatever was on the radio. His voice had rhythm, like a young preacher in the making. He challenged Melvin, argued with conviction, and dreamed with wide eyes. Underneath the chatter was a boy trying to find his place, eager to prove himself—on the field, in the room, in the family.

Gladys, age 5:

Gladys was sensitive and unsure, a child who had already seen too much. She often stayed close to Juanita, trying to be brave but not always succeeding. When the house grew loud or uncertain, she shrank back. She watched more than she spoke and held her fear tight. The world hadn't shown her much kindness, and it made her cautious. But in quiet moments, she reached for comfort, and that achieving mattered.

Me, age 2 going on 3:

As the knee baby, I was small and still finding a place between the big kids and the baby. Quiet by nature, I was always watching, always absorbing. I clung to Juanita's side, trailed behind Johnnie, and stared up at Melvin with wide-eyed curiosity. Both in the way and wrapped in love. A shard meant for me cut her face and left a scar. The memory lingered in late-night stories and the silence that followed. Subtle shifts in the house carried its weight. Words hadn't yet come, but memory was already taking root.

Gloria, age 1:

The baby of the house, Gloria, didn't speak yet, but her presence shaped everything. She demanded attention, disrupted sleep, and drew tenderness from the tired. Momma carried her, Juanita soothed her, and everyone adjusted around her needs.

She was a symbol of both hope and exhaustion. A reminder that life pressed on, even when it felt too heavy.

In her smallness, she reminded everyone of what they were trying to protect.

CHAPTER 5

THE WEIGHT OF THE FIRST GOODBYE

Momma married Dad in 1932, at nineteen, and stepped into a hard life. Grief came early, but there was no room to pause or feel sorry for herself. Each day demanded strength just to keep the family going.

Marrying Dad meant stepping into a life already shaped by absence. A woman had passed, three children looked for care, and he carried the weight of loss. It was not a fresh start, but a continuation of an unfinished story. Life didn't slow down. What was broken had to be faced and rebuilt without delay.

After the wedding, Dad found work doing maintenance at a hotel. As their first child's arrival approached, Momma returned to Georgia to be near her parents. That visit gave her space to rest and breathe. Dad joined later. The older kids stayed with family in Jacksonville, a rare break from daily responsibilities. Time with Grandma and younger sister Eunice brought a sense of calm before life picked up again.

When the day came, Dad made it in time for Melvin's birth. Melvin entered the world healthy— small, by Momma's memory—but full of life. Joy filled the house.

Eunice stayed close, eyes fixed on her new nephew. Wherever Grandma moved, that little hand kept reaching for Melvin's tiny fingers.

Not long after, Grandma began urging Momma to let Melvin stay in Georgia with her and Mr. Holmes. She said a newborn needed full attention. Back in Jacksonville, Dad's older children still needed care, making everything more complicated.

The decision weighed heavy, but Melvin stayed in Georgia so his life could open with a stronger foundation. Along with the choice came a promise: to write, to call, to return soon. A piece of the family was torn away that day, leaving an absence that could be felt in every corner of the house. The decision was heavy, guided by love, not comfort or ease. The hardest paths are often the most loving ones. This was one of them.

Momma pressed a final kiss to Melvin's forehead, tears soaking the blanket as a soft prayer rose

from trembling lips.

Eunice stood on the porch, hands gripping the railing. Her eyes were wide and uncertain, looking up for answers. Momma knelt beside her and spoke gently. Her voice broke with sorrow, each word spilling out like grief too heavy to contain. This change was only temporary, and love would remain strong—words that needed to be believed. Trust in family staying close mattered more than where anyone lived.

Eunice made a quiet promise: Melvin would be reminded each day that they both loved him. Her lips quivered, eyes filled with tears. She wrapped her arms around Momma's neck and wouldn't let go.

Dad stood by the car, silent, looking away. After a pause, he climbed inside, cleared his throat, and tried to stay steady. Mr. Holmes waited to drive them to the train station. There was no time to linger. At the door, Momma adjusted her coat, hands shaking.

Grandma rocked Melvin, her gaze calm and focused. Momma asked that he be loved like one of their own. A nod followed—clear and certain. According to Dad, this was one of the hardest decisions he ever faced. Doing what felt right didn't ease the pain. Leaving a child, even briefly, leaves a deep mark.

Eunice stood at the edge of the yard, watching the dust rise as the car pulled away.

Tears marked the ride back to Jacksonville. Faith held what hands could no longer keep close.

This memory, shared by both my parents, remained vivid over time. A lasting reminder of the weight they carried. A reflection of love at the heart of their decision. And proof that love can stretch across years and distance.

In 1940, two years later, a new light entered the home: Juanita. Laughter filled the space, spilling out from the midwife's house. This one child shifted the flow of the household. The entire structure adjusted; one child became a symbol of healing.

Back in Georgia, the bond between Melvin, Grandma, and Mr. Holmes deepened. One question lingered: Would Melvin return to his parents?

In Jacksonville, Juanita added warmth to the home and gave Momma something steady to hold onto. That moment helped ease the strain of caring for three stepchildren shaped by loss and change. The tension that had been building began to settle.

The joy of that moment didn't erase the struggles. The house was still full, emotions often close to the edge. Bringing Melvin home too soon could upset a balance still finding its rhythm. Life in Georgia gave him structure. Another move might bring more confusion.

No easy answer came with this choice. The family had pushed through more than most. Juanita's presence lifted spirits, but that alone couldn't fix everything.

CHAPTER 6

THE FIFTH BORN AND THE FUTURE

One night, the soft glow of my table lamp lit the room. A message came through from my cousin Gregory. Attached was a photo of my mother, one I hadn't seen in years. Youth showed on her face—calm, at ease, and with a soft smile.

That image stayed with me—not just in Boston, where everything ended, but back to where my life began.

The days leading up to my birth brought excitement, nerves, and questions with no easy answers.

Ohio Valley Hospital marked a shift. Pain rose and fell in waves, while a cold November wind swept through the night. Thanksgiving was approaching, but the hands that usually cooked would now be caring for a new life.

What was once familiar had been left behind—the sounds of home, the comfort of women who had done this many times. The hospital brought safety, but felt distant because there were no humming voices, no gentle hands with towels or whispered prayers. There were only nurses in pale uniforms, blinking machines, and a still room. Joy and fear stood side by side, with faith holding steady. Even with support, doing it a new way added pressure.

For the family, giving birth in a hospital wasn't just practical; it marked a turning point. The shift from home births and long-held customs to trained medical staff and structured care signaled a break from tradition. Having a doctor present brought reassurance—someone ready to respond, with the knowledge and tools to act if anything went wrong.

Holding her fifth born under hospital lights brought relief and marked a break from tradition. Choosing the hospital over home birth embraced change. What had been left behind made room for what was next. In Jacksonville, births usually took place in bedrooms with midwives. In Ohio, trained professionals guided the moment, and the presence of a doctor added a layer of safety no one could overlook.

Light filled the room, one final push came, and a cry followed. "It's a boy," the doctor

announced, marking a new beginning tied to all that had led to this moment.

Later, a nurse placed the newborn into open hands—warm, breathing, and full of new life.

That moment spoke louder than words. Life emerged not only from pain, but from years of strength passed down through generations. In that room rested more than a newborn; it held the connection between the past and what was still to come.

CHAPTER 7

A HOLIDAY BEGINS

This section of the memoir shares memories passed down through stories told by various family members over the years.

Over nearly 30 years, my dad worked in one of the hottest parts of the mill. My oldest brother, Newton, operated a crane in another section.

The day I came home from the hospital was filled with joy and exhaustion. Momma stepped out holding me, wrapped in a soft blanket. Newton stood by the car, ready to take us home.

She always smiled when telling the story—Daddy, worn out yet proud, bent down and said I had been worth every moment. Newton opened the car door, crouched beside us, and grinned as he greeted his new baby brother.

Gratitude lit up Momma's face. Newton's presence eased her nerves. Support came naturally; he helped her get settled, closed the back door, and took the driver's seat. One glance in the mirror said more than words ever could.

For Momma, Thanksgiving was never just a meal; it was the heartbeat of family. The smell of sweet potato pies carried warmth through every room as laughter and conversation filled the air. In those moments, closeness wasn't spoken—it was lived.

With a newborn in her arms and Daddy working long shifts, she wondered how to manage the holiday meal.

Newton asked if she had any plans. The question caught her off guard. Worry had already started to creep in about how to make the day feel special.

Daddy, always steady, reminded her that Ruby Nelle would step in and everything would come together. Still, the pressure weighed on her heart.

After talking with Janie, Newton shared that help was on the way. Janie, willing and understanding, knew how much the holiday meant.

Some wondered if she could manage it all while caring for Junior and Yvonne.

Newton gave a simple nod, letting everyone know they'd be just fine.

In the kitchen, Janie and Ruby Nelle would move in steady rhythm, their teamwork shaping the day. Together, they will make sure everything runs smoothly. This day held all the makings of a moment to remember—a time when love could once again fill the house, and when the moment came, everyone would be there.

Dad gave a slight nod as Newton turned the key. The engine rumbled to life, a quiet signal that everything was in motion. It carried the sense that the plan was unfolding just as it should. But for Newton, it was more than just a ride home. It was the sight of Momma holding me close, her body finally at ease, while Daddy settled back into his steady rhythm. To Newton, that picture was proof that his baby brother was safe in her arms. There was pride in his smile, the kind that comes when you know deep down that your family is going to be all right.

Cradled in Momma's arms, I lay quietly as Daddy leaned back, rubbed his eyes, and admitted that sleep was finally catching up to him. That part never changed. The baby always drifted off first, and Daddy never lagged far behind.

I was born into a house already moving to its own rhythm. Daily life carried a steady hum, shaped by routines of care and the unspoken tempo of a family in motion. And just like that, Dad, without missing a beat, stepped right back into the familiar flow he knew by heart.

As the car rolled down the road, the hum of the engine and the soft rattle of pebbles filled the silence. My steady breathing blended with the quiet hopes and whispered promises riding alongside us.

As Thanksgiving approached, challenges lingered in the background. Yet strength rose to meet them, the kind that always appears when people choose to stand together.

Momma glanced down at me, noting the lightness of my skin. A gentle smile crossed her face, not out of surprise but from knowing. For the first time, she saw herself reflected in me more than in the others. That ride home carried more than a new arrival. It carried love, tradition, and the quiet beginning of something new.

Juanita stepped in proudly and without hesitation. She held me close, her hands firm and gentle. The comfort she gave was simple and real. At 15, Ruby Nelle had turned her focus toward school and the future, stepping away from the duties she once carried so effortlessly. Yet on the day we met, her face lit up with joy. Her hands, gentle and sure, cradled me with a warmth that needed no explanation, no words—just presence.

My name, Alvin James, carries deep meaning. It was chosen in honor of Momma's father, James. It held the weight of family history, values, and a deep connection to those who came before. But I've always believed Melvin, my older brother, played a part in how she landed on Alvin.

There was a rhythm to it—Melvin and Alvin—like steps in a line, one following the other.

Maybe Momma liked how the names echoed each other. Or maybe she hoped it would tie us together in a lasting way. Whatever the reason, it wasn't just a name—it was a thread. James tied me to the past. Alvin, to the present. Together, they carried a quiet promise that what we shared would last, woven into both our lives and the life of our family. Ruby Nelle filled Momma in on how things had gone while she was away. Johnnie refused to settle down at night, dragging out bedtime with endless complaints and questions. Gladys had been extra clingy, needing more patience and reassurance than usual. Juanita worked hard to steady the household, cooking meals, tidying up, and keeping things in order. She carried more than her share to help hold everything together. Sleeping arrangements placed me in a bassinet beside Momma and Dad.

Juanita and Ruby Nelle shared a room. Gladys and Johnnie slept in the front room with blankets pulled around them. Gladys approached slowly, curious but open. She accepted her new baby brother almost immediately. Juanita rushed in after school, eager to hold me. Johnnie, less interested, cracked jokes about dinner instead.

CHAPTER 8

PRAISE IN THE WIND

As Daddy got dressed the next morning, Momma spoke with calm determination. Her voice steady, she let him know they needed to talk. Thanksgiving was near, and she stressed the importance of getting the shopping done that day. Daddy nodded, pulled twenty dollars from his wallet, and placed it in her hand. Momma gave a small nod in return, satisfied she had enough to move forward.

She planned to stay home, so Ruby Nelle would handle the shopping and ride with Newton. Daddy, ready to lie down, reminded her to wake him before his shift. Not long after, the house filled with the steady rhythm of his snoring.

Wheels crunched in the driveway. Newton's voice called from outside, letting them know he'd arrived and needed help unloading. Juanita gently placed me into Momma's arms and hurried out to assist.

Ruby Nelle entered with a spark in her step, announcing a deal on the turkey. The house came alive with the sound of footsteps and opening doors. Each person moved with quiet purpose, falling into their roles without a word. The day before Thanksgiving, plans took shape at the counter. Newton, Janie, and the others were expected soon, and extra chairs would be pulled out to make room for everyone. Melvin was still in Georgia with Grandma. His absence hung in the air, but attention shifted toward making the day meaningful.

Neckbones and rice with okra simmered on the stove—a house favorite. The aroma drifted from room to room, stirring appetite.

Chairs scraped the floor as everyone found their place. Juanita cradled the youngest. Ruby Nelle and Johnnie took their seats. Gladys clung to Momma's skirt before climbing into the high chair. A place was ready for each person. Silence fell as heads bowed in thanks. Then came the sounds of forks clinking, voices rising, and laughter filling the room. The meal began, served with care. Elbows stayed tucked in, not from scolding, but from habit.

Family stories flowed easily, passed between Momma, Ruby Nelle, and Juanita—tales told so often they'd become part of our shared identity.

My first night at the dinner table came wrapped in sound—laughter, clinking forks, and voices carrying down what mattered. Held in Momma's arms, too small to speak and too young to follow the conversation, I sat at the edge of history being passed down.

Momma's memories filled the room—growing up Black in the South without frills or silver trays; washboards clanged, and biscuits rose in cast-iron pans. One look from an elder could still a room without a single word.

Sunday dinner meant structure—sit up straight and speak only when spoken to. It wasn't about putting on a show; it was about knowing how to act and showing respect.

Daddy added stories shaped by long days, worn-out shoes, and nights spent chasing work. He joked about hoboing—jumping trains, slipping past conductors, men losing fingers or sometimes their lives. To him, it was a story; to others, it was survival. One man said, "I'm gonna catch this next train or go to hell trying."

When the train came, he ran beside it, leapt for the open door, and slipped beneath the wheels. His life ended there, a harsh reminder of Proverbs 14:12: *"There is a way that seems right to a man, but in the end it leads to death."* "The danger was always there, but so was the strength to endure. Like it says in Isaiah 40:31, *"they that wait upon the Lord shall renew their strength; they shall mount up with wings as eagles."* Sometimes Dad would include a mini sermon at dinner time.*

Voices moved from one seat to the next, weaving experience into the air. Held close in the arms that brought me into the world, I was part of it all before I even knew what it meant. Not through words, but simply by being there—a beginning written into the rhythm of the table.

Midday settled in. Momma sang *His Eye Is on the Sparrow* while rocking the baby, her voice steady and full. The chair creaked gently beneath her as she kept him still. Juanita gathered the laundry and stepped outside toward the washbasin.

From the kitchen window, Momma kept watch. Juanita moved with purpose, lifting, scrubbing, rinsing. Inside and out, the day carried on as it always did. No fuss. Just the work getting done. Hands scrubbed cloth against wood while the warm November sun touched the yard, lifting steam from the basin.

Clothes found their place on the line. Sheets waved in the breeze—a quiet sign of care. Peace settled in the nursery. The walk to the clothesline was slow and steady.

Praise came in a few simple words—"Job well done, honey."

They exchanged a nod and a small smile as the laundry moved with the wind. Juanita wiped the sweat from her brow, and together, they walked back inside.

CHAPTER 9

THE RITUAL OF PREPARATION

The kitchen filled with the rich smell of roasted spices and baked dishes. Gladys stood beside her sisters, quietly taking it all in. Juanita sat on a stool, watching the older woman work with practiced purpose. Momma held me in one arm, guiding it all with quiet authority.

Her eyes stayed sharp on every detail. Ruby Nelle worked her seasoning mix, promising the turkey would be the highlight. Janie, steady in her work, tended to the sweet potato pies. She was determined to match the flavor that had always come from Momma's hands. Chopping, sizzling, and soft laughter blended into a rhythm that brought the kitchen to life.

Momma moved with ease, guiding each step. Juanita learned to chop collard greens, adding the potlikker ingredients just as instructed. Janie, ever steady, turned her attention to the ham, hoping to make it just right—something Daddy would truly enjoy.

The door creaked open. Newton stepped inside, tired but smiling. Pies cooled on the counter, and lunch for the road was packed and waiting. After kissing Janie in greeting, he looked toward the back room. The children were already asleep, worn out from the day's excitement. The kitchen brimmed with the warm scents of dinner—roasted turkey, yams rich with butter, and a blend of simmering spices. Newton lingered in the doorway as Janie reminded him to get some rest before dinner at 4:30. After a short hug, he headed back out to work.

With the final touches in place, Janie turned to Momma and mentioned she needed a little rest. Momma nodded and motioned toward the closet for extra blankets. Janie curled up beside the sleeping children and wished her mother-in-law a peaceful night.

CHAPTER 10

THANKSGIVING DAY

At 1:00 p.m., the family came together for dinner. A golden turkey rested at the center of the table, surrounded by the full spread of the feast. Desserts sat off to the side, ready for later.

Momma wiped her apron, growing a little frustrated. At 18, Amos had been spending too much time at Moore's Inn catching up with his drinking.

Daddy sighed while slicing the turkey, shaking his head at boys who thought they were grown but didn't have the sense to go with it. Ruby Nelle muttered that nothing good had ever come from hanging with that crowd. Momma kept glancing at the door, still hoping he'd show.

Standing at the head of the table Daddy's presence commanding yet calm, the hum of conversation fading as we all prepared for grace. The air was thick with the scent of collard greens, cornbread, and roasted turkey, each dish a labor of love. Around the table, Ruby Nelle, Janie with baby Yvonne, Juanita, Johnnie, Junior, and little Gladys in her highchair filled the room with life. In Momma's arms, I rested quietly, cradled by the warmth of family and the comfort of home.

The house grew still, the kind of quiet that comes before something sacred. Daddy's voice rose steadily and sure, carrying the rhythm of reverence that filled every corner of the room. It was a sound I knew well, equal parts strength and surrender, gratitude and grace. His words flowed like a prayer stitched from years of faith, work, and family—a reminder of where we came from and what held us together.

When the final "Amen" swept through the room, a warmth lingered in the air. Momma's smile was soft, her eyes alive with pride and knowing. The spell of silence lifted, replaced by laughter, the clatter of spoons, and the music of family. Plates passed, hands reached, voices overlapped. It was more than a meal—it was belonging, the kind that roots itself deep and stays with you long after the table is cleared.

Eventually, Amos walked in—late again. He was told to wash up before sitting at the table. With a quick apology, he took his place among his siblings. Daddy raised his hand and began the prayer.

Right after, the teasing kicked in. Ruby Nelle joked about her brother always showing up last. Laughter rippled through the room as dinner began.

The conversation stayed lively with jokes and stories. When Johnnie tried to join the grown-up talk, a glance from Momma quieted him for a moment. Then came a bold declaration: one day, he'd cook a meal like this himself.

Ruby Nelle teased him, saying he'd better learn how to cook first. Johnnie fired back, saying that Momma would teach him. More laughter followed, filling the room with the kind of easy comfort only family can bring.

CHAPTER 11

WHEN PATIENCE ROCKED THE CRADLE

On June 5, 1949, eighteen months after I was born, Momma brought home her sixth child, Gloria, from Ohio Valley Hospital. With a newborn to care for, she needed an extra hand. Juanita stepped in, promising to watch over me so Momma could focus on the baby. Her calm, steady way always made things feel easier.

Ruby Nelle pitched in with the cooking and cleaning, while Gladys waited patiently for a chance to hold her baby sister. Momma welcomed the help, knowing it would take all of us to keep things running.

One afternoon, Ruby Nelle asked if she could meet up with friends at the high school carnival

before it ended. Momma agreed but told her to fix her daddy's lunch before leaving. Ruby Nelle gave her word, packed Daddy's lunch, and rushed outside to join the others already waiting.

Most of that day passed with Momma in the bedroom—rocking, feeding, and changing Gloria. The rest of the house moved with its usual rhythm: pots clinking in the kitchen, floors being swept, and me, too restless to sit still, bouncing from one room to the next.

Whenever things got too quiet, Momma would call me over. One sniff as I came near was all it took—she already knew I needed changing. I was still too young to manage it myself, so I had to rely on Johnnie. Only eight years old and never thrilled about the task, he helped anyway, though not without frustration.

Every trip brought a groan, especially on cold nights when the job felt even worse. There wasn't anything fun about it, but it fell on him all the same.

Momma reminded us often—I had to learn, and Johnnie had to help. That didn't stop the grumbling. Too many times, I hadn't made it to the outhouse in time.

A sharp glance from Momma ended the arguing. We made another trip to the outhouse. Johnnie was reluctant, but she went without complaining.

Then it happened again—another accident, another door slammed. Holding Gloria in her arms, Momma shook her head and laid down the rules: no more slamming doors in this house. Johnnie got a warning—Momma said she'd be telling Daddy. I got a reminder to speak up next time. I made a quick promise, eager to please.

While Johnnie fumed, Juanita stayed calm. She came over, wiped my face, picked me up, rocked me to sleep—handled everything without a fuss.

Patience, Momma always said, came naturally to Juanita. On the hardest days, she stepped in without a word. She cleaned, helped, and kept the peace just by being there. The moment Juanita showed up, my face lit up. A small laugh slipped out. Without missing a beat, she gently reminded me to speak up and tell Johnnie when I needed to go.

At night, she sang *You Are My Sunshine*, and that tune became our ritual—the last sound I heard before falling asleep.

On trips to Mr. Jenkins' store, folks often joked that Juanita must've been my mother.

Carrying me on her hip, she heard it again and again. People swore I had to be hers. Juanita always played along with a laugh, and Momma never corrected them.

I was too little to understand all the comments, but her care stuck with me. She was always nearby, and I followed her everywhere. Caring for me came naturally to her—it never seemed like a burden.

Nothing she did was rushed. Every move had a purpose.

With steady hands and quiet focus, she worked as if caring for others had always been her place. It was a rhythm she seemed to know by heart.

Mornings went smoothly, but nights were harder. After the lullaby, after being tucked in, tears came. Daddy lost sleep. Momma tried everything. Nothing seemed to help.

That story came up often during dinner. Momma would shake her head, remembering Daddy pacing the floor—worn out and half-asleep. The memory always brought a few laughs to the table.

A visit to the doctor finally brought answers. The milk alone wasn't keeping me full, no matter how often I was fed. It just wasn't giving my little body what it needed.

At the time, baby formula was too thin for some babies. A spoonful of Karo Syrup made the difference—thicker, sweeter, more filling. After that, the crying stopped, and the house could finally rest.

The syrup wasn't just a fix for feeding; it showed how Momma handled things. Her careful attention led her to make small changes that brought big results. That moment revealed her practicality and strength. She always found a way to figure things out and make the needed adjustments.

CHAPTER 12

WINTERSVILLE WAS ENOUGH

My dad worked long hours at Weirton Steel as a general laborer. At home, my mother held everything together, raising us with faith, structure, and a firm sense of right and wrong. Daddy carried his load without complaint, setting an example through actions, not words.

Back then, nine of us squeezed into a two-bedroom shotgun house. It was clear that the setup couldn't last. Tired and looking for something better, Dad started asking around at work. One of his coworkers, Charlie, owned some property and offered advice: renting wouldn't give us anything solid, but owning could change things.

Charlie described a place: It was just an old shack in Wintersville, sitting off a dusty road about thirty miles out. The place was in a part of town called Silver Stream Knolls, where Black families were expected to liveEven without written laws, segregation still decided where people could and couldn't live.

In the 1950s, owning a place to call your own seemed nearly impossible for most Black folks. Things like redlining and housing restrictions shut people out of entire neighborhoods. Still, Charlie offered to sell Dad two lots in Wintersville for seventy-five dollars each. One had a rundown two-bedroom shack, and the other was an empty piece of land.A trailer was available to rent for two dollars a month. It gave the family a place to stay while repairs on the shack began. Without hesitation, Dad gave Charlie six bucks as a down payment, with plans to bring the rest the next week.

A shift happened in that moment. This wasn't just about money; it was about having space, gaining control, and beginning a path with real meaning.

Over the next few weeks, confidence started to grow. The move to Wintersville became more than talk. The place sat way out and looked worn, but it offered freedom. A fresh start. A real chance to build something better.

CHAPTER 13

A STAKE IN THE GROUND

Early that Wednesday, after finishing his shift, Dad met with Charlie and paid off the rest. In return, Charlie handed over the key to the place in Wintersville.

Now, it truly belonged to him—no more hoping, no more relying on someone else's say. Having something in his name brought a deep sense of pride and purpose. There was no hesitation, no looking back. It was clear this was the start of something better. He knew it was up to him to make it happen, one step at a time.Mr. Jeter gave Mom and Dad a ride out to take a look. The house had seen better days—faded siding, cracked windows, flaking paint. Every part showed signs of age. Still, they stepped out of the car, took it all in, and started thinking about what came first.

Nothing caught them off guard. Just like before, there was no indoor plumbing. Water had to be carried in from a well, and an old outhouse sat out back. Not ideal, but it was a start—enough to build a new life.

Momma gave it a once-over—direct, not sentimental—assessing the task ahead. Daddy moved around the house, checking loose hinges and peeling paint. Tired floorboards creaked underfoot but held strong.

On the ride back, Mom and Dad talked about the old house. Dad said the roof had to come first, while Mom thought the windows needed fixing before winter. They agreed the floors could wait.

The house had potential, but it would take patience and hard work to make it livable. The next day, Mr. Jeter drove them back out. Dad stepped out with tools in hand, already thinking about what needed to be done. It wasn't much, but it was theirs and ready to be fixed up into something better.

The house was small but full of possibilities. In one corner sat an old potbelly stove, blackened from years of use but still working. Dad got a fire going, and the steady heat pushed away the cold, filling the room with a soft orange glow.

Nearby, a chipped enamel sink bore signs of heavy use.

While Mom and Dad got things in order, they made a mental note: Johnnie and I would sleep in one room. Ruby Nelle, Juanita, and Gladys would be in the other, with Gloria—almost two— sleeping in a crib. Mom and Dad would stay in the small trailer they planned to rent.

Dad made mental notes as he walked through—loose hinges, patched-up walls, and peeling paint all needed attention.

The next day, Charlie delivered the trailer, a plain metal-sided unit. It was parked in the shade of an oak tree beside the shack. Inside, a simple bed rested against the wall, enough for comfort and rest at night. The trailer stood as a quiet promise of new beginnings—small but sturdy.

The next morning, Newton drove them back to Wintersville. Dad climbed onto the roof with a hammer, steadying it one nail at a time. Inside, Momma went from room to room, humming Mahalia Jackson as she worked. She hung curtains and placed pictures of Jesus on the walls, giving the house its first sense of home. Momma settled into a natural rhythm. While Dad rebuilt the structure, Momma shaped the spirit of the home. Little by little, the house changed— cleaner, warmer, more theirs.

One afternoon, after hanging the last curtain, they stood back and took it all in. Not much, but steady. A photo of Johnnie hung near the front room—braids down his back, proud and stubborn. When the time came, Momma cut them off and placed them between the pages of the family Bible.

A quiet reminder of the boy he used to be and the life they continued to build.

The day came when we would move into our own property. Deacon Smith drove the truck, loaded with our household and family belongings. Dad sat up front with ten-year-old Johnnie and me, almost five. The three of us squeezed together on the front seat beside Mr. Smith.

Sister Smith followed behind in her station wagon, carrying Momma, eighteen-year-old Ruby Nelle, eleven-year-old Juanita, six-year-old Gladys, and little Gloria, just two. As the car approached the turn onto the second lane, Momma pointed toward a distant high school, her voice rising with excitement.

Ruby Nelle took in the view of where her classes would begin. Gazing out the window, she was impressed by the size eager for the year ahead. Momma pointed out the elementary school we'd passed earlier, where Gladys and I would go.

Dad, looking ahead, said our new home was just down the road.

The truck and car pulled up to the property, where a modest shack and trailer sat at the bottom of the lane. A tall tree stood nearby, its shadow stretching across the yard. Ruby Nelle looked around, quiet but curious.

Johnnie's eyes lit up. "This ours, Daddy?"

Daddy nodded, taking in the view. Johnnie grinned widely, satisfied. Ruby Nelle, still adjusting, studied the scene, her mind already turning over ideas. Juanita grabbed Gladys and Gloria's hands, pulling them forward, eager to explore.

Little Gloria laughed, trying to keep up as they ran toward the big tree. Their laughter filled the air, light and free.

With the door open, Johnnie stepped inside and said with certainty, "This is ours now." He jumped onto the bed and claimed a side like it had always been his. I climbed up beside him— still a little unsure, but the closeness brought comfort. A grin broke across my face, followed by laughter. For the first time in a while, it felt like something close to normal.

Johnnie, always full of ideas, shared his plans—hidden treasures buried in the backyard, secret passages behind the walls. His excitement stirred something in me, too, a sense of wonder about what this new place might hold.

Life began at the bottom of the second lane on Ellsworth Street.

There was no indoor plumbing and no electricity for the first few weeks.

CHAPTER 14

SHE WORKED BY FAITH

Morning broke, releasing a soft light that crept over the horizon. Momma began her day. Her worn boots crunched against the earth as she stepped from the shack. A weathered bucket swung at her side as she moved toward the well, a daily task.

Women handled household responsibilities like cooking, cleaning, and caring for the family. Fetching water was essential for cooking, washing, and other daily needs.

Momma walked to the well with steady purpose. Work had shaped her body, but she carried the weight without complaint.

She fixed the rope to the crank and let the bucket drop, the rope scraping as it slid down. A splash came from deep below, and she began to turn the handle. Her arms and back tightened with the rhythm, sweat gathering on her brow as the bucket rose, heavy and full. She set it down and carried it back toward the shack, already moving to the next task.

Behind the house stood the outhouse, plain and rough. In winter, the cold slipped through the cracks, and the wind pressed against the walls. Every trip out there felt longer than it was, the chill cutting straight to the bone.

The shack itself needed the most work. Dad started with the roof, patching leaks that stained the ceilings. New planks quieted the floors, and he kept at it, steadying the foundation and fixing what had worn thin.

Little by little, the house began to change. White curtains hung in the windows, and pictures of Jesus went up where Momma wanted them. Her touch was in every room, softening what was bare and making the space feel alive.

It wasn't just a shack anymore. It was a home—a place where we could rest, where laughter had room, and where love settled into the corners.

In the back stood the outhouse, a simple structure that served as our toilet. A seat rested over a hole in the ground. On cold winter nights, with the wind howling through the cracks, every trip to the outhouse tested your endurance. The moment you stepped inside, the cold cut through you, settling deep into your bones as time slowed. For now, it was the roof of the shack that drew the most concern. That roof covered our main living space, and every crack or leak meant trouble.

My dad patched it first, sealing the leaks that had stained the ceiling. Fresh planks silenced the creaks in the worn floorboards. He carried the load, digging into the foundation that kept everything upright. From there, he moved through each worn corner time had left behind. What he built back was more than a house—it was a kind of holding us together. The house didn't match our early hopes, but little by little, it began to take shape. White curtains hung in the windows, and pictures of Jesus were placed on the walls. They brought a solemn touch to the plain rooms. Our home was transformed—not just through repairs, but through Momma's nurturing touch. She left her mark on the house, from the hand-sewn curtains to the warmth of the kitchen. It was more than four walls, carrying the smell of food cooked with care and the sound of footsteps that gave it life. Laughter filled the corners, and even on hard days, love held steady. Every object carried a piece of our story, turning a plain house into a home.

CHAPTER 15

SILENCE, BLOOD, AND THE COLT .45

At first, Momma's excitement about joining a new community turned to agony as we faced the harsh reality of being outsiders. The warm welcome she hoped for vanished, replaced by cold stares and subtle hostility from our neighbors.

On Second Lane, everybody knew everybody, and ties ran deep. My family's arrival stirred both curiosity and unease.

With fewer than six families living on the lane, each new arrival threatened to disrupt the delicate balance of existing connections. We first moved into a two-bedroom shack, then later into a trailer. Neighbors watched with suspicion, quick to mark us as different. To them, our place in the community was measured by what little we had. Years later, Dad said Wintersville only accepted certain families. Backgrounds decide everything, regardless of a person's actions or intentions. His words carried the weight of hard experience.

Wintersville's unspoken rules often came up in conversation, where family ties held more sway than character. As a child, I didn't fully grasp what belonging meant. In time, I began to see how the patterns worked. Family names carried weight, opening doors at the mill and shaping respect in the church. Even the guest lists at community gatherings seemed to follow the same lines.

Others—like ours—met closed doors, missed job offers, and little neighborly kindness.

Growing older changed that. Legacy held no power over the person shaped by choices and convictions. The town clung to its old bloodlines, but true worth came from within.

That night, Dad led our family in prayer, offering thanks to Jesus and asking for protection. As sleep crept in, the kerosene lamp—the only light in the house—threw its faint glow across the walls. Its flicker was steady, signaling the day's end. Shadows shifted with each tremor of the flame. The house stayed quiet, worn but holding firm. In that stillness, we settled into rest.

The initial excitement about the new town soon gave way to cold realization. Neighbors grew distant, their actions subtle but sharp. A quiet message echoed: outsiders don't belong. One evening, Momma set down the kerosene lamp. Then she spoke the truth—this place didn't feel like home. Dad placed a steady hand on her shoulder, promising they'd face whatever came together.

Another day, Juanita took me outside to play. Thick air clung to the yard as neighborhood kids gathered nearby, their faces tight with suspicion. No laughter—only silence, stretched thin like a storm about to break. Eyes stayed fixed, ready to spot trouble before offering kindness.

At first, they kept their distance, sneering and whispering. Then rocks and bits of trash flew at us.

A boy stepped closer, mocking Juanita's hair and calling it "nappy."

A step ahead of me, her body became a shield as he told us we didn't belong and ordered us to leave. Juanita's fingers gripped mine, pulling me close as the first stones hit the ground nearby. Danger escalated with every shout. Then she lifted me and sprinted toward the house.

The crowd behind us grew louder. Flying glass replaced the stones, slicing through the air with a deadly whistle.

A shard caught Juanita just beneath the eye. A sharp cry escaped her lips as blood streamed down her cheek. Everything inside me froze—no words, no movement, only the chill of helplessness.

We burst through the doorway together. The door slammed shut behind us, sealing out the chaos for now.

Momma hurried to Juanita's side, pressing a cloth against her face. Her touch was calm and sure, but her eyes told a different story. They burned with a fury that carried something deeper, something fierce. Evening settled in, heavy and still. She sat on the couch, her body stiff, every muscle tight. The room carried a quiet edge, sharp and waiting. When Dad walked through that door, it would all break loose. At 4:10, the door creaked open. Heavy boots struck the floor with slow, deliberate steps. When Daddy got home, she didn't wait for pleasantries. She laid out what had happened. If that piece of glass had struck me, it might've killed me. I was mall—barely more than a toddler.

The cut was deep enough to scar and dangerously close to blinding her. For Momma, that was the last straw.

She told Daddy that we needed protection, that what happened couldn't happen again— especially not while he was at work. Her voice carried the kind of quiet strength that said she wasn't making a suggestion. She was laying down the law.

Daddy didn't argue. He listened, nodded, and quietly left the house.

A few hours later, he returned with an old long-barreled Colt .45. He didn't say much, but the message was clear. He intended to protect his family—no matter what.

Hands rose to grasp the weapon, lifting it with care as if weighing not just the steel, but the responsibility it carried. The grip settled into her palm, firm and familiar, like it had always belonged there.

A heavy silence filled the room, thick with everything left unsaid: anger, urgency, and the slow shift of power.

Nothing between them offered comfort or ease—only steady resolve. Juanita's blood had long since dried, but the moment stayed etched into the walls like a warning. A decision was made in that room. There was no ceremony, no fanfare. No more pleading. No more waiting for the storm to pass.

Momma no longer stood in quiet endurance. A readiness to confront each threat had taken hold. The house, once weighed down by unease, now carried a sharpened clarity. Dread hadn't vanished, but it no longer ruled the space. With cold steel within reach, intention took its place. Anyone who came again would face a woman no longer asking for protection, but ready to deliver it.

The shift was unmistakable: vulnerability gave way to vigilance, exposure to empowerment. The home hadn't turned violent—only prepared.

Dad inspected the Colt, then tucked it beneath their mattress. A silent guardian. A symbol of their will to stand their ground in Wintersville.

A few days later, after Momma and Daddy left the house, Johnnie revealed a secret: a gun hidden in the trailer. Despite warnings, curiosity pulled us in. Tense, we stepped inside. The room sat tidy, carrying a faint scent of flowers. Johnnie reached down and lifted the bedding, revealing the gun and a few bullets tucked beneath. Stunned and frozen, fear kept our hands from moving. After a pause, he put everything back, trying to leave no trace, though the shift left a mark.

When Momma returned, something felt off: the lock was open, and the room seemed just a bit different. She asked who had gone inside. Ruby Nelle, standing nearby, pointed straight at Johnnie and me.

Johnnie spoke first, claiming he was looking for a toy, but the lie hung in the air, thin and heavy. Without a word, Momma grabbed a shoe and struck him across the back and legs. Each blow was a clear warning: don't cross that line again. Cries echoed through the trailer, raw and unrelenting.

Then she turned toward me, anger still burning in her eyes. A warning followed—next time, I'd face the same punishment. Tears gathered as my gaze dropped in quiet understanding. Then came the instruction: clean up and come to the table.

Dinner came with heavy hearts and quiet minds. The lesson settled in, but the image of that gun stayed vivid in my memory.

CHAPTER 16

A SPOONFUL OF SUGAR, A JAR OF PEACHES

Later that week, the neighborhood changed. Laughter faded from the yards. Screen doors stayed shut. Footsteps on gravel no longer moved through the neighborhood.

Daddy sat at the table, stirring sugar into his coffee, eyes fixed on the window. "Something's off out here." His voice came steady, even. The spoon tapped the cup, breaking the stillness.

Silence pressed in, thick with expectation, as if the neighborhood held its breath.

Dad pushed back in his chair and finished the last of the coffee. Then, he broke the quiet. In a low, steady voice, he said. Started after Ruby Nelle overheard them."

His eyes drifted toward the doorway, sharp and focused. "That moment changed everything. Folks haven't looked at us the same since."

A small nod. "Their faces tighten when we walk by. That kind of distance doesn't happen by accident."

The cup touched the table with a soft clink. "So, what's it gonna take to ease this tension?"

The question settled between them, heavy with the sense that nothing had ended—only paused. Momma set the shirt she finished ironing aside, her eyes were steady with quiet strength.

They couldn't control others, but their own behavior was still within reach. A simple gesture—a warmer smile, a kind word—might begin to shift things.

At dawn, the neighborhood came alive—children's laughter mixed with the hum of daily routines. In the kitchen, Momma selected a jar of homemade canned peaches before walking to Mrs. Thompson's house.

A knock on the door preceded a forced smile, steadying her nerves. Mrs. Thompson answered, surprised but polite. An introduction followed, along with the gift of preserved peaches—a simple offering meant to bridge the distance.

Inside, they sat facing each other, the tension beginning to ease. The recent attack on Juanita and Alvin came up, framed as part of an effort to build trust and kindness among neighbors.

Mrs. Thompson listened.

Her caution came from old wounds—mistrust, discomfort, and the weight of neighborhood divides. At first, it kept her guarded, measuring every word and glance. Over time, that edge began to soften.

When Momma first approached, she braced for confrontation, judgment, and blame—the kind that comes when conflict lingers. Her body held the caution, stiff in every move. Even her words came measured, careful not to spark more fire. As the conversation went on, she realized support was being offered instead of criticism. Little by little, her guard came down. The shift marked a turning point: from suspicion to possibility.

After a pause, Momma admitted to jumping to conclusions and seemed more open than before. Support was extended—not just for her, but for the whole community.

By the time the porch steps creaked under retreating feet, the weight between them felt lighter.

The problem hadn't vanished, but something had begun to shift—a small beginning.

Back from the visit, a different energy filled the room. A jar of peaches served as a gesture of goodwill, followed by coffee that helped ease the edges of old tension. The exchange showed promise—a step toward softening strained ties with the neighbors.

Later that day, Daddy walked through the door, work behind him. An excited smile greeted him, full of quiet hope. Pride marked his face, an acknowledgment of the strength it took to lead with grace in a tense moment.

That evening, dinner brought a lighter mood. The table stood ready, and stew filled the room with warmth. Daddy bowed his head, offering thanks for the meal, the family, and a fresh start.

Despite Dad's efforts, cold crept through every crack in that old house, cutting through even the thickest blankets. Yet in that moment, warmth still found us.

Wrapped in layers of whatever we could gather, the family huddled together in the small living room. Light from the kerosene lamp flickered, casting shadows that danced across the walls. The scent of kerosene hung in the air, blending with the wind's howl outside. Inside, something different took shape.

Juanita, wrapped in a blanket, grinned as she told the story of Johnnie getting stuck in the chicken coop. Smiles spread around the room. At the stove, beans simmered while heads shook at the image of Johnnie flailing through feathers. Ruby Nelle bent over, wiping her eyes. Gloria clapped along, swept up in the moment. Even Daddy leaned back, the scene vivid in his mind.

Gladys babbled something that sounded like agreement, sparking another wave of grins.

The stories kept coming, each one stacking on the last, drawing us closer. Warmth floated through the air, softening the cold and thickening the space between the walls. The roof leaked. The wind howled. But none of that touched what we built inside.

CHAPTER 17

WHEN LAUGHTER TURNED MEAN

One sunny afternoon, Gladys and I joined some neighborhood kids outside. Laughter floated through the air, and for a while, everything felt light and easy. My sister wandered off to play with a group of girls, while I hung back with two boys about my age who introduced themselves as Peewee and Clarence.

Peewee suggested we play Cowboys and Indians. Everyone agreed, and I hoped it would be fun. But the game resisted my desire. Specifically, Clarence grabbed me from behind, locking his arms tight around me while Peewee pulled out a rope!

In less than a minute, they had me tied to a tree—arms pinned, body cinched against the bark. My hands twisted helplessly against the rough cords that held them in place.

Clarence smirked. "It's just a game," he said.

But my gut instinct sent an alarm: *This is fun at my expense only.*

They made their point, then took off running. Their laughter hung in the air as they disappeared. I was left alone, scared, and humiliated.

Tears stung my eyes as I cried out for help, voice cracking in the wind. Just when hope started to slip away, Gladys came running. She didn't ask questions. Without a word, she knelt and worked the knots loose, fingers fast and angry.

"That's why you can't trust those fools," she snapped, her voice hot and sharp.

"What made you think messing with them was a good idea? Stuff like this can't happen again."

I walked beside her, head down, shame burning in my chest. The scolding landed sharp, leaving no room for debate. It carried a lesson I knew would stick. "Don't do stuff like that again. You gotta think first, okay?"

I nodded, words too heavy to say out loud. By the time we reached the porch, her tone had softened. The frustration was still there, hard to miss. But underneath it was something protective, holding steady. The screen door stood open, a silent message: learn from this, and move forward.

Inside, Momma greeted us. The scent of simmering greens filled the kitchen. Fresh biscuits cooled on a folded dish towel, and a pot of oxtails bubbled gently on the stove.

She glanced over. "What y'all been up to?" Gladys shrugged. "Took care of something."

Momma gave a quiet nod, returning to her stirring. No more questions followed. The moment was left to settle, like steam rising from a pot—unspoken, but understood.

Later that day, Juanita shared what had happened—how some neighborhood kids had tied me up and teased me. The concern was real, but the focus quickly shifted to what needed to come next.

Ruby Nelle questioned if I truly belonged in first grade. She thought my shyness and quiet nature might stand in the way. Momma replied without hesitation: School was still the path forward because being around kids my age might help—even with the growing pains it would bring.

After Gladys promised to look out for me, the weight on Momma's shoulders seemed to lift.

CHAPTER 18

CROWNLESS AND DROWSY

The first day of school remains vivid. The bus didn't serve the children of Silver Stream Knolls. Families like ours, without a car, made the daily walk on foot through bitter winters and sweltering summers.

The morning sun cast a warm glow over the neighborhood as we made our way up the hill on Second Lane to Route 22. Ruby Nelle, Juanita, and Johnnie headed west toward the larger brick buildings, while Gladys and I walked east toward the elementary school.

As her hand reached for mine, we crossed the busy highway, the sound of passing cars fading into the distance.

While buses carrying white children passed by, walking remained our only option. Rain or shine, in the cold of winter or under the hot summer sun.

We grew up untouched by the idea of race, never seeing ourselves as different from anyone else. Our parents shielded us from the harsh reality of racism. With the hope of letting our childhood stay innocent. I walked beside my older sister, our steps steady. Her hand stayed wrapped around mine, her eyes steady and watchful.

Blacks and Whites attended the same schools, but the journey told a different story. —The path carried the same name, but not the same experience.

That difference revealed more than just access to transportation; it showed who the system was built to serve and who was expected to adjust. The same classrooms held both Black and White students, yet the journeys began miles apart, shaped by an unspoken inequality that said plenty without ever being named.

Spoken with calm defiance, Gladys voiced the truth of the moment. It settled between us. A seat on that bus remained out of reach, but the message rang clear: the right to learn mattered just as much for us as for anyone else. Harsh realities came into view, but we didn't surrender to them.

The lesson came in walking through those truths, recognizing them without letting them break us or define our worth.

Each step on the walk to school carried both tension and hope. The brick building rose ahead, its shadow stretching long across the path. At the entrance, the teacher introduced herself as Mrs. Davis.

She gave a small nod and, with a gentle motion, pointed us toward our classrooms. No fuss, only calm and quiet direction.

Inside the first-grade room, the air buzzed with unfamiliar sounds—voices overlapping, chairs scraping. The teacher's voice rose above it all, calling the class to order.

Each glance from a stranger came like a challenge, and a wave of discomfort tightened the chest.

Life at home flowed smoothly, shaped by Juanita's care and the comfort of familiar spaces.

Here, the walls felt heavy, their chipped paint and stale air closing in. Each detail made the distance from home feel even greater.

The room stirred with hushed motion—feet shuffling and whispers drifting. Sharp instructions from the front cut cleanly through the noise. We were told to sit and place our folded hands on the desk. Small fingers rested on rough wood as the teacher wrote her name on the blackboard with crisp strokes.

Mrs. Davis stood near the board, arms folded, rarely blinking.

Her presence carried a firmness I hadn't seen before. Her neat dress and tapping heels announced her presence. A shiny pin on her sweater marked her as someone not to cross. Whether stern or simply unfamiliar, her presence set a tone no one dared challenge.

I sat up straighter without thinking, hoping she wouldn't call on me. Everything about her said, *Don't play in here.* With my hands folded on the desk, uncertainty crept in. The classroom rules had been given, but my place among them remained unclear.

An instruction came from the front, prompting us to rise and turn toward the U.S. flag hanging near the blackboard. With our hands over our hearts, we recited the Pledge of Allegiance. For a moment, I felt a flicker of belonging. The rhythm of voices moved around me, and in their sound a small spark of connection took hold. The faces were unfamiliar, but they didn't feel quite as distant. The words we shared seemed to form a fragile bridge, reaching across the space between us. In that instant, the strangeness of the room eased. Even in the middle of uncertainty, I caught the trace of acceptance.

A moment of calm settled as I took my seat. The routine of standing and reciting the pledge gave me something steady to hold onto.

The teacher called on a couple of students to hand out the day's coloring assignment. That sense of calm began to slip. Sheets slid down each row, smooth and unbothered. One hand to the next, as if the rhythm had always been theirs. No one paused to ask questions or check directions—

just quiet momentum, steady and sure. That rhythm carried a sense of belonging, one that didn't come easily to me.

Minutes stretched as stillness settled over me. The pages in front of me blurred until I couldn't focus. My eyelids grew heavy, fighting to stay open. I thought about home, with its familiar voices and light through the windows. The safety I wanted felt far away. Words from Mrs. Davis cut through the haze—faint, but enough to pull my focus back bit by bit. Eyes lowered to the desk, the weight of being out of place settled in—unseen, but heavy.

Time crept by, slowed by strict rules and steady corrections, each one quietly chipping at my confidence. The classroom felt colder, the walls pressing in. My thoughts slipped back to the refuge of home. Sitting at the desk felt endless, every instruction weighing on me. I wondered how I would ever survive this place.

Mrs. Davis announced that recess was about to begin—a twenty-minute break for play. The news sparked a burst of excitement, just what was needed. We rushed to the door, eager to get out. The teacher stopped us cold, saying no one was leaving until we settled down. A silence fell, tense but quick. Then the door swung open, and we spilled into the air outside. Outside, the playground burst with color and life. Bright red slides twisted like fiery rivers, and blue swings creaked as they soared.

Laughter rang out as kids darted across the worn asphalt, their joy rising and falling like waves. Eager hands clutched the rust-speckled stairs. Shrieks followed as they shot down the slide.

Finding a place among the others was a constant challenge. No invitations came. I stood off to the side, watching the line form step by step. Bodies climbed higher, voices rising with excitement. Following behind, the climb up the eight metal steps grew heavier with each attempt. Whatever sense of belonging the morning's pledge had offered faded quickly. At the top, the slide brought no cheers, and at the bottom, no voices were calling out in support.

By the time my feet touched the ground, the others were gone. They had scattered to the merry- go-round without a glance back. The quiet that followed felt sharp and unwelcome.

Standing at the edge, silence clung to the air. My chest tightened as I took it all in. The laughter wrapped around me like a song inviting me to join, but I didn't understand how to accept the invitation.

Despite wanting to be part of it, I struggled to interact with the other children. Every attempt at conversation felt forced, my gestures lost in the chaos of the playground.

A boy dashed past, calling out to another as a group gave chase. I stood off to the side, watching them disappear, the distance between us growing. The playground, full of energy and joy, only deepened my sense of isolation.

When recess ended, I dragged myself inside—tired, uncertain. Everything seemed overwhelming and strange. But deep down, I told myself I would figure it out. Not that day, but soon enough.

All I had to do was keep moving, one uncertain step at a time. The classroom grew quiet as the teacher announced a letter-tracing exercise. Pencils moved carefully over the outlines, but exhaustion tugged at me. My eyes grew heavy, the shapes on the page blurring with each blink.

Sleep crept closer despite every effort to resist. Mrs. Davis knelt nearby, asking if everything was alright. Rubbing my eyes in a futile attempt to clear the haze, I mumbled that I was just tired.

And I was tired—not from running, or playing, or even thinking too hard, but from somewhere deeper. A heavy tiredness settled inside me, more than just sleep. It felt like something unspoken had curled up in my chest.A kind of tiredness that settled inside me, like the weight of something unspoken had curled up in my chest. I didn't yet have the words to name it.

I fought to stay awake, but my body wouldn't listen. A full stomach and the low hum of the classroom pulled me under.

Before long, my head dipped forward, and the tracing assignment sheet lay abandoned on the desk.

I drifted off without warning, head resting on folded arms. The pencil remained in my grip, as if the drawing had simply paused. The classroom settled into a still hum, soft and steady. It blurred the line between waking and dreams, pulling me under. From somewhere distant, Mrs. Davis's voice cut through the fog: "Wake up, Sleeping Beauty, you can't sleep here!" Playful, but just firm enough to pull me back.

Laughter rippled across the room, harmless and warm, filling the space with gentle teasing. Heat rose in my cheeks as I sat up, the weight behind my eyes still lingering. Even so, the teacher's voice carried no edge. It was just a gentle nudge, giving a worn-down boy a moment to breathe. Grabbing the pencil to disappear into something familiar, I hoped to write over the sting of embarrassment.

The bell rang at 1:30, marking the end of a day already too long. Feet moved quickly toward the door, eager for a way out. At the threshold, Gladys stood scanning the crowd. A pause lingered in the space between us. I spoke of lagging at recess and dozing through class. The teacher's light remark stayed with me longer than I expected. Gladys laughed, unaware of how heavy it had been. That laugh erased the comfort that had started to build. One glance at my face held her still. She leaned in close, voice low. "Don't go telling Momma you fell asleep in class."

The way she said it made it clear—bringing it up would only bring trouble. Not the kind worth stirring.

CHAPTER 19

THE YEAR I WALKED ALONE

The next day, recess brought a new push of courage, my legs carrying hesitant steps toward a cluster of classmates. I turned to Jason, hoping to join in. A glance—then nothing. The game kept moving, and the silence that followed gave its own answer.

Looking back, that moment at recess was more than childhood rejection. It was an early lesson in how the world moves for Black folks in white spaces. At five years old, I didn't have the words to explain the weight of it, but Jason's silence spoke volumes. It wasn't only about a game; it carried a message. One that would return in many forms over the years.

That playground reflected the workplaces to come. During work hours, White colleagues might smile, make small talk, or even share a laugh. But once the day ended, so did the connection. The friendliness stopped at the parking lot, never stepping beyond surface lines. That same divide existed back then, too, though I didn't yet know what to call it.

Recess taught me what no book ever did. Inclusion was selective, bound by rules no one had to say out loud.

The game kept going without me, like I hadn't asked to play at all. No confrontation. There was no explanation. Only the sense of a door that had always been closed. Indifference lingered louder than words.What I took as a child to be personal became clearer with time. That distance, subtle and unacknowledged, was part of a larger truth. Proximity didn't mean acceptance.

Participation didn't mean belonging. And silence, in moments like those, became a language of exclusion.

A hard bite to my lip held back the sting in my eyes as a tight knot rose in my throat, thick and unmoving.

Laughter and shouting filled the playground—not malicious, just indifferent. Each joyful sound echoed like a reminder of distance. My shoes dragged slow lines through the dust. It was proof I was elsewhere, even while standing in the middle of it all. Clusters of kids darted and leapt through games, voices light and limbs loose, as if play came easily.

The rhythm moved smooth and certain. No questions asked, no space left for outsiders. That ease drifted just out of reach, like an unspoken language.

The squeak of the swings caught my attention, cutting through the noise of the playground. An open space led me toward them, and my feet followed without much thought. Gripping the cool

metal chains, my small hands held tight as I settled into the seat. I pushed with my legs and rose into the air. The breeze brushed my face, and for a moment, everything else slipped away. The swing carried me higher, then back again.

In that rise and fall, I felt a lightness I couldn't name. Forward, then back; it offered something close to freedom. Not belonging, maybe, but escape. No explaining, no pretending, just the wind and the arc. As the motion slowed, that lightness faded, replaced by the same ache that had been waiting. A scuff of the shoe stirred a little dust, as if movement alone might hold the heaviness back.

All around, activity carried on—tag, bouncing balls, kids calling out across the yard. The whole scene pulsed with life, just out of reach.

The bell rang, and my feet touched down. The walk back toward the building began, each step bringing back that familiar dread. Another stretch of the day waited—another round of trying, watching, and wishing.

CHAPTER 20

THE WEIGHT THAT LIFTED ME

As the isolation dragged on over the next two weeks, I found myself yearning for connection amid a sea of unfamiliar faces.

One day, a shift in the routine caught my eye—a little girl in a white and brown polka-dot dress. She looked delicate, almost timeless, as if someone had stepped out of an old film reel. She reminded me of Annette Funicello from the Mickey Mouse Club, a face I knew from the glow of early television. From across the yard, the light danced in her eyes, and her hair shimmered like polished liquorice. A gentle charm lingered around her—soft, unspoken, tugging at something deep inside me.

Her presence lit a small flicker of hope, the first since school began. It felt like the connection I had been longing for in all that loneliness.

For two days, distance offered a sense of safety, though the pull remained strong. On the third, footsteps closed the space between us. Her voice held more curiosity than kindness when the question came: "Why you starin'?"

Flustered, the words tumbled out. I liked her. No hesitation. Just a steady-eyed frown.

"Don't like you. You're ugly," she said, then turned and walked away.

The words landed like a slap—no visible mark, but heavy all the same. My chest tightened as she left, her words delivering that first sting of rejection. No teasing, no lead-up—just something sharp and cold, thrown without care.

Later at recess, Ms. Brown called me over. My silence must have spoken for me. She leaned in and asked what had happened. I told her what Darlene said. Her lips pressed into a thin line, disapproval clear, but she offered comfort just the same.

Smiling, she said, "Don't worry. Go over and play."

But I didn't. I couldn't. That afternoon, something dimmed inside. I sank deeper into silence.

The classroom's colors faded; lessons blurred. I moved through the day like a ghost—present yet untouched.

The playground, once noisy and full of motion, became unbearable. Classmates ran wild, laughter filled the air, and I stood off to the side—unseen, unwanted. Each day chipped away at my spirit.

Then the final blow came. As the year wound down, the teacher sent a note home. Her words were plain and heavy. She recommended I repeat the first grade. Holding that folded paper brought a weight hard to ignore. Everything I'd tried to push through—every failure, every silence—seemed carved into that single page.

The note came home like a weight too heavy to set down. At the front door, I handed it to Momma. She read the paper, but no hardness settled in her face. Her eyes met mine—not with disappointment, but with something steadier.

She sat beside me, her voice calm and encouraging. "Life don't always go the way you want, baby. But that don't mean it's over."

Shame crept in—failing the year, not fitting in, getting left behind.

"Being dumb is not the case. You weren't ready. Each person grows at their own pace. Been knocked down too but still standing."

Those words grounded me, like roots settling into uncertain soil. Darlene's rejection still lingered, the sting of being unseen. Now came this, piling on what already hurt. Every sign pointed to failure.

But Momma's voice stayed firm. "This ain't about them. This is about you. Go back, and next time, be ready."

CHAPTER 21

"YOU GONE LEARN THESE WORDS TODAY"

I sat at the kitchen table, hunched over workbooks and scraps of paper. My shirt clung to my skin in the thick summer heat. No overhead fan. No breeze. Just the weight of the day pressing down.

Through the window, I watched kids racing up and down the street. Their laughter carried over the dirt road like stones skimming water. I wanted to be out there with them. Free, chasing clouds and sunlight like the rest. But inside, I had catching up to do. Momma had already lived a full day before ever sitting beside me. Before sunrise, water was hauled from the well, breakfast cooked, and laundry scrubbed in the metal tub with the washboard. By midmorning, clotheslines out back sagged under the weight of wet garments. Daddy's lunch still waited to be packed, and dinner had to be started.

The floor needed sweeping, and there was always more to do. Each day filled itself before we even noticed. At just twelve, Juanita had stepped into a grown woman's shoes without being

asked. While work continued in the kitchen or another load soaked, Gloria remained in Juanita's care. Dishes were dried, and smaller items hung with care. Small hands moved through each task with purpose, carrying more than their size suggested.

By the time Momma sat down next to me at that old table, her arms were tired and her feet sore, but her focus never wavered.

"Gone learn these words today." The voice was steady and calm. Fingers worn from years of labor guided mine across the paper. I mouthed the letters, struggling at first. Never once did they rush me. Their patience was shaped by long days and a love that ran deep.

Outside, laughter erupted again. A boy hollered. A jump rope slapped against the dirt road. The world spun on without me. My eyes drifted toward the door, but her pencil tapped the paper. The message was clear: stay with it.

Each afternoon settled into the same rhythm: lessons given, effort returned. Juanita's quiet presence—doing chores to lighten the load—made those moments possible.

The lines stopped looking like confusion. Words began to make sense. The numbers added up. My voice found more confidence with each sentence read aloud.

That summer, we built more than skills. Belief took shape—layered between sounds, letters, and the rhythm of hard work.

I missed the games, even the sting of summer heat while running down the street. But in their place, something deeper began to take hold.

I returned to first grade with more than a second chance. I carried lessons etched deep at the kitchen table—lessons shaped by a mother who gave only love and hard work, and a sister who stepped up long before being asked.

Together, they gave me the space and strength I needed to rise.

CHAPTER 22

BENEATH THE KICKBALL SKY

On a radiant September morning, the schoolyard buzzed with the energy of excited children reuniting after the summer hiatus. Lunch pails in hand, their voices rose in a symphony of chatter and laughter, brimming with anticipation for the adventures ahead.

This year began differently. I stepped in with steady confidence, ready for a fresh start.

As the bell rang and students filed into the classroom, the hallway pulsed with movement and chatter. Among the sea of unfamiliar faces, one smile stood out.

I made my way over to Billy, the kid who'd moved in over the summer. As we shook hands, the year no longer seemed so lonely.

The uncertainty of starting over began to fade, replaced by the promise of friendship and the strength I carried within me. As the day went on, I moved through the classroom with a steadiness I hadn't felt before. A quiet assurance began to take hold. The hard work of summer

had paid off, and with Momma's steady guidance, I faced first grade again—this time, ready.

With each passing day, I grew more sure of myself, not just in the classroom but in how I carried myself among others. The friendships I began to build felt real, anchored in a trust I hadn't known before. The support and love from Momma, combined with my own resilience, laid the foundation for a bright future.

The schoolyard, once a place of uncertainty, now felt like a canvas full of opportunities to learn, grow, and thrive. And it all began with Momma; her encouragement and her unwavering belief in me.

In a blink, Billy and I formed an instant connection, bonding over shared interests and experiences. Our camaraderie solidified—a friendship formed with the ease of something ancient and unspoken.

Days blended into weeks as we moved through school life. Laughter carried us across the playground, from games of tag to fierce rounds of kickball. With every moment together, the bond grew stronger.

One sunny afternoon, my friend and I waited in the school parking lot. The creaking swings and distant bursts of laughter filled the background as we joined the others on the grass. We threw ourselves into the game, every kick and chase fueled by raw energy. The air rang with missed catches, bursts of laughter, and cheers that carried us forward. Each moment pulled us closer.

During one match, while we were mid-celebration, a group of rowdy kids wandered over. A redheaded kid with freckles snatched the ball from my friend and bolted. Our eyes locked, and the chase stretched across the grass.

Near the lot, it ended. One quick move, and I took the ball back, lifting it high in triumph.

Before any celebration could begin, the one I'd tackled and his crew swarmed us. Fists flew. In less than a minute, everything unraveled.

Then came the word—spit out like venom. The slur cut through the noise: the N-word, hurled with malice. No explanation was needed. Its weight hit harder than any punch, freezing everything in its path.

A teacher stormed over, voice raised, demanding answers. The bully pointed fingers. Billy pushed back, firm and clear: "Took the ball while we were playing a game. And then they called Alvin a nigger."

The teacher interjected. "Fighting and racist language will not be tolerated. One more incident, and your parents will be brought in."

All of us nodded our heads, but something inside shifted.

What changed went deeper than mood. Unfairness had always lingered in the background—easy to ignore, easy to swallow. Being overlooked, passed by, or held back seemed normal until that moment.

This one cut deeper than all the rest, not from wanting to belong but from being struck at the core of who I was. The insult wasn't about choice or effort—it was about identity, fixed and undeniable. That word did more than sting—it opened my eyes to a divide I hadn't seen before. It was a line drawn long ago, setting me apart from the rest. Some people wouldn't care about my effort or friendship; they'd only respond to my skin.

From then on, the world pressed in on me. I moved through it with sharper edges and quieter steps. A fire sparked beneath the surface: a vow to rise beyond anyone's limits or slurs.

As the teacher marched the other boys away, I stayed beside Billy, that word still ringing in my mind. I asked what it meant. He shrugged, brushing it off, his attention drifting back to the unfinished game. His promise to reteach kickball the next day came easily, his tone warm enough to keep the door open.

Later that week, Billy brought me to his mother's diner. The air inside held a soft warmth, wrapping around me as soon as I stepped through the door. Something sweet lingered between the booths and stools, faint but inviting. Sliding into a corner booth, I watched as his mother worked behind the counter. A quick hello, two Cokes, and a plate of fresh donuts arrived without a word needed.

She moved through the room with calm, steady ease. Nothing in the place shouted welcome, yet every detail offered peace. It wasn't much—just a booth and a couple of donuts—but it gave me a place to breathe. In that small pause, the sharp edge of the slur started to dull.I sat across from Billy, sugar on my fingertips, soda bubbling between us.

The world eased up. I wasn't the kid from the playground anymore, or the one pushed to the side. I was just a boy with a new friend, doing my best to make sense of it all. The question about that word didn't disappear, but it no longer held all the weight. Billy's mom offered more than a treat; she gave us a place to land. And that meant more than anything shouted under the schoolyard sun.

Trading kickball stories, rewinding the chase and the catch, both of us laughed like it ended in victory. That little diner, alive with clinks and low voices, offered us something steady. It was a place untouched by the chaos of the schoolyard. Time passed in the warm haze of the diner, thick with coffee, donuts, and comfort. Stories passed between us, laughter exchanged like currency.

For a while, nothing else mattered—not bullies, not questions, not school. Just two boys settling into a friendship that was solid and real.

CHAPTER 23

THE LINE BETWEEN US

A few days later, Billy asked me over to his house to play with his toys. It felt like a welcome break from school, especially with my parents away. Billy's house overflowed with toys— soldiers, building sets, and miniature cars scattered in every direction.

Excitement buzzed between us.

Toy soldiers took the field, lined up for epic battles. Knocked down, rebuilt, and rearranged—the scene played out over and over. Each skirmish burst with sound effects and wild commentary, our voices rising and falling like battlefield commanders. The carpet transformed into rocky terrain, the couch stood tall as a cliff, and a pair of cushions became enemy strongholds. We launched attack after attack, toppling armies and building them back again without pause. Time slipped away, lost in the clatter of plastic soldiers and the rhythm of our imaginations. For those hours, nothing else existed but the war we created and the bond it quietly built between us. forts.

As the day wrapped up, I thanked Billy for the time together. A smile met me, along with a warm invitation to return anytime. I walked home with a lightness in each step. A quiet joy lingered after the fun faded, warming the space just behind my ribs.

But soon after, our friendship would face a challenge—one that would change everything.

The next day brought the usual meetup at school—jokes traded, races challenged, the rhythm unchanged. But something shifted that afternoon.

Billy mentioned a conversation with his uncle the night before.

His uncle had seen me at their house, used the N-word, and threatened to burn the place down. The same word that redheaded boy had spat on the playground. The weight of it fell on me again, heavy and sharp, cutting deeper than I could name. Cruel in a way I still couldn't fully grasp, it lingered long after the words were gone. It was hard to understand how someone could carry that kind of hate, let alone speak it aloud.

Billy's hands trembled as he told the story. The words came out in pieces, his voice cracking. His mother's shout tore through the room as she ordered the uncle out. She slammed the door hard, locking it as if to keep the whole world away. Then she moved through the house with a restless energy, guarding what she held dear.

The air between us changed. What once was light and easy now hung tangled in fear.

His uncle's words echoed long after they were spoken. Doubt crept in. Were we still friends?

Billy ran off to the monkey bars without a word, leaving me rooted in place, alone and unsure.

When the bell rang, recess ended. And something else did too. The ease we'd shared unraveled beneath a weight neither of us had chosen.

The next day, we walked the hallway in silence. Tension hung between us like a veil—thin, invisible, but unyielding. What once came naturally now felt forced. We kept pace but avoided each other's eyes. The bond had loosened.

That slur his uncle used didn't just land; it stayed. It drew a line between us that neither of us crossed.

When the bell rang again, we split off to separate classes. The friendship we had faded into silence.

I didn't have words for what had happened—no lessons in history or talk of systems to explain it. All I knew was the impact hit hard and left its mark. Hatred aimed at something unchangeable, something stitched into who I was—enough to make a mother bolt her doors and raise her voice.

The sound of it rattled through the house, sharp and unyielding. And something inside me cracked too: the sense that trust and play lived safely beyond harm's reach. That crack stayed with me, small but deep, a reminder that the world could turn without warning. The weight settled on Billy too, though neither of us named it. Nothing had to be spoken—the message carried itself, sharp and undeniable. It passed between us like a shadow, heavy and lingering. Maybe the monkey bars gave him space. Feet off the ground, rules loosened, gravity less certain.

A place to pretend nothing had changed.

But once something cuts that deep, it doesn't vanish. It settles in and burrows deep. It changes how the world looks. Over time, whispers shape how worth gets measured, even when you try to block them out.

That day didn't just shake a friendship; it exposed something raw. Childhood can crack fast, joy slipping away in a blink. Even the strongest bonds can bend under the weight of a world that keeps pressing in.

The moment passed without another word. No language, no space, no permission to name what had happened.

But even now, years later, I still wonder what Billy remembers. If that moment ever came back to him, I can't say. Maybe he mentioned me once, the friend who showed up and brought more than he expected. Or maybe it drifted away, tucked into the blur of childhood days. For me, the memory stays close. Not sharp or bitter, just present. A quiet reminder of how early life begins to shape us.

CHAPTER 24

SHE HEARD, BUT DIDN'T STOP

A typical evening—the TV cast a soft, flickering glow across the room, shadows dancing on worn but familiar furniture. Family photos lined the walls, quiet witnesses to the lives unfolding beneath them. The air carried a hum of tension—the kind that never quite settled.

Dad, split between long hours at the mill and his duties as assistant pastor, left most of the day- to-day to Momma. The line stayed firm—steady, sharp, and unshakable. With Momma at the helm, nothing fell apart.

That night, Johnnie strolled in wearing that crooked grin—the one that always meant trouble was coming. Sprawled on the floor with Gladys and Gloria, eyes locked on the TV. Then a smack landed on the back of my head. No warning, no reason. Johnnie came at me like always— pushing me aside. It was a pattern I knew too well, one that never seemed to change. I rubbed the spot, confused and irritated. Then came the swing—his face lit up, as if this was the moment he'd been waiting for.

Wrestling never meant laughter or fun for me. It was always one-sided pain. Johnnie's laughter echoed above, but nothing about it felt like a game.

In the kitchen, pots clanged, drawers slid shut. Ham simmered, green beans bubbled on the stove. Familiar warmth moved through the room, but none of it reached me, suffering on the floor.

By the stove, Momma stood still, wooden spoon in hand, and gaze fixed straight ahead. There was no turn of the head and no step taken to stop what unfolded in the other room. Silence held the space; not the kind born of peace, but of choice.

Johnnie grunted, pressing harder. My teeth sank into the inside of my cheek. I knew better than to expect anyone to step in, so I braced myself the best I could. That moment marked something. Not just bruises, but a shift deep inside. There was no rescue, no voice, and no hands reaching in. Just absence—heavy and sharp.

Pain didn't end with the grip. Something small shifted—stopped asking for protection. Kitchen noise carried on, covering the sound of a child pinned to the floor. No one moved toward the struggle. No raised voices. Only stillness, carrying its own message.

To Momma, this wasn't violence. This was something else. Something boys had to go through. I hit the floor again, caught in Johnnie's grip, heat rushing to my face. My body stayed pinned.

Every motion met a block. Every effort fell short, always trailing, never breaking through.

Hurt and frustrated, yet somewhere in the struggle, a small understanding began to take shape. I was learning how to take a hit and keep going. Taking a beating didn't mean quitting; it just meant another day was waiting. Showing up still counted, even when stuck in the struggle.

Maybe that was the point.

This wasn't just a scuffle. It was an early lesson in holding your ground, even when the odds didn't line up right.

Momma called out for us to wash up for dinner. I stayed down a moment, catching my breath, while Johnnie walked off like nothing had happened. My sisters dashed to the bathroom, laughing and pushing to be first, as if beating the others actually meant something.

When they were done, I pulled myself up and made my way in. Damp towels clung to the rack, heavy with the day's use. The sharp scent of soap hung in the air as I stood at the mirror. My neck throbbed—faint red marks from Johnnie's grip already rising on the skin.

But the lesson reached past the soreness. It wasn't just about the sting or the scuffle. That moment shaped something deeper—holding your own didn't always mean standing tall. Some days, real strength showed up in the rising.

By the time I took my seat at the table, tension from the match still clung. But the truth sat clearer now. Johnnie wasn't out to cause harm. Something was being tested in me. A lesson was unfolding—how to carry myself through hard moments, even when the teaching lacked tenderness.

As plates passed and conversation picked up, the noise of the day settled into the hum of family. Beneath the clatter and motion, an unspoken truth held us together. Love didn't always come gently, but it stayed.

CHAPTER 25

MOMMA STAYED, BUT SO DID HER RULE

Whenever Johnnie left the house, Momma's words followed him like a shadow: "Don't forget to take your little brother." Not a suggestion—more like law, drilled in so many times it became routine. Johnnie hated it—not because he didn't care about me, but because it was a responsibility he never signed up for.

The sky stayed dark, the ground crusted with frost. Johnnie bundled into a heavy coat and scarf, ready for his paper route. Momma stood in the open doorway, framed by the warmth of the house, watching as cold morning air curled just behind her.

Johnnie shot me a frustrated glare, like I was the problem—like dragging me along made everything harder. A groan slipped out as I sank deeper into the couch. The warmth wrapped around me, too good to let go. The thought of leaving that comfort for the bitter cold twisted my stomach.

Johnnie hovered beside me, his presence pressing in as he waited for a reaction. I held still, but Momma's sharp glance cut through, telling me my time was up. The weather didn't matter; I had to go.

With a sigh, I stood. The chill seeped in before we even stepped outside. Coat and boots went on with slow, stiff movements. Johnnie muttered under his breath and stormed out, the door slamming behind him. I followed, only to be met by a slap of cold that stole the breath from my lungs.

He was already in motion, moving fast. A stack of newspapers landed in my arms without warning, nearly tipping me over. My fingers, already numb, struggled to hold on. He didn't look back—just kept his steady stride, always ahead.

The house faded behind us as we made our way up Second Lane. Wind sliced through every step. The cold pushed past my coat and settled deep inside. Each step grew heavier. The stack tugged at my arms, slipping more than once. Johnnie never looked back. If I slowed, he walked faster, eyes locked forward like I wasn't even there. When he did glance behind, it was only to groan or shake his head if I stumbled or said something.

At the top of the lane, Johnnie hopped on his bike without a word. I climbed onto the middle bar, gripping the papers tight as wind slammed against my face. My fingers burned, but he kept pedaling, focused on finishing, dragging me along.

I stayed quiet because complaining wouldn't change a thing. His eyes were locked on the road.

Each turn of the pedals made one thing clear: to him, getting done was all that mattered.

He lifted a finger toward chimneys where smoke curled into the sky, mumbling something about doughnuts. That made him pedal faster. At the first house, the scent hit strongly. A kind older woman opened the door and, seeing me shivering, handed Johnnie a warm bag of doughnuts. He stuffed them into his coat pocket without offering me one. My fingers throbbed. I wished I'd stayed home.

We moved on, cold biting at my hands, and now, my feet. The next house was rundown, snow creeping through broken weeds. An elderly woman grabbed her paper, muttered something, and shut the door without a thank-you.

At another house, a woman in a robe with a cigarette dangling from her mouth stared at us, then blew smoke in our faces. No tip. Just a hard stare.

Then came a house where a grumpy old man snatched the paper from Johnnie's hand and barked about folks making noise too early.

Johnnie didn't answer—just nodded and turned. His eyes caught mine for a moment, like even he couldn't believe it.

We kept walking—not much talking when Johnnie's at work. The bag of doughnuts swung between us. The warmth from that first house lingered like a memory.

By the time we were heading back, the last house sat at the edge of the route—a squat yellow place with a little dog barking in the window. The door creaked open, and an older woman peeked out, bundled in a thick robe. She smiled and gave a small bag of ginger cookies to Johnnie, nodding some respect in the process.

The cold bit into my fingers and face as I clung to the middle bar, hands tight at each push of the pedals. As soon as our house came into view, I moved to get off. The bag of treats swung against Johnnie's coat, just out of reach. At the top of Second Lane, my feet hit the ground—legs stiff, cheeks stinging, hands gone numb. Johnnie bolted ahead, pedaling fast and leaving me to jog behind. When I finally caught up, our eyes met—mine worn down, quietly hoping for a break. A sigh and an eye roll came first, then the doughnut was handed over—not out of kindness, but because the game of holding out had run its course. I took a bite, letting the sugar calm the mood just enough to soften the edges. We finished the route, helped along by warm treats and a few kind folks who didn't mind the knock at their door.

Coming home was a relief, but he didn't say a word. Shaking off the snow and cold as we stepped inside, he muttered something and disappeared without looking back. There was no doubt about it. Having me tag along felt more like a burden than a choice.

CHAPTER 26

FIGHTS, STATS, AND ROOM TO GROW

As the years passed, Melvin settled into the care of his grandmother and the steady presence of Mr. Holmes. Back in Ohio, Dad stood at the kitchen counter, eyes fixed somewhere far off.

Melvin had been with Momma's family in Georgia for twelve years. Now the moment had come. Dad reached for her hand. "Time to bring him home. "Momma nodded. Melvin belonged with them now.

A few days later, Momma called Grandma to say Melvin needed to come to Ohio.

Hesitation came through on the other end. The change meant a hard road ahead. Melvin was close to Mr. Holmes and leaving wouldn't be easy.

Momma reminded Grandma that Melvin should be with family—in the house Dad was building for all of them.

Grandma agreed. She knew the move wouldn't be easy, but she understood that sometimes love meant letting go. She believed Melvin's bond with them would hold, carried by years of care and quiet moments. Even with miles between them, that tie would not break. Momma made the arrangements. Melvin would arrive on Friday. Saying goodbye would sting, but the time had come.

Back then, when Melvin lived with Grandma, life felt different. He had a room to himself, a bed untouched by others—no need to share or compete for space. The house stayed quiet most days, just him and Grandma, with Mr. Holmes around, and Aunt Eunice was away at college.

By the time Melvin turned five, Aunt Eunice was deep into her teenage years, wrapped up in her own world. She crossed his path only in passing. Life unfolded like that of an only child—no squabbles, no cramped quarters. His belongings stayed where he left them, untouched.

Momma pulled Melvin into a long embrace, her face pressed against his shoulder. She didn't let go right away, holding on as if to make up for the years he'd been away since birth. "You're home now," she whispered. Dad stood nearby, a rare smile easing across his face. "Good to have you here, son."

Melvin stepped inside, seeing our family together for the first time. Gladys spoke first: "We've been waiting on you." Johnnie stayed by the doorway, watching quietly. I shifted on my feet, then finally said, "It's good you're here." Melvin nodded, still silent, still taking us all in, as if trying to measure what this new life might mean.

"In our crowded Ohio house, privacy was scarce, and Melvin discovered that the very first night. Johnnie and I already shared a bed, so adding him meant three boys stacked in like laundry, head to foot, the old mattress groaning for mercy. Georgia had given him his own room; Ohio gave him two brothers, no space, and a blanket that never seemed wide enough.

Melvin tried to stay still on the edge of the bed. Every small movement drew a sigh from Johnnie, heavy with annoyance. "Sorry," Melvin muttered, like he was apologizing for existing.

He stared up at the ceiling as if waiting for it to explain how this counted as progress.

Being in the middle, I was always covered. Melvin shifted at the edge, Johnnie sighed beside me, and somehow, we fit. The memory stays with me, present in a way that time has never been able to erase. What I remember isn't comfort, but the sound of Melvin settling into our chaos.

Every night, once we found our places—feet pointed different ways, elbows kept close—Johnnie and Melvin would get going.

Baseball first, then boxing, sometimes basketball. They had strong opinions, didn't mind going back and forth, like a game of catch with words. Melvin was more measured. Johnnie got worked up, but that's just how it was.

One night, Johnnie said nobody could touch Willie Mays. Melvin answered with Jackie Robinson, steady and unshakable in his eyes. They traded names and stories like cards, each one laid down with pride. Then Johnnie brought up Joe Louis and that first loss to Schmeling. That set Melvin off. "You talking about the rematch? How Louis came back and laid him out in the

first round," he scoffed. He said all the Black folks in the South gathered around their radios, waiting and praying for the outcome. And when Louis won, the shout that rose up carried through the streets like thunder. That punch, Melvin said, carried more than a man's victory—it belonged to everyone who needed it.

I stayed quiet, but I wasn't just lying there. I was part of it, folded into the talk, hearing how their voices turned sports into lessons about pride, strength, and what it meant to belong.

One night, after they finished another long back-and-forth, Johnnie nudged me. He told me I'd better start keeping up with the numbers if I wanted in on the talk. Melvin said it wasn't just about what a man hit or how many runs he scored. It was about what those moments stood for. Melvin said it wasn't just about how many hits a man got or how far he could knock the ball. It was about the way folks talked about him after, like it meant something bigger than the game.

Those nights in that bed weren't comfortable, not by any measure. But something about those voices in the dark stuck with me. I listened as they argued, remembered how they cared, how they made room for me even when space was tight. That bed didn't just hold three boys—it held lessons.

Later that week, we huddled near the radio, listening to a game. Satchel Paige came up. Johnnie didn't think much of him. He said Newcombe threw harder. Melvin said Paige had finesse, and that made all the difference. They argued as usual. But then Melvin told us what Mr. Holmes said—stories from the Negro Leagues, where

Satchel and Newcombe had to play through hate and still kept their heads high.

Johnnie grew quiet, like something had settled in. He asked, not real loud, "What if they don't let me on the team 'cause I'm colored?" Melvin didn't raise his voice or say much. Just said if they didn't want him, he'd play so well they wouldn't have a choice. And that was that.

The night rolled on. The radio faded into crickets outside. But their voices stayed strong. Talking ball, talking life, and telling me, in their way, what it meant to belong and stand tall.

CHAPTER 27

TRYING TO BUILD, WANTING TO LEAVE

Daddy was busy building our new house by the road, and Melvin was meant to be helping. But his mind was somewhere else entirely. His movements were slow and distracted, as if his body was in Ohio but his thoughts hadn't made the trip from Georgia.

The hammer slipped, the nails bent, and the boards never lined up quite right. At first, Daddy kept on, hoping Melvin would settle into the work. But finally his voice cut sharply with frustration: "Pay attention, boy."This house won't stand if it's built like what you're doing."

Melvin mumbled an apology, eyes down, hammer still in hand. "Trying... just thinking about things back in Georgia."

Daddy sighed and walked over, rubbing his forehead. He tried to steer Melvin back into the moment, reminding him this was work that mattered. Every nail counted, he said, because this house was going to be ours. But Melvin couldn't shake the weight in his chest. Georgia stayed with him, especially thoughts of Grandma. He missed the slow, familiar rhythms of a life once lived. No matter how many boards they lifted or holes they dug, he couldn't build fast enough to outrun that homesickness.

Still trying to stay patient, Daddy gave him a choice: either join him and Mr. George or head back inside. Melvin chose to retreat, his longing for Georgia clear in the way he walked back to the house. Daddy sighed again, then turned back to the task with quiet resolve, nodding for Mr. George to hand him the nails as they kept working.

CHAPTER 28

WHEN LOVE MEANS LETTING GO

Even with the noise and laughter in Ohio, Melvin missed Georgia. Momma and Daddy had brought him north, but his heart never caught up. Down there, he had space, his own room, and a quiet that felt steady and sure. In Ohio, the noise and closeness of our crowded house left little of either. Up here, he had to squeeze into a bed with me and Johnnie, in a house that already moved to its own beat. Nothing about it felt like his.

One evening, the house was still. No dishes clanging. No voices rising. Just Momma sitting at the table with her Bible open, the light above her throwing long shadows across the floor.

Melvin stood by the window, arms folded, looking out like he expected something to show up in the dark. After a while, Momma called him over.

He sat down slowly. No words at first.

"What's wrong, baby?" she asked.

He didn't look up. "I miss Georgia," he said. "Miss having my own bed. My own space." Momma didn't try to talk him out of it. She listened. Then said, "You had twelve years with Grandma. And when your daddy finishes the house, you'll have your own room again. But right now, you're with your family. That counts for something."

Melvin nodded, but it didn't land. Georgia was still pulling at him. You could see it in his face.

Momma reached across the table and took his hand. "Missing something don't mean you don't love what you got. It just means part of you's still down there. And that's alright."

Then he said it—quiet, but clear. "I wanna go back."

Momma didn't flinch. Just said, "I'll talk to your daddy."

Later that night, the kitchen was quiet. Daddy sat at the table, nursing a mug of coffee. Momma dried the last plate and told him straight: "Melvin wants to go back. He's homesick."

Daddy didn't say anything right away. He rubbed his hands together, thinking. Then nodded. When Melvin walked in, they didn't sugarcoat it.

"You still wanna go back?" Momma asked.

Melvin nodded.

Daddy stood up, walked over, and put a hand on his shoulder. "Alright," he said. "We'll get you there."

Melvin didn't cry, but something in him let go. You could see it in his shoulders. The tension eased, just a little.

That night, he told us. Said Momma and Daddy were letting him go back to Georgia. Not because they didn't want him. But because they loved him enough to let him be where he felt right.

At first, no one spoke. Then the questions came.

Ruby Nelle folded her arms tightly across her chest. Johnnie's face went slack, like he'd just been hit. Gladys and Juanita stared, unsure of what to say. The air thickened with confusion and frustration.

"Leave?" Ruby Nelle snapped. "Just like that?"

Johnnie shook his head. "So, Melvin gets to go back? Back to Grandma, back to Georgia? I've never even been down there. This place, this is all I know. But he gets to leave like he's the only one that matters? That ain't right. Nobody else even gets a say."

Gladys looked down at her hands. Juanita added, "Ain't family here too?"

The anger went deeper than just Melvin leaving. It came from being the ones left behind.

One person's happiness felt like it cost the rest of us something. We were left adjusting, squeezing into corners, doing what we could to make this new life work. Melvin didn't argue. He just stood there—no bragging, no smile. He hadn't expected this part. The weight of leaving wasn't light.

His voice dropped low. "Didn't ask for any of this. Just... don't feel right in here."

He tried to reassure us, but it met resistance. Then came a question, directed at me—was there any way I could go too? I shook my head and gave a quiet no. Tension wrapped the room. Ruby Nelle, still fuming, said nothing more. She sat in silence after that. The steady pop of the stove filled the space where words no longer reached. The next day moved slowly toward a bittersweet evening as the family prepared for Melvin's return to Georgia. Momma wanted the farewell to mean something, so she baked her signature peach cobbler.

It was more than just dessert. That cobbler carried connection, love, and a gentle challenge to Melvin's grandmother—an unspoken message in every bite.

As night fell, the house grew quiet. Mom and Dad's decision to send Melvin back to Georgia hung heavy in the air. Sensing the tension among her children, Momma stepped in. With a firm but gentle voice, she called us all together, leaving no room for disagreement.

She offered an explanation—Daddy needed rest before his shift. Then came a prayer. Hands joined, heads bowed. She asked for guidance, steadying us for the conversation ahead. Her words carried weight, setting the tone and making clear how important this moment had become.

Afterward, Melvin expressed his gratitude, promising to stay connected. Though still upset, his siblings agreed to write and keep in touch. Plans were made for visits and letters, with quiet faith that the bond would hold, even across the miles.

Johnnie, trying to lighten the moment, cracked a joke about baseball. Laughter followed, a small spark that softened the edges.

Despite the sadness of the decision, the family drew together, united in support.

Later, as the family gathered for dinner, Melvin sat quietly. His presence spoke louder than words. Before the meal, Momma pulled him into a hug, her voice warm and steady—reminding him that no matter the distance, he'd always be part of this family.

At the table, Melvin didn't speak. But his eyes moved slowly from face to face, memorizing each one. No words were needed. His gaze held everything: sadness, gratitude, connection. The silence between us was full, rich with emotion. In that look, we saw what couldn't be said: thanks, sorrow, and a quiet understanding that we were all still bound, even as one of us prepared to leave.

CHAPTER 29

FATHERS DON'T ALWAYS SAY IT STRAIGHT

Years later, during a family reunion in Boston, Dad and I sat on the swing on Ruby Nelle's porch. The swing moved slowly, the wood beneath us creaking in rhythm. The air carried the scent of fried catfish, garden soil, and late summer warmth. Laughter floated from the kitchen, but out on that porch, something quieter took hold.

Without warning, Dad's voice softened, slipping into memory. His words turned to Melvin—to the time he and Mom left him in Georgia with her mother to raise. That decision was always there in the background, never spoken yet never far away. We lived with it in silence, each of us knowing more than we said. Now, it cracked bit by bit. Regret showed up, not loud or dramatic but heavy. Carried for years, finally spoken.

It was the first time past choices were named without defense. No stiff posture. No excuse. Just truth.

He said Melvin knew the love had been real—that the effort had meant something. Whether it was truth or mercy, the words gave us what we needed. Peace followed—quiet, steady, and just enough. A smile softened his face. His shoulders relaxed. Then came a small nod—not to me, maybe, but to whatever he had finally let go.

Then came the shift. "Stay in tonight," he grinned. "Quit chasin' after them girls."

Laughter broke through. I promised to behave for now. The swing creaked again, settling into its old rhythm. But something had changed.

That swing carried more than two bodies; it held a kind of quiet healing. It asked for no speeches, only space between us. In that space, honesty could surface, given just a little time

CHAPTER 30

BETWEEN THEIR STORM

Early evening in 1951. Light from the setting sun cast a golden hue through the Harris windows. The room was thick with tension.

Juanita stood her ground—fiery and tense, fists clenched tight, eyes locked on Johnnie.

Across from her, Johnnie stood still, arms at his sides, a smirk tugging at the corner of his mouth—stubborn, unshaken.

I stood between them—small, teary-eyed, arms stretched out, trying to calm the storm. Hoping the shouting would stop, that everything might return to normal. But the tension ran deeper than words.

The fight hadn't come out of nowhere. Frustration had been building for weeks. Ruby Nelle, though the oldest, had started pulling away—her mind elsewhere, drifting from the family. With her attention gone, Momma leaned harder on Juanita, who picked up the slack as best she could.

But Johnnie didn't want to hear it. Being a year older didn't make Juanita the boss, not in his eyes. Orders didn't carry respect when he didn't believe it had been earned.

Still, Juanita stepped in when things got tense. That role landed on her shoulders, and the pressure kept growing until Johnnie snapped.

This wasn't about dishes or sweeping. It was pride. Power. The push and pull of growing up in a house too small for all that emotion. Everything pressed in from every side—too much to carry alone.

Frustration boiled over. Juanita tried to take control. Johnnie mocked her. Then came the shove. The punch. The two of them locked in a struggle, falling to the floor.

My small hands reached out, desperate to stop what had already gone too far. But the yelling, the blows, the chaos; it was more than I could stop.

Ruby Nelle stepped in because someone had to. Her grip was firm, her words sharper. She yanked them apart and made it clear: fighting fixed nothing. Before walking off, she shot me a quick nod and reminded us all—family doesn't tear itself apart. Family sticks together.

Juanita and Johnnie were still fuming, but the storm had passed. Ruby Nelle told them to clean up before Momma came home. The quiet that followed wasn't peace, but it was something close.

Johnnie stormed out in a huff and jumped on his bike. I asked if I could come along, but he brushed it off and pedaled away. Left standing there, tears welled as I watched him disappear up the road.

Still upset but trying to hold it in, Juanita pulled me close. Her voice was softer now, steadier.

She promised that one day we'd all understand each other better. Things had to change; this fighting was pulling us apart. And the weight of it? It didn't just fall on her or Johnnie. It reached all of us, even me, Gladys, and little Gloria.

CHAPTER 31

AFTER THE BENEDICTION

The old church carried the sharp scent of pine cleaner, and sunlight streamed through the high windows, casting a warm glow over the polished pews. The space felt alive in a way I had never known. It wasn't only the music or the preaching that gave it life. It was the people, carrying their hopes, troubles, and joys inside those walls.

Daddy stood tall at the pulpit, his voice booming as he wrapped up the fourth Sunday service. The room moved with him, words rising and falling like waves, holding every ear with ease. Folks leaned in, hanging on every word.

He preached with his usual fire, pointing to people one by one in the congregation. His words pressed them to serve, to commit, to answer God's call.

Sister Brown clapped with enthusiasm from the third row. In the back, I stood as Momma moved quietly along the side of the sanctuary, guiding the little ones. Her calm presence settled the room. No raised voice—just a gentle touch that brought everything into order.

After service, the women gathered around Daddy, praising his sermon. Momma moved through the side room in silence, gathering Sunday school supplies. Her eyes held the weight of exhaustion, not envy, but the quiet strain of always standing behind him. While the congregation lifted him up, her burden remained unseen.

Later that night, tension hung thick in the kitchen. Momma scrubbed the counter in short, sharp motions. Daddy loosened his tie and spoke, trying to soothe her, but his words didn't land. At church, he soaked in admiration. At home, she faded into the background.

The argument didn't erupt; it settled in, slow and heavy. Momma's voice shook slightly but held firm. An apology came, followed by a promise to do better. But Momma said words weren't enough anymore. What she needed was honesty—spoken plainly, not brushed aside.

Daddy's silence toward Momma's sacrifices cut deep. He overlooked her pain, her strength, and her need for respect. It showed itself not only in front of the church but also within our home. His private apologies weren't enough. What Momma needed was steady, visible recognition, not just quiet words behind closed doors. Change required more than promises; it demanded action. She deserved more than silent support and unspoken gratitude. But no one offered a solution.

The hurt between them had settled in long ago. What she needed was something Daddy had never learned to give.

The house fell still. Juanita wrapped her arms around me, holding tight as voices behind the walls rose, then softened. And then Momma's voice rang out—raw, steady, and demanding the respect she was owed.

The quiet that followed settled like weight across the room. Then Daddy spoke, his voice low, admitting she was right. The tension cracked. Juanita took my hand and led me outside. A faint smile crossed her face. The worst had passed for now.

CHAPTER 32

BOSTON BOUND, WINTERSVILLE BRUISED

The next Sunday, soft murmurs spread among the women at church. Smiles lit their faces, but their comments cut deep. Some called Momma lucky to have Daddy, questioning why a man like him stayed with someone so reserved.

Momma held her head high—shoulders squared, steps steady. Without saying a word, her presence alone delivered an answer stronger than any sermon Daddy ever gave.

Rumors swirled about Daddy and another woman, but nothing was ever proven. There was occasional flirting, but no signs of actual infidelity.

After church, Ruby Nelle gathered the family. The house hummed with its usual sounds—the creaking of Daddy's rocking chair. She stood in the center of the room, fists clenched, voice shaky but firm.

Ruby Nelle announced she wanted to move to Boston.

Momma's hand flew to her chest, stunned. Daddy's jaw tightened, though his eyes softened as he took in the news. She explained that Uncle Willie B and Aunt Sarah had given her a place to stay. It came with the promise of opportunities Wintersville could not offer.

Momma's voice cracked as she told Ruby Nelle how much she'd miss her. Daddy paused before speaking, his voice filled with pride and quiet support. Still, the strain on his face showed the weight of the moment.

Juanita froze. Johnnie scoffed, brushing it off as a passing phase. Gladys's voice trembled with worry. Ruby Nelle stayed calm as she laid out her reasons. More jobs, better schools, and the chance to grow beyond what our small town could offer all weighed in her favor. She spoke like someone who had already made peace with leaving.

When Gladys pushed back, worried about how we'd manage without her, Ruby Nelle held steady. She reminded her of her own strength and said Juanita and Momma would still be there to guide them. The pain didn't stop her from standing firm.

She crouched beside Gloria and me, wrapping our hands in hers, warm and steady. Her voice stayed soft as she gently explained her reasons for leaving. Gloria tugged on her hand, asking why. The question came again: why not stay?

Ruby Nelle smiled, tears brimming but held back. Some people needed distance to grow. Still, letters, calls, and stories would always find their way back. She pulled us into a tight hug, promising we were bound by blood—no matter the place, no matter the miles.

That evening, Momma pressed her hair near the wood-burning stove. The fire hissed, filling the room with the scent of dinner and hot hair grease. As the comb moved through her thick hair, steam rose in thin clouds. Ruby Nelle sat upright, gripping the chair, flinching when the comb grazed her scalp.

"Stay still," Momma said firmly. This wasn't just a visit. It was the beginning—the first step away from Wintersville. In a place like Boston, first impressions mattered.

"No need to ask if it hurts. Your face says enough," Gladys said softly, eyes on Ruby Nelle. Then she lowered her voice. "That kind of burn only stays for a little while; it doesn't let go easy."

Ruby Nelle chuckled. "My scalp's always been tender."

Ruby Nelle brushed it off with a half-laugh and a surface-level response. It wasn't a real answer; it was a deflection. A prime example of how detachment often shows up: not in anger or rebellion, but in subtle refusals to connect. No admission of pain, no opening up, no chance of leaning into Gladys's softness.

When the last strand was done, she checked the mirror—hair smooth, neat, grown. One remark claimed she looked like a woman ready for the world. Gladys nodded. Ruby Nelle smiled, thankful and ready.

She wasn't just receiving attention now; she was stepping into a new role, both visually and emotionally. She had become someone expected to lead, carry poise, and leave childhood behind. Emotional distance was the only way she'd learned to handle the pressure.

Before bed, she tied her scarf to protect her hair, glanced once more in the mirror, and took a slow breath. This next step wasn't just hers; it carried meaning, something she took on for everyone back home. The care still showed, like when she straightened Gloria's collar or folded the towels just right. But the patience behind it all was beginning to wear thin.

The girl who used to hum while brushing her own hair now moved in silence, jaw tight, eyes already elsewhere.

CHAPTER 33

BOSTON WAS THE BEGINNING

The next morning, we kept to ourselves. Juanita didn't say a word. Even Johnnie moved slowly and carefully. Ruby Nelle was getting ready to leave for Boston, and no one had the words for how to handle the moment. The thought of her being gone hung over us, too heavy to name.

She stood at the door with her suitcase in hand, dressed in a bright yellow blouse and a pressed black skirt. She moved like someone stepping into the unknown—hopeful yet carrying the weight of goodbye in every crease.

She'd stayed up late the night before, folding and refolding, checking the bag again and again. Each item packed felt like a quiet promise. Leaving that morning wasn't just a trip—it marked a change for all of us.

Juanita stayed off to the side, arms crossed, her face set like stone. The others moved around, saying what needed to be said. No one asked her anything, and she didn't offer.

Bags zipped shut, with one last glance sweeping the corners for anything left behind.

Ruby Nelle knelt beside Gloria and me, told us to behave and not give Juanita any trouble. A promise to write and visit remained, though the farewell carried a finality that couldn't be ignored.

Juanita's tears came as the cab rolled in—first a shimmer in her eyes, then a steady flow down her cheeks.

Ruby Nelle's step off the porch marked more than a goodbye. It marked the beginning of the future she had been reaching toward for so long. Momma had always believed it was possible, even if believing meant learning to let her go.

One last hug came—tight, silent, full of everything words couldn't say. Ruby Nelle blinked back tears and promised to stay in touch. Something changed in that moment. The road ahead belonged to all of us.

She was the first to walk through that door with a suitcase in hand, but the pattern had already taken root. Momma understood—others would follow. Not right away, but in time. The Great Migration, here we come.

We stood together as the cab eased down Route 22, its outline shrinking until it disappeared from view. Once gone, the house grew quieter—like something essential had slipped out with her.

The silence she left behind filled every corner. No more soft humming in the kitchen. No more quiet hands settling the younger ones when tension rose. Ruby Nelle had been our steadying force. With her gone, the weight of her responsibilities shifted to Juanita. Thirteen and still finding her way, she now had to carry more than just her own growing pains.

The rhythm of our home changed like a song missing a verse that once held us together.

Letters arrived every few weeks, brimming with stories of Boston. Crowded sidewalks, towering buildings, and a new job at the nursing home filled the pages.

Momma read the letters aloud, and for a moment Ruby Nelle felt close again. Her voice carried across the miles, steady and sure.

Those letters stirred something deep in Momma. Boston stopped feeling like a faraway idea and started sounding like an open door. With each one, a quiet shift took place—Momma began thinking about joining her.

Ruby Nelle's absence changed the way things moved in the house. Rooms stayed quieter, and routines shifted. Still, the thought of her chasing something better gave the rest of us quiet encouragement.

CHAPTER 34

THE PROTECTOR WE DIDN'T EXPECT

One peaceful summer morning, our family walked home from church. The sun warmed our backs, and birds called from the trees. Momma led us, tilting her hat to block the light, and we talked about the sermon.

Then, out of nowhere, a woman rushed at Momma, her face tight with anger. She shoved Momma hard. None of us saw it coming or noticed the signs beforehand, so when it happened, it caught us off guard.

Juanita didn't hesitate. Though small, she launched herself at the woman and locked her arms around her neck. The woman gasped, legs buckling, but Juanita held on. After a tense moment, she let go. The woman staggered back, panting, red in the face.

Daddy arrived with slow, deliberate steps. He placed himself between Juanita and the woman, standing tall as the tension grew. The woman pointed at Juanita, her hand shaking. Juanita stayed ready—eyes steady, chest rising fast.

Momma raised her voice, demanding answers—why bring this chaos to her doorstep, to her family? Her words trembled with fury and disbelief. Beside her, a voice stayed soft but firm, declaring they'd face it together. The time had come for the truth to stand in the light.

Still shaken, the woman stepped forward and apologized. But Daddy didn't accept it.

His response came fast and sharp, leaving no room for doubt. He followed it with a promise to speak with the Bishop and make sure she'd never return to the church.

The message rang out beyond its target, landing on every ear nearby. Any shame that tried to creep in through the back door was sealed off for good.

Her hands trembled as she gathered her belongings. The crowd stepped aside, their silence cutting deeper than any word.

Juanita stood still, jaw tight, stance unshaken. Momma leaned in close and offered a soft thank you. Daddy placed a hand on Momma's shoulder, steady and calm, though neither of them had answers for what lay ahead.

Later, I thought about that day. The woman's attack didn't stand alone. The silence around us had already started to loosen the seams. Glances and stiff smiles spoke louder than words. When Ruby Nelle left, the last shield disappeared, and old tensions crept in. The moment shook us, but more than that, it revealed a truth we hadn't wanted to face. Spite had been sitting quietly, even inside the church. What once felt steady had begun to give way. When one protector stepped back, Juanita rose without hesitation.

She stood tall, alert, fierce in her defense of the family. Momma, still trembling, managed a nod of thanks. We left the church in silence. The storm had passed, but something had shifted.

Momma walked ahead, her face unreadable. Daddy stayed close, his hand on her back. The rest of us followed, quiet, each carrying the weight of what had happened.

At home, everything felt different. In the kitchen, Momma and Juanita moved with purpose, but the usual rhythm was gone. The sound of dishes and water faded under the weight in the air. I sat off to the side, trying to make sense of it. Juanita had stepped in to protect us, but the reason behind it all still floated out of reach. The world felt tilted, like something beneath us had shifted. In the next room, Gladys and Johnnie whispered with more urgency than usual. The church no longer felt like home. The warmth had vanished.

From the kitchen, Momma's voice cracked as she wondered aloud what had become of the place that once gave her peace. Daddy answered gently, more confused than reassuring. Then Juanita spoke—clear, certain—saying no one would lay hands on us again.

During dinner, we bowed our heads to pray, but the words didn't reach. Food was left untouched. No one had an appetite. Momma's face looked drained. Juanita, steady and watchful, sat across from her. Something unnamed had broken loose, and no one knew how to stop it.

The house stayed still, thick with things no one could say. Momma stood at the window, gripping the curtain, staring into the yard. Her body leaned forward, heavy with more than the day's work. Daddy sat at the table, fingers tapping a slow rhythm against the wood. In her mind, the woman's rage replayed—shouts, shoves, hatred poured out in front of the congregation. That anger hadn't come from nowhere. The worst part wasn't the attack—it was the eyes that turned afterward, the silence that followed.

That church had always given her space to breathe. But now, its foundation had cracked. Kindness turned shallow. Glances turned sharp. The refuge had become a test. Daddy kept looking over, trying to read her, not fully grasping what she carried. To him, it seemed like gossip that would fade. He believed people would move on. But for Momma, trust was gone. Every whisper, every look pulled her deeper into doubt.

They sat in silence. Nothing was said, but everything was felt. The space between them filled with distance neither could cross. The outburst and what followed weren't something Momma could dismiss. It touched something sacred. Daddy, steady as he was, stood in the middle of something falling apart, unsure of how to stop it.

Looking back, the attack wasn't the deepest wound. The real damage came from the silence that followed. That silence cut sharper than words. The woman's rage wasn't hers alone. It had been growing behind handshakes and hymns. When Ruby Nelle left, it gave others room to let it loose. Without her presence, they saw an opening—and took it. No one stepped forward. Their silence spoke volumes.

That day drew a line we hadn't seen before. The church looked the same, but the spirit inside it had changed. It no longer held the peace we once trusted. Resentment had settled in. Even now, the image that lingers isn't the chaos. It's Juanita—small, but certain—stepping forward. One protector stepped back. Another rose, steady and unshaken, even as everything else fell away.

CHAPTER 35

THE WEIGHT SHE NEVER SET DOWN

The Great Migration swept millions of African Americans from the rural South between 1916 and the mid-1970s. They fled racial violence, segregation, and lives boxed in by limited choices, heading north, west, and into the Midwest in search of freedom, stability, and the hope of something better. Wintersville didn't need signs to make the rules clear. Everyone knew where Black families could live and how far their dreams were allowed to reach. Momma faced Boston with quiet determination, seeing a chance to raise us in a place where her faith could grow and opportunity wasn't cut off at every turn.

After the dinner dishes were washed and put away, Momma and Daddy slipped into the trailer. The stillness between them hung heavy, pressing down like a weight too much to lift. Momma settled into her worn chair, clutching a tissue, her eyes shimmering with tears that hovered but never fell. Her hands trembled as if stirring something unspoken deep within. Daddy sat across from her, rough hands clasped together, gaze fixed on the floor. After a long pause, his voice broke the silence, soft and rough, carrying the burden of years spent holding back.

Years later, Gladys shared what passed between them that night. Daddy had told Momma he hadn't fallen in love with her before they married. Help was needed to raise Ulysses, Amos, and Ruby Nelle. The truth came out just before our move to Boston, along with his apology for the silence he'd kept all those years.

The story shifted something inside me. I had always pictured their marriage as one built on love that deepened over time, but after that confession, the foundation felt less certain, like something solid beginning to slip. When I asked why Momma never spoke of it, Gladys said she chose to carry the pain alone, knowing we couldn't fix it. Instead, she focused on raising us, setting her own hurt aside.

Sitting with that truth, I began to understand the depth of her giving. No breakdowns in front of us, no sign of how hard it had been. Steady every day, pushing through, holding the family together in silence. A quiet nod settled inside me—not from having all the answers, but from the understanding that they managed with what they had, and somehow, through it all, gave us everything they could.

CHAPTER 36

FROM HOLDING ON TO LETTING GO

Momma stood at the edge of the porch, arms crossed over her chest, her red-rimmed eyes worn and tired. Something stayed locked inside—grief, frustration, and the cold Ohio wind biting at her. No glance backward when words came. Her eyes fixed beyond the quiet yard, past Ellsworth Street, toward a future she believed could hold more for all of us.

That moment stirred something deep within her that had built up over the years. Daddy's confession only confirmed the truth. Nothing remained here but routine and resignation.

Momma thought of Ruby Nelle, who had left for Boston two years earlier during the second wave of The Great Migration. Ruby Nelle's letters painted pictures of a life far beyond Wintersville's reach—a life filled with promise. With each letter, the idea of Boston settled deeper in Momma's mind, like a suitcase packed and waiting by the door.

Boston was a way out of a cycle she refused to pass down—the smallness, the quiet shame, the limits hidden behind tradition. Wintersville made sense to me—the creeks, the schoolyard, the endless Sundays at church. But Momma believed in something more for us. Ebony magazines stacked on the table, stories about jobs in shipyards, better schools, and neighborhoods that welcomed folks like us. Ruby Nelle's voice over the phone carried a lightness, as if something heavy had lifted from her.

Boston didn't just keep Ruby afloat; it gave her space to expand. She started with babysitting and kitchen work. Then came Bobby

Sutherland—religious, calm, steady, and kind. The two were a good match, growing and building a life together. Valerie was born into a life shaped by opportunity, not restriction.

Valerie became the reason to settle down, stay focused, and keep moving forward. No child deserved to grow up stuck in survival mode. After getting married in Boston and giving birth, leaving Wintersville became less about escape and more about building something solid from the ground up.

Momma never painted Boston as a dream. She spoke of it without rose-colored promises or illusions. For her, it held more options than Wintersville ever would—more doors cracked open, fewer nailed shut. No fantasy—only forward motion. Not just surviving, but living.

Daddy used to sit with his Bible open, fingers pressed to the pages as if the answers might rise up from the print. Maybe he believed the right verse would speak to him, guiding him to keep the family anchored. But by then, Momma's course had already taken shape. The heart had moved long before any words were spoken. A new path had already begun, traced quietly and steadily.

The choice to leave wasn't born of bitterness. No hatred for Wintersville fueled the decision. It came from something deeper than anger—a quiet insistence that life held more than what this small town offered. She stepped away because she believed in more—for us, for herself. The hope was for her children to grow up with possibilities, not patterns. That decision came from a place of deep hope, not resentment.

Talk of The Great Migration often centers on the miles—how far families traveled. The focus stays on the distance between where they were and what they left behind. Every step forward carries the weight of that in-between space.

But the journey stretched beyond geography—it carried belief. Belief that something better existed beyond what had always been. That something more waited past the edge of what they'd lived through.

That morning, Momma's hands rested still on the counter. Her face was calm. No tears came. No explanation followed. None was needed. The message was clear: her mind was made up.

The decision didn't appear out of nowhere. It had formed over the years, built through sacrifice, daily compromise, and strength that never wavered.

The full plan hadn't formed, but the direction was certain. Departure was coming.

In that steady, unspoken choice, their footsteps joined millions of other Black families—not just fleeing the past but reaching for something more. A life where dignity had room to grow. Where doors opened. Where survival led to something like joy.

Perhaps it began with Ruby Nelle's letters, filled with city stories and pride hidden between the lines. Clarity struck during the church outburst—a sharp moment of reckoning. Love alone no longer shielded her children. Or the heavy pressure of staying pushed her to let go.

She had held everything together. But the life surrounding her had grown too tight.

Daddy, shaped by hardship and routine, placed his faith in the steel mill. To him, that life was familiar—steady, fixed, and easy to follow.

But Momma looked past all that. The Navy Yard and railway jobs in Boston were waiting for him. Boston opened doors that Wintersville couldn't offer. Not some far-off dream, but a real step forward. A clear move toward something better.

Ruby Nelle had left with little more than a diploma and determination. Something real took shape—work, love, a home. Momma took it in, steady and measured. No chasing dreams—just making room for a new, better life to take shape.

No argument came outright. Silence stretched between them, but Momma had learned how to read it. Waiting no longer made sense. The kitchen table held the standoff—one rooted in what was, the other reaching for what might come. One stayed still. The other moved.

Clarity rose from within, not from anyone else. Silence didn't grant permission—it marked a line. And one step crossed beyond it.

There was no flinching and no begging. Just forward motion and letting go of what no longer fit. A step into something broader—no map, no spotlight, only steady courage.

The mill offered steady wages, but no real future. Not for the children. Not the kind of future that feeds dignity, growth, or purpose. That truth needed no debate; it stood firm. Eyes locked on a place with more promise. Once the vision formed, the move came with no hesitation. Strength gathered, a choice made, carried through with full resolve.

Leaving wasn't just a family decision; it echoed a larger shift. Black families walking away from the familiar because staying meant shrinking. And some lives were never meant to stay small.

Moving ahead—not with all the answers, but with the hope of something better than what was being left behind.

CHAPTER 37

THE PROMISE IN THE DIRT

Seven years old, I was playing with Peewee and Clarence beside the house when Juanita called out. Her voice carried a seriousness that made clear this wasn't teasing or fussing.

I brushed dirt from my small hands and ran toward her. Juanita crouched down until our eyes met, speaking in a calm, steady tone. The decision had been made Boston would be our next home. Momma had already decided, and turning back wasn't part of the plan.

The word "Boston" stopped me cold, as if we were stepping into a life that didn't belong to us. The picture didn't fit. Wintersville held everything familiar: our church, our backyard, our people.

Why? Juanita said Momma wanted something better. Folks in town didn't treat us right. Jobs paid more up north. Schools had more to offer. Ruby Nelle had already started building a life there.

I didn't ask any more questions. My voice stayed small, but my thoughts were loud. The news felt too big to carry and too heavy to set down.

After Juanita walked away, I drifted toward the ditch between our house and the Blackwell family. That patch of ground always gave me something steady to lean on. I picked up a smooth rock, turned it over in my hand, then placed it gently at the edge where grass met soft earth, whispering a promise to myself that someday, I'd come back for it.

That promise became my way of holding on. Even if everything around me started shifting, that stone would stay put.

As I walked back to the house, I glanced over my shoulder again and again, holding tight to that ditch, that rock, that small piece of life, just a little longer.

CHAPTER 38

A FATHER'S QUIET PLAN

Remembering the family reunion in Boston back in '87. The yard overflowed with laughter, music, and plates of food. Dad pulled me aside, face calm, though something heavy weighed on his heart. He motioned for me to follow. We stepped away from the noise, seeking a quiet corner. His eyes moved slowly, searching for the right place to begin.

He took a seat, hands resting on the table, voice soft. Momma's move to Boston hadn't been easy. That choice carried weight, especially for the one who stayed behind. Distance unsettled us; the unknown added to it.

But love for the family pushed past all that, even if it meant separation for a while.

Not much was said in that moment, yet the silence between words carried more weight than anything spoken aloud.

I nodded steadily, absorbing everything without speaking.

Dad leaned forward—the kind of movement people make when memories surface and details sharpen. Every effort had gone into keeping the family safe, even when the words remained unspoken. Behind the silence was the full weight of provision. Before leaving Wintersville, they'd made a hard decision. Dad would stay behind to provide support, planning to join us later, once Momma had us settled.

My thoughts turned to life without a familiar presence—Momma navigating Boston's crowded streets, new schools, unfamiliar faces.

Dad moved deliberately, not rushed, following a plan already laid out. He wrote down a number—the number of Bishop Mason, national presiding bishop of the Church of God in Christ. That name carried weight in our world. Doubt crept in, but the promise made to Momma—that the family would have a real chance—pushed him forward. When he finally reached for the phone, his grip remained steady.

Once Bishop Mason answered, Dad shared the story—the move, the reasons, and the role he couldn't immediately fill. His words were careful, leaving no room for doubt. Bishop Mason listened, then offered reassurance and a name: Elder Young, a steady leader with a congregation in Boston, known for helping families find their footing.

The next call came soon after. Dad sat at the table, the slip of paper in front of him, the number waiting. His hand hovered over the rotary phone, not hesitating for permission, but waiting for the right moment. Asking for help didn't come easily. Always the one who others leaned on, he was now on unfamiliar ground.

The call went through. The introduction came first, simple and direct. Then the request followed—help Momma and the children settle once they arrived. Elder Young didn't hesitate. His voice, warm and steady, promised the church would be ready to welcome them.

After hanging up, the room stayed still. The call had done more than arrange logistics; it offered reassurance. Distance hadn't diminished responsibility. A way had been found to ensure the family would be supported from the moment they stepped off the bus.

Dad leaned back, a small smile tugging at the corners of his mouth. In soft, quiet moments—just as I remembered—his eyes would close. Satisfaction settled in without words. The balance held steady: loss met hope, vulnerability met strength. Uncertainty was answered by careful planning. Choosing to remain behind while supporting Momma's move reflected deep responsibility, quiet resilience, and a faith-driven optimism rooted in the church.

The support from his faith community provided essential emotional sustenance, guiding him through this challenging crossroads.

CHAPTER 39

HER VISION, HIS RESTRAINT

The morning sun slipped through thin curtains, casting a soft glow across the living room. Momma's bags stood neatly by the front door, packed and ready. The house held a quiet stillness—the kind that settles when something important is about to change.

Momma stood in the center of the room, purse over one shoulder, steady and sure. Her move to Boston came from vision, not fear. This wasn't about escaping trouble; it was about reaching for something greater. Like many Black families during The Great Migration, ours sought more than what places like Wintersville could offer. We wanted growth, opportunity, and a life defined by more than hard work and sacrifice.

This shift went beyond geography. It expanded possibilities. Familiar routines were left behind intentionally, not hurriedly. The goal remained clear—better schools, steadier jobs, and a community moving forward.

Our family joined a bigger movement than ourselves—not as escapees, but as builders— choosing a future beyond the limits of small-town life.

Daddy sat nearby, hands clasped, eyes tracking every move. He made no attempt to stop her. Understanding had already settled in. The agreement was clear: he would stay behind with the boys. Johnnie was fourteen; I was seven. We'd wait until school started in the fall. The girls— Juanita at fifteen, Gladys ten, and little Gloria, only five—would go ahead with Momma. Our belief was rooted in preparing the landing before taking the leap.

Before leaving, Momma knelt in front of Johnnie and me, voice calm, eyes steady. The plan was clear: she'd go ahead, set things up, find a place, and then send for the rest of us. Johnnie nodded while I fought back tears. Daddy came over silently, resting his hands on our shoulders—a quiet anchor in the uncertainty.

Juanita stood nearby with quiet strength, her suitcase resting firmly at her side. Daddy's gaze lingered on her, recognizing his daughter rising to the occasion, ready to support Momma by watching over the younger children. In that brief moment, he entrusted her with a silent yet weighty responsibility.

Gladys, impatient and already halfway to the door, rolled her eyes at the quiet emotions swirling around her. Gloria clung to her Raggedy Ann doll, rubbing sleepy eyes as she leaned against Momma's leg.

Momma straightened Gloria's beret, kissed her forehead, and stepped outside. Newton waited in the car, engine humming softly. Daddy opened the screen door, holding it as Momma led the girls out. Each step he took toward the car seemed drawn from a deeper well of strength.

After the bags were loaded, Newton gave a small nod, the engine purring gently as they climbed in. Momma turned once, eyes scanning the porch—taking in Daddy, then us—before slipping inside. There were no long goodbyes, only one final glance filled with quiet urgency and love. No kisses passed between Momma and Daddy— only an unspoken restraint, shaped by personal pride.

The car pulled away toward the bus station in Steubenville. Johnnie and I stood beside Daddy on the porch, watching until it vanished up the road. This marked a significant emotional milestone, the fracturing of the family unit unfolding before our eyes. Left behind was the silent weight of absence, confusion, and longing.

The house became a holding place for grief, loneliness, and everything that had shifted. A heavy emptiness settled immediately, impossible to ignore. The first wave of confusion hit hard— difficult to explain, and even harder to manage. Stillness offered no comfort; it only amplified the absence.

Ruby Nelle's move had set everything in motion. Our family's place in the long river of The Great Migration had been shaped by Momma's will and a reluctant Dad who never intended to leave. A promise lingered—that Boston held something better.

CHAPTER 40

BROTHERHOOD IN A SHIFTING HOUSE

The next day, Newton brought his son, Junior, over to stay with us. He was ten years old, short— but taller than me—athletic, and full of loud, boundless energy shaped by Little League baseball. I liked him immediately.

Johnnie, already standing at the edge of young adulthood, saw an opportunity for leadership. Attention always pulled him in, and with two runts—one seven, the other ten—it made for a perfect setup for fun. Never once were we left behind.

Much later, Junior confided in me that he'd always admired Johnnie as an older brother. But I kept pace. We moved as one—close, steady, ready for whatever lay ahead.

Junior's arrival brought fresh energy, shifting the rhythm of our days. He carried himself with lively confidence, quick on his feet, disciplined by Little League. The bond formed almost instantly. Looking back, our connection felt natural—two kids quietly seeking steady ground during an uncertain time.

My quick attachment to Junior wasn't just about finding someone new to play with; it revealed a deeper need for connection, for something familiar to hold onto amid so much change.

CHAPTER 41

THREE BOYS, ONE HOUSE, TWO GOODBYES

When Momma set her sights on Boston, the ground beneath us began to shift. But before the full move took place, Johnnie and I remained in Ohio with Daddy while she headed north to get things in order. For about two and a half months, it was Daddy, Johnnie, Junior, and me. At nearly eight years old, those weeks stood out as a rare calm amid so much shifting. Childhood offered few moments as warm and steady as those.

By the time Momma decided it was time to leave Wintersville, things in Boston were already coming together—housing lined up, church connections reaching out, and a sense that a new chapter was quietly waiting for us.

My Uncle Willie B. had moved to Boston in 1945 shortly after his military service ended and well before Momma headed north. He found steady work at Bilt-Rite Rubber, and by the time she arrived, roots had already been laid, and a solid life had been built in the city alongside Aunt Sarah.

Uncle Willie B. joined the Nation of Islam and opened a small restaurant with Cousin T.J. A promise followed: they would help Daddy find work. He and Aunt Sarah planned to support Momma and my sisters as they adjusted to their new surroundings. But with limited space, everyone couldn't live together, so they had to spread out.

Momma and Juanita stayed with Cousin T.J. and his wife, Eula Bess, in another part of the city while Momma searched for an apartment. Gladys and Gloria moved in with Uncle Willie B. and Aunt Sarah, who lived in a different neighborhood. That was the only way to make it work—too many people and not enough room.

At the heart of this decision to split the family across separate homes stood a familiar truth of The Great Migration made in pursuit of something better. Each move carried meaning— resilience shaped by experience, resourcefulness passed down through generations.

Hope remained tucked into every transition. Uncle Willie B.'s promise to help Daddy find work, and Aunt Sarah's offer to support Momma and my sisters, reflected how Black families leaned on extended kin to navigate unfamiliar cities. That kind of support offered more than shelter. It created connections and steadied those trying to find their footing in an uncertain place.

Still, separation had its own costs. Beneath the surface, a growing awareness took hold. Our world had started to stretch apart. The split ran deeper than housing limitations; emotions quietly intensified, identities shifted, and each of us began negotiating our place in a family learning how to stay together while living apart.

CHAPTER 42

WHAT JUNIOR BROUGHT

One evening, Daddy sat at the kitchen table, his Bible open in front of him, hands folded as if he had just finished a prayer. Without Momma and the girls, the house grew quiet and heavy, and that stillness allowed Daddy to take charge in his own way. Not much was said, but when words came, they carried weight.

Dad kept Johnnie, Junior, and me busy—cutting grass, cleaning, handling whatever chores needed doing. That summer became a stretch of waiting, working, and growing up a bit faster than expected.

Life shifted after Momma and the girls left. Johnnie kept the family thread intact through letters. Momma described the Boston church as open and full of life—the folks greeted her kindly, the choir carried the songs, and the preacher held everyone's attention. She spoke of it as a place that felt steady, welcoming, and real. As a preacher himself, Daddy didn't simply listen. Hearing about another man's delivery sparked a familiar fire. The message mattered, but so did the way it moved people.

Mentioning that preacher's style wasn't just sharing information; it served as a subtle challenge, and Daddy was never one to back down from a challenge.

Juanita wrote about the pace of life in Boston—how fast everything moved compared to the calm, familiar days in Wintersville.

Daddy worked long shifts, returning home carrying the weight of the day. Although we missed Momma deeply, his steady presence brought structure. Trust rested in Momma's ability to build our future, while preparation on Daddy's end ensured we'd be ready when it was finally time to leave.

CHAPTER 43

PORCH LAUGHTER, DIRT ROADS, AND BERRY JUICE

During overnight shifts, one rule stood firm: don't leave the house. The bedroom door closed at sunrise, and after a quick bite and tea, he went to bed. We sat down at the table once the house was quiet. Most mornings, there were only biscuits to eat. On rare mornings, there was also a slice of ham. Those summer mornings made even a plain breakfast feel like something worth remembering.

After eating, Junior and I would burst through the front door like the day had been waiting on us. The dirt road came alive, dust rising behind us like smoke. Laughter filled the air—bold, loud, untouched by worry.

Johnnie stayed behind most mornings, leaning on the porch post, arms folded like he had better things to do. A little half-smile would creep in, pretending to be too old for our nonsense. But his eyes gave him away. The urge to run tugged at him, too—he just wouldn't give in.

He was still a kid, truth be told, trying hard not to look like one. He had some responsibilities. But that same pull—to race up the road and lose himself in the day—never let go.

Later, we'd sprawl out in the grass, staring at the sky, turning clouds into lions, dragons, or whatever else we dreamed up. Junior once pointed to one and claimed a lion was chasing a wagon across the sky. No one questioned it, not for a second.

While Dad slept, Johnnie, Junior, and I turned the yard and the countryside of Wintersville into our kingdom. Kids on an adventure, building forts from boxes and inventing games until nightfall.

Then we'd go back inside, remembering Dad's rule. Daddy wasn't a cook like Momma, but no one complained. Nothing fancy—just solid, stick-to-your-ribs comfort food. Hot dogs, boiled or pan-fried, served on two slices of bread with mustard. Johnnie would open canned pork and beans, heating them in their own sauce.

We helped Dad with the yard, mowing grass and trimming hedges. That summer, the work didn't feel like chores. Each of us stayed focused, doing our part to keep things moving.

Freedom came with rules—Dad made sure of that. Boundaries were clear, and we were expected to follow them. But long summer days and fewer eyes sometimes made it easy to stretch those lines.

One evening after dinner, just before dark, the family was ushered outside. The sky glowed with soft shades of pink and orange. Daddy took a seat on the porch while the yard filled with laughter and motion, chasing lightning bugs. Junior caught one and held it up like a rare jewel.

That tiny blinking light drew all of us in. Plenty of lightning bugs had danced through summers past, but something about that night slowed time. Daddy's deep laugh drifted from the porch, wrapping around us like a blanket. That stretch of evening held a kind of peace I didn't recognize until much later.

One bright afternoon, the three of us—Johnnie, Junior, and I—walked to the berry fields with empty baskets. Under the hot sun, our hands reached for the fattest blackberries. My fingers and mouth were stained purple from eating too many. Juice ran down my chin, and I didn't care. The flavor burst in my mouth and made everything else fade away.

Johnnie laughed as he picked, tossing berries into his basket without much aim. Sometimes he hit, sometimes he missed, but he never seemed to care.

Junior picked a little, then slipped back into fooling around.

His eyes stayed busy, always searching the field for something else to mess with. After a while, we wandered into a nearby meadow and lay down on the grass, since a blanket was something we never thought to bring.

Blackberries got passed around, along with bologna and cheese sandwiches. Not long after, a stomachache hit—I'd eaten too many berries. I curled up in the grass, tears welling fast. Johnnie and Junior just laughed, shaking their heads like they'd seen it coming all along.

CHAPTER 44

AUDIE MURPHY AND THE MUDDY ADVENTURE

One fateful night, temptation got the best of us. Fueled by the thrill of being unsupervised, our audacity pushed us too far. The line between harmless fun and real trouble faded fast, and soon enough, we were knee-deep in something we hadn't planned.

The drive-in down the road had a new movie, *To Hell and Back* with Audie Murphy, and the pull was strong.

Daddy had already left for his overnight shift at the mill, same as always, leaving the house in the hands of Johnnie, Junior, and me. Boredom took over—too much time, nothing to do, energy spilling in every direction.

Johnnie, never short on ideas, tossed out a plan: sneak off to catch the movie. A promise hung in the air—we'd be back before anything could go wrong. Still, hesitation lingered.

Daddy's rules weren't fuzzy: No one was to leave the house after sundown.

Junior hesitated, weighing the what-ifs, especially with Ms. Yetts watching. Trouble never stayed hidden long on that block.

Johnnie shrugged. "Stories over. She's on *Gunsmoke* now. Long as we move quick, we're good."

Silence filled the room like a stop sign, forcing second thoughts. What if we took too long? What if something stopped us on the way back? Not many words were said, but the ones that came stuck.

Johnnie didn't flinch. He brushed off the doubts like dust, saying it'd be quick—no harm done. The chance to do something bold, off-limits, and grown was too tempting to pass up.

He leaned against the kitchen counter, his arms crossed like his mind was already made up. "Audie Murphy's gonna die a hundred times on that screen tonight. Wanna hear about it tomorrow from somebody else—or say you were part of it?"

He glanced at Junior, who stood there biting his lip—the usual sign he wasn't so sure.

Johnnie pushed on. "In and out, that's all. Nobody's checkin' for us this time of night. Daddy won't be home till morning, and with Momma in Boston, the house is ours every night he works the over-night shift.

What's the worst that can happen? Just a movie, nothing more."

Junior shifted in his seat, still thinking it through, but he didn't say no.

Johnnie smirked, already heading for the door. "Alright then. Y'all can sit here bored stiff, or you can come watch a real hero on the main screen."

Junior didn't push back, and with Johnnie already reaching for the door, I followed.

The road called, dirt underfoot still holding the day's leftover warmth. The sun had just slipped behind the hills, and the sky glowed deep purple and burnt orange. Johnnie kept our spirits up with jokes, including one about a scarecrow.

It took me a second to get it, but I laughed right along with him.

Walking in step, our shadows stretched long across the dirt road, pulled by the sinking sun. A few cars rolled past, headlights sweeping over us like stage lights. Each mile pushed the world behind a little more, like we were stepping into something wild and wide open.

After the two-and-a-half-mile walk, the glow of the screen appeared like a lighthouse. Just seeing it sparked something inside. The whole moment felt bigger, like more was happening than we could see.

Then reality hit: none of had a penny to our names. Johnnie, always quick with a plan, didn't miss a beat. Out back, a chain-link fence stretched low to the ground. A corner lifted—just enough space to slip under. He went first, heart pounding. Junior followed, laughter low and quiet. Johnnie brought up the rear.

We dropped onto a patch of grass, just close enough to catch the screen. The movie's sound drifted from speakers clipped to car windows.

A light drizzle started—no problem at first. But it grew heavier, and soon, the ground turned to mush. Junior squirmed, then leaned over and said we should head back. That got quick agreement. My shirt clung to my skin in the heavy air. But Johnnie shook his head, saying it wasn't that bad.

The rain only got worse.

Finally, Johnnie gave in, and we headed for the fence. Crawling back undertook more effort this time—mud clung to everything: our shirts, our shoes, our skin. The long walk home began— soaked and silent. The earlier rush had drained out somewhere along the way.

A grumble rose among us about the mess we'd landed in—it all felt like a waste. Junior didn't argue. Just said he wanted to dry off. Cars sped past, splashing us and adding insult to injury. But right there, in the mud and cold, soaked to the bone—we cracked up. Couldn't help it.

What started as an escape turned into a soggy march home, heads full of a story we'd be telling for a long time.

Laughter echoed through the night as we trudged through the mud. Even the worst parts felt lighter with the three of us in it together. That misadventure—soaked, cold, and ridiculous— brought us closer and left a lasting memory.

The muddy walk home carried laughter and camaraderie we'd never forget.

CHAPTER 45

NOT EVERYONE GETS WHIPPED

The next morning, the phone rang just as Daddy came in. He picked up and heard Ms. Yetts on the line. The call didn't take long. When he hung up, he looked different—his jaw tight, his eyes sharper. I could tell that the call had changed his mood.

No words were needed. His expression said it all—the line had been crossed. Ms. Yetts had already done her part.

Daddy locked eyes with me. "Go on to your room."

His voice was calm but firm, leaving no room for excuses. No argument followed—just a turn and a walk back, nerves tightening with each step.

I glanced at Johnnie and Junior, then turned toward the room. Behind me, Johnnie started with an apology, but I didn't stop walking. A knot had already formed in my chest.

The sound of the belt sliding through the loops snapped through the house. The first crack of leather on skin shattered the silence, followed by another, then another. Johnnie didn't make a sound, but the pain showed in the way he braced himself.

Afterward, Daddy told him to go to his room. Footsteps echoed down the hallway, and the door clicked shut behind him.

A moment passed. Then Junior spoke up. Daddy's voice dropped, but the tension didn't budge. The belt came down again. Junior's voice trembled under each blow, his cries bouncing off the walls. I pressed my hands over my ears, trying to block the sound—no use. The helplessness settled in, a cold weight in my chest, fear climbing with every crack of leather.

Adrenaline surged. Muscles locked. I couldn't move—just frozen, listening to the sharp cracks echo from the living room, each one a countdown.

Daddy stood over Junior, his face looked hard as stone. Each strike made Junior flinch, his small frame jolting with every blow. Silent tears streamed as he sobbed into the stillness. The belt kept coming, time stretching into something slow and brutal, a moment that refused to end.

Finally, Daddy's breath grew heavy, shoulders heaving. "Go to your room, Junior." His voice was rough, final. "Think about what you did."

Junior moved stiffly, wiping his face with the back of his hand, shuffling down the hall. Daddy didn't move; he just stood there, his expression locked in place—cold, unshaken.

Junior reached Johnnie's door and knocked softly. A pause, then the sound of slow footsteps. Johnnie looked up, pain still etched into his face. He sat on the bed, eyes dark with a mix of anger and concern. Junior closed the door behind him and dropped down beside him.

The house held its breath. Junior's footsteps faded into silence, and all that remained was stillness. Then the floorboards creaked— Daddy's steps, coming closer.

I sat rigid on the bed, heart pounding loudly in my ears. Eyes locked on the door, I waited. The knob turned. Daddy stepped in, his face still flushed with anger. I stayed still, unsure of what to do. Then came Daddy's voice, low and even, calling me closer. My feet moved forward, heart pounding with each step. The stern look on his face softened as he knelt, his voice calm now. No blows coming—just a quiet acknowledgment that following Johnnie and Junior had been punishment enough.

When his eyes met mine, something shifted. I saw calm understanding there. The belt didn't rise. Instead, he let out a long, heavy sigh that settled into the room like a cloud. He knelt, his voice gentle and steady. The hard lines of his face, shaped by sadness, showed restraint in that quiet, steady moment. There was no rage beneath it—just care, worn thin by stress. The tired sadness in his face told its own story. Parenting under pressure carried a quiet burden. The move, the money problems, trying to hold everything together—it wore on Daddy in ways I couldn't begin to understand.

I hadn't led Johnnie and Junior into the mess, and Daddy knew it. No words passed between us, but I could tell he wasn't going to punish me.

Sometimes the youngest doesn't need a whipping—just to be seen, to be understood.

Relief washed over me, slow and quiet. The tension I'd carried all morning began to melt. No words were spoken—just a small nod, and the weight lifted all at once. Daddy stood, said he was heading upstairs to rest, and left the room. I lay back on the bed, still shaken, but grateful.

Spared, this time.

At its core, Daddy's response marked a shift—from strict, reactionary discipline to something more deliberate, more aware. Instead of lashing out or repeating what he'd done with Johnnie and Junior, he paused. Took a breath. Looked at the full picture before doing anything else.

His footsteps faded up the stairs, and before long, the soft strains of Hank Williams' *Your Cheatin' Heart* drifted from the radio. The song moved through the house like a breeze, a signal that the worst of the day had passed.

In the other room, Johnnie and Junior sat quietly on the bed. Their voices were low, worn down to whispers. Both had felt the sting of the belt, both trying to settle. Johnnie seemed to be comforting Junior, though the pain lingered on their faces.

I stayed on the bed, thoughts turning slowly. No whipping came—something I hadn't expected. Part of me was relieved. Another part felt unsure, even a little guilty. So I stayed silent and let the moment pass.

The house held still, save for Hank Williams' voice, filling the space where all that tension had been. The music brought a calm that settled deep.

A few minutes later, Johnnie opened the bedroom door. His face was still tight with emotion, but the sharpness had softened. Junior followed close behind, his eyes swollen and red from crying. They both paused in the doorway. Our eyes met and held for a long moment. The room was quiet, thick with unspoken things. Then Johnnie finally spoke, his voice low, still working through everything.

He said Daddy hadn't whipped me.

Junior looked away and muttered that I was lucky. His voice was flat, but the sting was clear. Johnnie's face twisted, frustration rising again. The morning had been hard on all of us, but something about how it ended made it feel even harder. Unfair in a way none of us could quite name out loud.

The bitterness hung there for a moment. Then Johnnie exhaled, letting some of it go.

"Anyone want breakfast?"

Junior gave a small nod, his voice a touch lighter.

We all stood up. The tension didn't go away, but it loosened enough to let us move. When breakfast was mentioned, it felt like a small relief. It was simple and steady, and it gave us something to focus on—something to do.

Johnnie headed to the bathroom first. Junior and I waited nearby, shifting quietly, the air still heavy around us. When he came out, he glanced into the kitchen and said he'd fix something for us. No one objected. We just followed, drawn by the need for routine. Junior went in next.

When he stepped out, his face was damp, a little less puffy. The water had helped. There was even the beginning of a smile—shy, but real.

I went in last and turned on the faucet, letting the cold water run.

Splashing my face gave me a quick jolt, a brief moment of clarity. It didn't solve anything, but it cut through the morning fog enough to breathe.

In the kitchen, the floor creaked beneath our feet. Johnnie and Junior stood by the fridge, quietly pulling out what was left: a few eggs, some bacon, half a loaf of bread. It wasn't much, but it would do. Johnnie took charge without saying so, grabbing the skillet and cracking the eggs like he'd done it a hundred times before. Junior stood beside him, dropping bread into the toaster, waiting for the pop.

I took a seat at the table, watching them move with quiet coordination. It felt strange—how normal the scene looked after such a painful morning.

The smell of bacon slowly filled the room. When the toast popped, Junior let out a small laugh— soft and unexpected. For the first time that day, something loosened in my chest.

Johnnie flipped the eggs with steady hands. Junior buttered the toast, his earlier tears already beginning to fade. No one said anything about Dad. No one brought up the belt. That silence felt like a choice, like a space we all agreed to leave untouched.

We just ate. Quietly. Gratefully.

Sunlight streamed through the kitchen window, casting warm light across the table. For a moment, we weren't thinking about the morning or the pain or what might come next. For a moment, we were just kids, sharing breakfast and trying to hold onto something that felt like peace.

CHAPTER 46

THE WEIGHT OF TWO HOMES

While Johnnie, Junior, and I were up at the Wintersville parade, my dad and Newton stayed back at the house.

The place, once alive with chatter and warmth, now sat quiet—too quiet. Since Momma and the girls had gone up north, a heavy stillness had settled into every corner. It clung to the walls, filled the spaces between sounds, and settled into the cracks like dust. Daddy sat at the kitchen table, his calloused hands wrapped around a chipped coffee mug. His eyes wandered to the window, past the swaying clothesline, to the empty yard where children once ran through summer light. The laughter was gone now. The yard was still.

The weight of two households pressed down on him—this one in Wintersville, the one he'd built with his own hands, and the one he supported in Boston. The mill wages didn't stretch like they used to. After the bills for both places were paid, there was barely anything left. Food, clothes, the smallest extras—everything had become a kind of luxury. He rubbed a hand across his face, fingers dragging down slowly, deepening the lines already carved into his brow. The silence around him only made the thoughts louder.

He promised he would go, even though leaving Ohio was never part of the plan. Leaving the home he'd poured his sweat into—every beam, every nail—meant letting go of more than just walls and land. It meant losing a piece of himself. Sometimes staying put feels like the only way to hold onto what's slipping away.

CHAPTER 47

WORDS THAT DON'T COME BACK

The front yard, once a place of laughter and play, carried a heavy tension that clung to the air. The sun beat down hard on the grass, drawing sweat and discomfort from everyone standing beneath it. Ricky, four; Lorraine, five; Yvonne, eight; and Patricia, six, stood close together.

I couldn't read their minds, but I could see the weariness from the long trip from Jacksonville. Their clothes were wrinkled, hair tangled, the kind of mess that came from hours of travel and missing luggage. The stress showed on every small face.

Inside, the house felt tighter than usual. The air itself seemed thick, like the walls were holding their breath. The summer heat only added to the pressure. Tension crackled between us like dry brush waiting to ignite. Janie stood in the doorway with her arms crossed, eyes sharp and unreadable. The four kids clustered behind her, their faces full of wonder, confusion, and caution. Whatever warmth could have been there never showed—it was cold and unfamiliar from the start.

I clenched my fists at my sides, tense and annoyed. The house already felt too full. Too loud. Too different.

Lorraine sat nearby, exhausted, slumped with a dazed look in her eyes. Without thinking, I made a sharp comment about her messy hair and wrinkled clothes. I hadn't meant to be cruel—it was just a reaction—but the words came out wrong, too harsh. Tears welled up in her eyes as she explained, quietly and ashamed, that her suitcase had been lost. All she had were the clothes she wore. The regret came fast, sinking into the silence that followed.

I turned away, eyes landing on Yvonne. She stood with her arms crossed, expression guarded.

The irritation flared again. Without thinking, I lashed out, accusing her of messing with my things, raising my voice too much, too fast. All the tension I'd been holding spilled out.

Yvonne didn't back down. She snapped that I wasn't in charge and shouldn't act like I ran the place. The words cut deep, sharper than I expected. Before I could fire back, Janie stepped in.

Her voice was firm. Her warning, unmistakable: don't talk to the kids like that.

I tried to shift the blame to Yvonne, brushing it off like she'd pushed first. But Janie wasn't having it. She shot back with a pointed reminder—that deciding who was in charge wasn't up to me.

The frustration surged again. Embarrassment flared hot in my chest. I shouted, unable to stop myself. Janie's expression changed—stern now, with a final warning. Newton would hear about this.

That stopped everything.

Without another word, she turned away and told me to go. The screen door slammed behind me, loud and final. Outside, the thick air wrapped around me like a weight. The heat, the shame, the sting of Janie's words—they all pressed down at once.

My chest tightened.

A soft voice floated out, steady and low, soothing the younger ones—gently working to mend what had been torn.

Out on the porch, Johnnie and Junior appeared with sly smiles, both shaking their heads. No words were needed; the trouble had been understood.

No smile came in return—only the image of Newton's face after hearing what happened. That thought weighed heavier than anything Janie could say.

Back on the bed, the weight of it all pressed down. The fight hadn't been about anything small or personal. Something deeper churned beneath it—a pressure I didn't yet understand.

That outburst hadn't come from nowhere. It had been building, layer by layer, waiting for the moment to break loose.

Later that day, the sun baked the yard, making the air shimmer. The house felt quiet and heavy after what had happened earlier.

Then the door opened. Newton came in, his boots thudding against the floor. Janie's voice cut through the room, sharp and clipped. The weight of the moment settled over all of us.

Later, Newton paced the floor, steps slow and deliberate. Janie followed, arms full of Ricky. Lorraine clung to the edge of her skirt while Junior, Yvonne, and Patricia stayed close, worn out from the long trip from Jacksonville.

Footsteps sounded down the hallway—measured, certain. With each one, the knot in my stomach pulled tighter.

The room filled with his presence before he even stepped in. When the door opened, his eyes swept the space, locking onto the figure in the corner. I didn't move. Hands stayed buried in my pockets, wishing I could disappear into the wall.

His jaw tightened. The look he gave landed like a blow—disappointment, maybe even hurt, sharper than anything he could have said. He let out a long breath, heavy with everything left unsaid.

I kept my eyes on the floor, the weight of shame pressing down, thick enough to choke on. Then came the question—direct and quiet.

"What did you say to the kids?"

I didn't speak right away. The words I'd shouted earlier came back like echoes in a cave. I repeated them—about them not belonging— and they sounded worse the second time. Uglier. More real.

His expression shifted, like something had cracked. Eyes closed for a second, and when they opened again, the light caught something wet at the corners.

He asked again, softer this time. "Those were your words? That they didn't belong?"

I nodded, the regret already deep. I said it was out of anger—that I didn't mean to make them feel like outsiders. The words had come out wrong, sharp and reckless. And now there was no way to pull them back in.

I wished there was a way to show how sorry I was—something more than just words. But all I could do was stand there, hoping he could see it in my face.

The apology didn't erase the hurt, and that was the point. Some words leave a mark, no matter what follows.

Being left out wasn't new, but the reminder cut deeper than expected. A memory surfaced:

standing alone at the edge of the playground, watching others play, pretending not to care.

Newton didn't raise his voice. He spoke evenly, explaining how the weariness had settled into every part of them. Like the weight of life had finally caught up and there was no place left to put it.

His words came gently: family sticks together. The kids were trying to adjust, still finding their place. What they needed was patience, not more pain.

Apologizing felt like the only place to begin.

At first, there was no response. Just a hand dragging slowly down a tired face, as if trying to wipe the day away. When our eyes met again, there was sadness there, but also a trace of understanding.

Then Janie appeared in the doorway, standing like truth itself. Her voice was steady. " Times are hard, but family gets through it by sticking together, not tearing each other down."

I apologized for the hurt I caused Lorraine and Yvonne, acknowledging that I should have been kinder, more patient, and more present. I carried the weight of that regret and promised to make things right.

Newton nodded slowly, then spoke. "Words can hurt," he said, "but they can heal, too, if you back them with something real."

CHAPTER 48

HE SPOKE TO GOD FOR ALL OF US

Later that evening, the house stayed quiet, the heat clinging to every wall and surface. After coming home and hearing what had happened, Daddy gathered us all in the living room.

We sat close, packed in tight, no one saying much. Daddy stood in front—calm, collected, his focus steady. He bowed his head, and the prayer began.

His voice was even, almost soft. He gave thanks—for family, for love and joy, for the strength we found in one another. Then came the request: help us learn from our mistakes, soften our hearts, and guide us forward together. He asked for patience, kindness, forgiveness, and the courage to keep growing.

His words shifted toward change—how life had been reshaped, how we were all adjusting. He asked for unity, for the kind of closeness that could hold through the hard parts. The prayer ended with blessings for Momma and the sisters back in Boston.

When he finished, nobody moved. The words hung in the air—thick with weight, thick with meaning. This wasn't just a habit. It wasn't routine. It was a call to repair what had been torn. A quiet but powerful reminder: no matter how broken things felt, we were still a family.

CHAPTER 49

NOT ALL OF US GOT ON THE BUS

The living room felt heavy that day—not just from the heat or Daddy's exhaustion after his overnight shift, but from something deeper, unspoken. When he called Johnnie and me in, the weight of what was coming pressed down on us. We sat on the couch, small and still, waiting.

Daddy sank into his favorite chair, quiet, like he was gathering strength. The birds chirped outside, but inside, the silence was sharp. Every second stretched, filled with things we couldn't say. I remember feeling that heaviness settle over all of us, slow and steady.

A call had come from Boston. Momma had found an apartment and wanted the family to join her before school started.

The news hit like a gut punch. Johnnie's jaw tightened, his brows drawn low. His eyes never left the floor.

It wasn't just about moving. It was about being swept into something bigger than ourselves—a story written long before we could read it. The Great Migration wasn't some far-off history lesson. It was here, in our living room, shaping our lives. Every plan, every good-bye, carried its echo. Momma had stepped into that current, leading us down a path familiar to so many Black families—chasing better, pushing past what the world tried to hold back. Step by step, she carved out something new. Boston promised more than Wintersville ever had.

Daddy had stayed, hoping she'd change her mind. But Momma had already planted her feet in Boston, and now the apartment was ready. He didn't have a choice. He had to let us go.

We were just kids caught in the current, leaving behind dusty roads, open fields, and the only version of home we knew. Stepping toward a future we never asked for.

Daddy gave a weak smile, then returned to his newspaper. Johnnie and I stepped outside with hearts pulled low in our chests.

Daddy told us we were moving to Boston, but not until Friday. Even so, the words hit me like thunder.

My eyes dropped to my worn-out sneakers. A lump rose in my throat. The wild summer days— the ones that felt like they'd never end—were slipping through my fingers.

In 1955, kids in our family didn't argue. We didn't question decisions. We didn't have a say. We went where we were told. I pulled the bag close to my side, the strap biting into my shoulder. The bright blue Sunday shirt clung too tightly for the weight of the morning. My pants didn't reach my ankles anymore, and my black shoes pinched just enough to remind me how fast I was growing.

The road was quiet that morning. A quick kick sent a pebble skimming down the path. Johnnie stood close, sleeves rolled up, khakis pressed sharp. His arms were crossed tightly over his chest, mouth set firm, not saying a word.

Junior stood off to the side in clean overalls and a tucked-in white T-shirt, his shoes neatly laced. He looked down, gently pushing at the dirt with his toe—quiet, still, like he wanted to freeze time before we left him behind.

Daddy walked up slowly, his boots crunching against the gravel. Long shadows stretched behind him, the weight of the morning pressing down on all of us. His shoulders sagged, carrying more than just the bags; he carried the end of something. A hand settled gently on mine. His eyes moved from face to face, searching, maybe for understanding, maybe just for peace.

Nothing needed to be said—our silence spoke loud enough. The time had come. We were heading north to join Momma and our sisters. Summer had run out.

A small nod passed between us, sharp in the chest. Johnnie sniffled once, quickly, while Junior wiped his nose with a sleeve, his lip quivering.

The question hung heavy—why wasn't Daddy coming too? But it stayed buried, swallowed down with everything else we couldn't say.

Junior reached into his pocket and pulled out an old baseball, worn smooth from use. He passed it to Johnnie without a word. That single motion carried everything they couldn't speak—brother to brother, goodbye to goodbye.

Daddy helped us lift our bags and carry them up First Lane toward Route 22. The sun rose higher, stretching shadows across the dusty road. We walked in silence, each step dragging, loaded down with more than just luggage. We were leaving behind a whole world.

At the bus stop, we set our bags down on the gravel. Daddy stepped back. The distant rumble of the engine grew louder, cutting through the stillness like a warning.

The bus came into view. Its approach was slow, but still too fast.

Lifting the bags took more than strength—they held more than clothes. Folded into the fabric were memories: nights on the porch, summer games, morning pancakes, and the sound of Daddy's laugh. They carried the sting of leaving, the weight of what came next, the ache of everything unspoken.

Every step forward brought those pieces along. The quiet goodbyes. The changing shape of family. The hope that this move—this leap—might lead to something more.

Junior moved slower now, shoulders low, glancing back one last time with a flicker of hope in his eyes. Daddy stood nearby, still and solid, just behind him. Close, but not stepping forward. Just close enough to say: I'm still here.

Dad looked at Johnnie, his voice steady but low. "Take care of your brother." Johnnie nodded, solemn and sure, the weight of that charge settling on his shoulders.

We boarded the bus and found our seats. I turned toward the window and saw them—Dad and Junior—standing outside, frozen in place.

No waves. No words. Just stillness. As if letting go had taken all the strength they had. That kind of quiet made everything feel more final—like saying nothing was the only way to keep from breaking apart. The weight of what we were leaving behind pressed in: home, the familiar, the version of ourselves that once made sense.

A tap on the glass. I whispered Junior's name. He gave one small nod, his lips tight, pressed into a line.

Daddy raised his hand. One slow, heavy motion. The kind that said everything.

The doors closed behind us. The bus lurched forward, and I pressed my forehead to the window, eyes fixed on their shapes until they blurred into the hills. Until the road curved and they were gone.

That moment burned itself into me. This wasn't just a simple goodbye. It felt like the end of a whole way of life. Something unspoken slipped away. A sense of freedom and wholeness disappeared with it. Even childhood felt marked, drawn through with a line.

The bus rattled on, its engine loud against the silence inside. My head filled with questions, none of them allowed to rise. No space for words. Just thoughts circling.

Momma believed Boston would be better. Better schools, better chances. A fresh start. But all I could think about was the empty space Daddy left behind. If this move was meant to be a step forward, why wasn't he coming, too?

Johnnie leaned back in his seat, eyes on the ceiling, somewhere far away. He didn't speak, but I knew the question troubled him too. Leaving felt like something done to us. Like the people stepping away became the ones left behind.

Without Daddy, the world felt off balance. The decision to leave had been Momma's, and Daddy chose to stay. We were only children who were caught in the middle, just along for the ride in someone else's plan.

Johnnie sat up, turning Junior's old baseball in his hands. Trying to hold onto something solid.

Something that still made sense.

This trip north wasn't just a move. It marked a fracture. Our family, once whole, now split across distance and silence. Not everything made sense back then. But one truth settled deep and stayed: Kids carry what grown folks leave behind.

Daddy never followed the promises of The Great Migration. He held tight to what was already his—faith, the land, the steel mill—anchors that grounded him in Wintersville. Starting over somewhere else didn't sit right. Maybe staying gave him a kind of strength.

Momma dreamed differently. She wanted more than survival and routine. She wanted opportunity, education, and a future where her children wouldn't have to choose between dignity and a paycheck. To her, Boston wasn't just a city—it was a possibility, a doorway to something better.

Maybe Daddy's love didn't fit with all the movement and change happening around us. His journey had started back in 1918, leaving a harsh home and hopping trains with a childhood friend, chasing his own idea of a better life. In Wintersville, he thought he had found it—steady work at Weirton Steel, a home of his own, land to tend, and faith at the center of everything.

That dream was simple: a roof over his head, food on the table, safety, and the Church. Holding onto that dream came with a cost. It meant leaving behind the ones who needed him in different ways. He chose what he believed was right, even if it left pain in its wake. But his decision left a quiet emptiness that only children could feel.

Johnnie believed something new could be built—something that didn't mean giving up everything that mattered. That belief was met with effort, with action. He tried.

I didn't have the words for it then, but something was becoming clear: some folks stay because they can't leave. Others go because staying would break them.

But no one walks away empty-handed. Even those moving forward carry the weight of everything they leave behind.

CHAPTER 50

THE DISTANCE THAT GROWS US

The bus pulled into the small Steubenville station just as the Greyhound for Cleveland arrived. Its engine rumbled steadily, like it had somewhere else to be. A short line of passengers had already formed, waiting to board. The station sat off to the side—a squat little building with chipped paint and a couple of wooden benches outside. Nearby, a food truck sent up a thick mix of grease and fuel into the warm morning air.

Johnnie tapped my shoulder, told me to hold our place in line, then walked off to buy the tickets. I dragged our bags forward—one in each hand—shoulders straining under the weight. The line moved slowly, nerves rising with each shuffle forward. It was our first time boarding a Greyhound.

Johnnie returned just as the driver stepped down and opened the luggage compartment. Without a word, we handed over the bags. Tickets got checked, a quick motion pointed toward the open door.

Inside, the bus was clean and orderly, soft gray seats lined in perfect rows down the aisle. The floor had been freshly swept. Empty overhead racks showed everything was ready for the ride ahead. Passengers spoke in low voices, the hum of quiet conversations filling the space.

Johnnie chose a seat near the middle. I slid into the window spot beside him. Fingers gripped the armrest, sunlight slipping through the glass, glinting off the metal rails. A faint vibration rose through the soles of my shoes.

Back straight, eyes fixed on the road ahead, Johnnie stayed focused on the view. As the bus pulled out, that view remained steady. Names rolled through my mind like stops on a map— Akron, Youngstown, Pittsburgh, Cleveland, New York, Boston. The wheels turned, and the journey began.

The station shrank behind us, slipping away without hesitation. Familiar streets disappeared, replaced by open fields, highway signs, and the long road forward.

I leaned my forehead against the window. Steubenville faded, and the smokestacks of Weirton Steel took its place. Thick smoke poured upward, curling into the sky. That place had always meant something—Dad had spent years behind those walls. My eyes scanned the clouds, wondering if Boston had anything like that.

Johnnie sat steady, seemingly untouched by the ride. His calm didn't come from ignoring what was happening—it came from stepping up. As the older brother, he saw I was struggling. Falling apart wasn't an option for him, so he held his composure.

That posture, firm and quiet, said what words couldn't: *You're safe. I'm here.* His strength showed not in what he said, but in how he carried the moment, for both of us.

Boston meant a new beginning, a chance to leave the past behind and build something better. But the weight of what we left pressed down hard. That calm beside the storm only made the contrast sharper.

Weirton rolled past the window. Red dust coated cars, rooftops, and sidewalks—a stain of industry, a reminder of where we came from. That dust belonged to Dad and everything he chose to stay with.

Dad remained, rooted in belief: the job, the house, the life. Momma moved toward something else—better schools, cleaner streets, real chances. Any agreement between them felt impossible to imagine.

The land kept shifting. Hills rose and fell beyond the glass. Weirton disappeared slowly, piece by piece. My thoughts knotted into questions—*What if Boston had no place for someone like me? What if the city didn't welcome, didn't offer a way in?*

CHAPTER 51

THE DISTANCE BETWEEN WHO WE WERE AND WHO WE'D BECOME

Johnnie leaned over and showed me how to adjust the seat back. The cushion gave a little, opening up just enough space to breathe. A small comfort—but enough for now.

Akron came next. The brakes hissed, the doors opened. A few passengers stepped off, others climbed aboard. My feet dangled just above the floor as I watched the shuffle of bags and faces. No words—just movement.

Stops blurred by: Youngstown, then Pittsburgh. We stepped off briefly— time to stretch, to eat. My stomach twisted, unsure if the ache came from hunger or nerves. The last meal felt distant, like it belonged to another day.

Inside the terminal, the air hung thick with fryer grease and stale coffee. In the corner, a small diner hummed quietly. A waitress jotted down the order without looking up—no steak, no extras, just something warm on a plate. The only meal for the day.

The food settled the stomach but left everything else untouched.

Chewing became automatic. The mind wandered—toward the life left behind, toward something not yet named, and toward whatever waited on the other side of this journey.

Then the bus call came, cutting through the low din of the terminal. Time to move again.

Back on the road. Each mile put more distance between me and Wintersville. Home started to feel imaginary—something that once existed but now slipped further from reach.

Somewhere along that stretch of highway, something began to shift. The road kept going, but nothing felt steady anymore. The kid who had boarded that morning already felt like someone else—fading, shape-changing.

Fatigue crept in and settled deep. My stomach stayed quiet, but the thoughts wouldn't stop spinning. Johnnie nudged my arm, just enough to pull me out of the spiral.

Next stop: Cleveland. The loudspeaker cracked overhead, a sharp voice calling us to move.

Johnnie stood, stretched his arms, and rolled his shoulders like he'd done this a hundred times.

By the time we arrived, my legs were stiff from sitting too long. The bus doors hissed open, and cold night air rushed in. The bus driver passed the bags down, one by one.

Inside the station, motion surrounded us—people weaving past, announcements echoing overhead, lights buzzing faintly. The scent of hot food hit like a wall—greasy, rich—but we didn't stop. No time. No extra money.

We found a spot near the wall and dropped our bags. They became makeshift seats while the crowd pulsed around us—people chasing buses, chasing jobs, chasing something they couldn't quite name. We sat still, watching. I scanned faces, wondering how many were carrying the same weight—uncertainty thick in their shoulders, caught between where they'd come from and where they hoped to land.

Johnnie sat beside me like nothing had changed. Calm. Steady. Watching him stirred something quiet and strong inside me—a deep, wordless admiration. There was no need to say anything. The understanding was already there. Same trip. Same unknown ahead.

We were different in how we carried it, but not in what we carried. Kindred—not in speech, but in silence.

Leaving Wintersville wasn't just about packing up and heading out—it was tearing loose roots I hadn't realized had sunk so deep. Now I sat somewhere in between, hungry for something I couldn't name, full from a meal that couldn't reach the parts of me still aching.

CHAPTER 52

THRESHOLD AT GATE 12: WHERE THE JOURNEY BECAME REAL

The loudspeaker crackled to life. The bus to New York was boarding at Gate 12. My chest tightened. Time to move.

Johnnie stood, grabbed his bag, and moved with a practiced ease, like he'd done it all before. I reached for mine, fumbling to lift it. A quick wave from him urged me forward. No room left for hesitation. The urgency in the terminal mirrored the churn inside me—the noise, the motion, the sense that everything was shifting fast.

Near the gate, the crowd thickened. Voices rose. Every step closer blurred into a kind of rush, too fast to keep up with. When I finally reached the line, the full weight of what was happening sank in. Something new waited just ahead—uncertain, unnamed, but pulling me forward.

Johnnie turned, calm and sure, and caught my eye. Over the noise, one sentence cut through everything: "Don't think too much. Just stay with me—Momma's waiting in Boston."

The bus door opened.

A blast of cool air greeted us, and the low hum inside offered a strange comfort. I closed my eyes for a second, trying to hold it all—leaving, longing, the fear of what waited next. For now, the bus was a buffer, a moving space between two worlds.

The road stretched ahead, wide and unknowable. Restlessness settled in—too many thoughts without clear names, too many questions without answers. This wasn't just a ride. It was a threshold. One life receded behind us, another waited up ahead, still forming.

Tickets exchanged. A punch. A nod. The doors shut with a deep thud.

The engine rumbled to life, and the station faded behind us.

We found seats by the window. Bags tucked beneath, shoulders still carrying everything that couldn't be packed. Outside, the city gave way to fields and sky. No clear picture of Boston in my mind—just the ache of what had been left behind and the fragile thread of hope pulling me onward.

The ride from Cleveland to New York stretched like forever. I hadn't realized how long ten hours really were. By hour two, everything ached—legs stiff, back sore. For a seven-year-old, a journey broken up by endless stops felt impossible. I wanted to rest, but my body buzzed too much to be still. Thoughts kept moving, even when I couldn't.

The bus rolled through the night, mile after mile peeling away from everything I'd known. My head spun with thoughts—too many, too fast—but the steady motion of the ride helped settle me, just a little. Still, even as my body begged for rest, sleep wouldn't come. My eyes stayed open, tracking every stop, every shift, every push farther from home.

When we reached New York, the city crashed in like a wave. Towers rose up on every side, cutting off the sky, swallowing the sun. The terminal roared with motion and sound—people rushing in all directions, lights flickering, horns blaring. The whole place buzzed with energy so thick it made the air hard to breathe. It was alive in a way that overwhelmed, like standing too close to something burning.

Johnnie, worn but steady, took the lead. His shoulders slumped from the long ride, but his steps never wavered. He moved through the crowd with purpose—eyes always scanning, steps sure and deliberate. He kept close, never too far ahead, always within reach. New York slammed into us with sound and speed, metal and glass reflecting it all back louder than before. But through it all, Johnnie carved a path, calm and constant.

That one steady presence made a difference.

A glance over the shoulder. A small pause. A pace chosen not for the city, but for someone still finding their feet. Every move he made left space—space for me to catch up, to breathe, to not fall behind.

The chaos swelled—bodies pressed shoulder to shoulder, bags knocked against legs, voices piled on top of each other, none of them stopping. My steps faltered. My eyes searched for something solid to hold on to.

Johnnie slowed just enough. No words, just a shift in stride. That small gesture said everything:

You're not alone.

He didn't talk much. No big speeches or drawn-out explanations. But his presence said more than words ever could. There was something in the way he walked, in the way he checked back

every so often to make sure I hadn't been swallowed by the crowd. I didn't fully get it at the time, but later, those quiet actions stood out. That kind of care doesn't need to shout to be heard.

We found a pause near the vending machines. A small break in the rush.

Johnnie dug coins from deep in his pocket—slow movements, as if even spare change carried weight. The ride had drained him, but his focus never drifted.

The machine clunked and spit out a bottle of soda. Johnnie popped the cap, took two long drinks, then handed it over without a word. No gesture made a bigger sound.

A laugh slipped out. That same move—first sip always claimed, like a rule passed down between brothers without ever needing to be explained. One swig at a time, like tradition.

The sweetness rushed in, more than just refreshment. For a moment, everything else faded. That sip became something deeper—comfort, memory, a reminder. In that small gesture lived something bigger: protection, unspoken and constant, stitched into everyday habits that didn't ask for recognition.

When it came time to board again, the rhythm stayed smooth. Johnnie snapped his jacket into place with a practiced shake, eyes sweeping the terminal to make sure nothing—and no one— was left behind. His steps cut through the noise, steady and certain, like the route had already been walked a hundred times.

The crowd surged. Lights flickered overhead. Exhaustion tugged at my body like heavy hands. But Johnnie stayed grounded, unmoved by the chaos. No need for dramatic gestures or soft words. His presence was enough—absorbing the weight of change, the fear of the unknown, and carrying it without being asked. Carrying it so I didn't have to.

That quiet strength—that calm under pressure—was everything I needed. In a world that felt like it might tip over, Johnnie was the anchor.

When we got on the bus again, our usual seats were taken. The only ones left together were in the very back. We took them without complaint. The bus pulled away, and the skyline of New York slowly fell behind us—loud, bold, flickering. In its place came quieter roads, trees lining the highway, and towns that blurred past like memories you're not quite ready to let go of.

CHAPTER 53

WHEN PRESENCE BECOMES HOME

Boston's skyline rose ahead, softer but steady, less intimidating than New York's towering sprawl. It didn't demand attention or dominate the sky. Instead, it stood there with quiet assurance, like someone who knows exactly who they are. Something about that felt right—like the city had been expecting us, holding space, keeping the light on.

The bus hissed to a stop. The doors opened, and a new kind of air settled in—not cold, just charged, like it carried the weight of everything about to shift.

Back in Wintersville, the fields, paths, and blackberry bushes had shaped the rhythm of my childhood. That land opened wide, inviting you to lean into it, to belong. But here in Boston, the buildings closed in tight. People moved fast, eyes forward, no time to notice anything small. The pace was unfamiliar. The ground felt different beneath my feet.

Still, the city hummed with quiet possibility—as if somewhere in all that movement, it had room for us, too.

Johnnie tugged our bags from under the bus, calm and sure, while I scanned the crowd. And then—I saw her. Momma.

A bright yellow dress caught the eye, glowing like sunlight against the dull backdrop of the terminal. A white Sunday hat perched perfectly atop her head. From one wrist swung a black patent leather pocketbook, and polished black shoes tapped a quiet rhythm against the pavement. In the middle of all that movement, one figure stood still—centered, grounded, a quiet glow that didn't try to blend in.

Her eyes lit up the second they landed on us. Arms opened wide, and that tight-lipped smile stretched across her face—cheeks lifted, eyes creased with joy tucked just beneath the surface. Her features, soft and distinct, gave a subtle nod to her Chinese ancestry. There was something unforgettable in the way she held herself—graceful, certain.

Beside her, Gloria bounced on her heels, one small hand locked into Momma's, the other gripping a well-loved Raggedy Ann. Her blue polka-dot dress fluttered as she skipped forward, white socks tucked into shiny black shoes, blue ribbons swinging from the ends of her neatly braided hair.

The second she saw us, Gloria broke free—laughter bursting from her like a song, feet flying.

Johnnie gave me a small nudge. No words, just that quiet, steady presence he always carried. Through the long miles and the weight of the day, his calm had been the constant—an anchor.

Gloria reached me first. Her arms wrapped tight around my waist—small, strong, and filled with everything she didn't know how to say.

"We missed you so, so, so much. It took forever!"

Then came Momma. The scent of lavender clung to her dress—faint, familiar, and deeply tied to home. Her hug wrapped around me like a shield. It wasn't just a welcome. It was a check-in, a quiet affirmation, a message passed skin to skin: *You're safe now.* My body softened into hers. The tightness I hadn't realized I was holding began to ease.

Her smile didn't fade, but something behind it dimmed. She kept looking past us, eyes scanning the crowd for someone who wasn't there.

Daddy's promise had been clear—he said he'd be there too. But when the time came, he wasn't. He chose not to come, and Momma's disappointment showed. His absence said everything.

The silence around it said more than words ever could—settling heavy in the space between us, filling it with what wasn't said.

Still, she held herself tall. When she pulled Johnnie into her arms, that same warmth wrapped around him. For a moment, his usual armor cracked. He leaned into her, allowing himself a brief peace.

With her arms around us and Gloria dancing nearby, the long miles began to lose their weight. Something in that circle—her presence, her effort, her love—held us steady.

Momma had carved out a life in Boston, joining The Great Migration with dreams too big for Ohio to hold. The city offered her a future—one she claimed not just for herself but for all of us. Somehow, she made space for us even before we arrived. In her arms, this strange new place began to feel like home.

All eyes turned to Johnnie—alert, always watching—and something in the chest eased. There were no words for it then, but that moment marked a shift. Not just relief. Not just exhaustion. A flicker of belonging surfaced in a place still unfamiliar, still earning our trust.

Arrival wasn't only about reaching Boston. The journey moved through more than miles. It moved through the break from everything known. Through a bus ride burdened with more than luggage—laden with Momma's vision, Johnnie's quiet strength, and a thousand unspoken questions.

Their roots ran back to Ohio, but they had stopped growing. Wintersville, with its hills and berry patches, couldn't hold the dreams Momma carried. Her steps moved with vision and courage long before understanding caught up. A yellow dress. Outstretched arms. A presence that said: you matter. That moment offered both comfort and challenge—a reminder that while the body may arrive, the heart takes longer to catch up.

In those first days, Boston rushed in—loud, fast, too much to claim as home. But space had already been made. Momma's presence made it real. No demand for attention, no need to prove anything. Just a quiet, steady strength that made room and held ground.

Johnnie stood in more than one role. Not just the one who carried bags but also the one who carried pressure, silence, and expectation. He had not chosen this role, but had accepted it. Without needing to be asked, he held steady for someone smaller, trying to make sense of the world—not by title, but by necessity. Stability came from that quiet strength, the kind that says: I've got you, even without the words.

Gloria, skipping with blue ribbons and a doll in hand, brought a lightness no one asked for but everyone needed. Her joy was untouched by the weight around her. It was a reminder that happiness still had room to exist, even after everything changed.

That joy became a thread of survival, proof that the spirit bends but doesn't break. Years later, that day stands as more than a memory. A crossing. A shift from what once was to what could be.

No promises waited in Boston. No guarantees lined the streets. But something lasting stood in that circle—Momma, Johnnie, Gloria. And that was enough to begin.

Home didn't live in walls or street names. Home lived in the hands that reached out when fear crept in. In the bodies that stayed close when the world opened too wide.

Understanding came slowly, but the truth held steady: arrival wasn't the end. That day marked the beginning.

CHAPTER 54

WHERE PROMISES UNRAVELED AND A MOTHER STITCHED A NEW BEGINNING

The first few weeks were a whirlwind—unpacking boxes, adjusting to city noises that never slept, and getting used to a crowded apartment. Momma stayed busy, her hands always moving: cooking, cleaning, ironing. But when she thought we weren't looking, she'd pause, gaze out the window, and sigh—almost lost in the hum of the city.

One evening, after I'd settled into the bunk bed I shared with Gloria, I woke in the middle of the night. The apartment was still and quiet, but faint voices drifted from the kitchen. I lay still, eyes closed, pretending to sleep while my ears strained to catch every word.

Momma sat at the kitchen table, Juanita beside her. The dim light cast long shadows on the walls. Juanita clutched a letter, its envelope worn and crinkled from being read and folded too many times.

Momma's eyes glistened, though no tears fell. Her voice—low and tired—carried the weight of everything she bore.

Juanita shared the same uncertainty, like so many others who had left the South during The Great Migration in search of something better. Momma stared at the letter, still holding on to the hope that Daddy would join us.

But as the months passed, Daddy's promise faded. He stayed in Wintersville, unwilling to leave the life he had built. Meanwhile,

Momma worked to build a new future for us in Boston. She prayed to Jesus with a quiet strength, trusting God to guide and protect us.

Daddy's absence grew heavier, his promise becoming a distant echo. Though strong, Momma struggled. But her prayers never stopped. She held on to hope, even as time passed and it became clear she was no longer waiting for Daddy. We were learning to move forward without him, and somehow, we would.

Momma had dreamed of a better life, but Daddy's fear of change kept him rooted. He gave her $500, not enough to cover the move, so she used her own savings to make up the difference. The months rolled by, and his promises remained unkept.

Though the future was uncertain, Momma stayed determined to make this new life work, drawing courage from her faith and trusting that we would be alright.

Momma had found a tiny apartment in Roxbury, a part of Boston where the sidewalks cracked and the houses leaned into one another like old friends. It was nothing like what we'd left behind. No yard, no trees, no open sky to breathe under—just brick, concrete, and the constant noise of the city.

Years later, Ruby Nelle told me a story that helped me understand what had been happening. Momma had confided in her, sharing how deeply Daddy's broken promise hurt—how betrayed she felt. The weight of abandonment and disappointment pressed on her as she struggled to accept that her husband had failed to support her and the children in this new chapter.

Momma's voice, filled with frustration, questioned why Daddy hadn't kept his word and had come to Boston. Months passed with no sign of him, and his promises began to lose their meaning. While he remained in Wintersville, clinging to what was familiar, Momma pushed forward—determined to build something new for us.

Our apartment on Sterling Street was small and modest. The icebox stayed cold with weekly deliveries of a block of ice, and the windows rattled when the wind picked up. Still, Momma made it a home with the warmth of her cooking and the strength of her spirit.

When Johnnie asked about having his own room, Momma gently explained that money was tight—for now, we had to make do. She arranged for him to stay with Ms. Johnson from church for a while. It was a hard decision, born from the need to give Johnnie some stability, even as she carried the weight of doing it all alone.

Johnnie's mention of Daddy's absence hit hard, but Momma didn't flinch. In that cramped apartment, she showed us that home wasn't about what we had—it was about the strength to

keep going in the face of it all. She kept moving forward, shaping a future even when the days felt heavy.

Her determination held us together. It made that place on Sterling Street something we could call home.

The living room glowed with warm, dim light from a vintage lamp, casting golden hues across the room. The air was thick with the cinnamon-sweet scent of apple pie baking in the oven. That scent wrapped around us like a soft blanket, offering comfort from everything beyond those walls.

Momma set the pie on the cooling rack, her hands moving with practiced grace. It was golden and perfect, just like always.

Momma's voice rang out—steady, authoritative—calling us to dinner. Gloria lit up at the mention of apple pie, her excitement more for the comfort it brought than the pie itself.

Momma kept working, the stew simmering on the stove as she directed the others to help set the table. Juanita, deep in thought, placed the plates with quiet precision. Outside, the schoolyard buzzed with the sound of children—a constant reminder that life was moving forward, with or without us.

Gladys glanced out the window, remarking on how unexpectedly cozy things had turned out, all things considered. Juanita, book in hand, asked Momma for help with a math problem she couldn't solve. She hadn't mastered it yet, but her persistence never wavered. Momma promised to help later, though her mind was already on the next task.

It wasn't love or sentimentality that kept us going. Momma rose early, tied her scarf tight, and moved through the morning like routine was armor—cooking, folding, straightening what little we had. Each motion was a refusal to fall apart. She never named the weight she carried. She just carried it. Somehow, we kept going. And that was enough.

CHAPTER 55

WHEN ABSENCE SAT AT THE HEAD OF THE TABLE

It was Christmas morning, 1955, our first holiday in the cramped rental on Ruggles Street. It was gray and quiet and cold, the kind of cold that made you draw your coat tighter and your hopes closer.

The sound of carolers filtered through the chilly air as I woke, rubbing sleep from my eyes. Gladys was already sitting up, eager and wide-eyed, while Gloria lay sprawled beneath her blanket, clutching her worn doll.

I was eight, and the distant laughter reached me—the unmistakable rhythm of Santa's voice, full of warmth and joy. We jumped out of bed, bare feet slapping the cold floor, and rushed to the living room. By the door stood Santa, flanked by members of the Salvation Army in bright red uniforms that cut through the gray morning like a promise.

Momma stood nearby, her hands clasped, her face a mix of surprise and relief. She'd been worried about how to make Christmas happen when money was tight, rent was overdue, and gifts felt impossible. The Salvation Army volunteers, singing carols and handing out small gifts, gave us something we hadn't expected—a Christmas worth remembering.

We had no idea the church had planned this surprise, or that Momma's silent prayers had set it in motion. Her quiet strength—reaching out to the community when everything seemed scarce— had made this moment possible.

The carolers disappeared as quickly as they'd come, and we gathered around the small tree. Momma had pieced together a simple display—just a few ornaments and strands of tinsel—but it was ours. Gladys tore open her gift, a tiny tea set, and screamed with delight. Gloria hugged her new doll, and I clutched my red tin truck, overcome by a rush of pure joy.

As we passed around our new treasures, I looked up at Momma, grateful for everything she had done, even if I didn't yet understand the weight she carried. She kneeled beside us and pulled us close, her presence offering quiet reassurance, reminding us that even in our toughest moments, something greater was at work.

I remember that first Christmas without him. Gladys had just turned eight. Gloria, five, lit up over her new doll. I sat on the floor, staring at the small tree in the corner, tinsel catching the light. It should've been a happy moment, but all I could think was: *Daddy should've been here, handing out gifts, cracking jokes like always.*

Juanita, fifteen, sat in the corner, watching with a serene smile. She didn't show excitement like we did, but the moment meant something to her, too. In her silence, understanding came through—an unspoken thank-you. Momma always made sure she was included, even if she didn't show it the same way.

That night, as we shared stories around the tree, I understood something I'd carry with me forever: we weren't rich in the way most people meant it. But in love, in family, and in the promise of tomorrow, we had more than enough.

I was always full of questions, even at that young age. So many things didn't make sense. Why did we move to Boston? What would life be like here? What about Daddy? I wanted to ask Momma everything, but every time I tried, the conversation shut down—fast, like a door slammed in my face.

One morning, as we sat at the kitchen table, Momma stirred a pot of oatmeal while I picked at my bowl. My eyes met hers, my mind crowded with questions.

All I understood was that something was missing. Daddy skipped birthdays, holidays, and the small moments like saying goodnight. We tried to fill the gap, but it wasn't the same.

We still celebrated, but a piece was always missing—like a puzzle that refused to come together. Momma gave everything she had, but sometimes the silence said more than words ever could.

It wasn't the same. It never would be.

Looking back now, I understand why Momma protected us from the truth. She didn't want to tarnish our view of Daddy, even if he wasn't around. She didn't want us to think less of him, even though he never made memories with us. Deep down, I missed him. We all did. No matter how much she tried to shield us, the emptiness lingered in our home.

I missed a great deal without my daddy around—he wasn't there for my birthday, or Momma's, Gloria's, Gladys's, or even his own. So many joyful moments that should've been filled with laughter were instead marked by his absence.

CHAPTER 56

WHEN HER PRAYERS
BECAME MY ARMOR

At eight years old, my world revolved around Momma and my three sisters. My father had broken his promises long ago. That left Momma holding everything together. Her strength came from her faith. Church was her compass, and her prayers were constant— soft and steady, like a hum that never stopped. I'd fall asleep to her voice and wake to it again. Her favorite song, *Take My Hand, Precious Lord*, drifted through our home, threading the days as she cooked, cleaned, and kept us going.

Then one night, everything shifted. Momma was mugged while walking home from church.

They didn't hurt her, but something in her changed. After that, I became her escort, even to late- night revival meetings. I was just a skinny kid, but I walked beside her with purpose. She trusted me. Not my sisters, but me.

The streets of Roxbury turned rough after dark. Momma walked fast, Bible clutched under her arm, scarf pulled tight against the wind. I stayed close, alert to every sound. She once told me the streets weren't safe for girls at night. That's why it had to be me. I didn't say much. I just walked taller.

The church was always a welcome sight. I enjoyed the light spilling through stained glass, the warmth, and the music waiting inside. Momma found her seat in the third pew and joined the singing without hesitation. Her voice blended with the others, strong and sure. I sat beside her, quiet, knowing this was her time.

After the service, Momma made her rounds. She greeted Elder Young and praised the sermon. He smiled at me and said I'd grow strong in the Word. Momma smiled too, proud and certain. Then came Sister Owens, and later Deacon Hardaway, whose deep voice carried through the sanctuary. Everyone in the neighborhood knew Momma. They respected her. It was a respect earned through years of kindness and quiet strength.

When it was time to leave, we stepped back into the cold night. I walked beside her, scanning the streets like always. Momma thanked me for walking her. Her voice was steady, but something in the way she said it stayed with me.

That night marked a change in me. I was no longer just the child she protected; I became someone she counted on. Her trust gave me strength. And looking back, I believe her prayers kept us safe. Those dark streets never touched us again. Momma's faith was like armor. God brought us through.

CHAPTER 57

THE DAY HUMILITY SPELLED MY NAME

Looking back, I didn't realize how much those early years would shape me and help me through struggles and quiet lessons in strength.

One moment that stayed with me happened in third grade during a spelling bee. I stood at the front of the room, nervous but ready. The word was *company*. I spelled it out: "C-O-M-P-I-N- Y." Then, I waited for Mr. Wilson to respond.

He just stared—eyes fixed, like he held a secret. Then came the verdict: wrong. My stomach sank. Embarrassment surged through me, draining whatever confidence I had left.

But instead of moving on, Mr. Wilson leaned back, arms crossed, and asked if I had a sister named Gloria in second grade. I nodded, still confused and burning with shame. I didn't understand how he made the connection.

Maybe it was our shared last name. Maybe he'd seen us arrive together in the mornings. Or maybe teachers just noticed things we didn't expect. In that moment, though, all I could feel was the weight pressing down in my gut.

Without much explanation, he walked out of the room. My classmates stared at me—some whispering. I wanted to disappear. A minute later, Mr. Wilson returned with Gloria. My little sister walked in, her eyes bouncing between me and him, unsure of what was happening.

He asked her to spell the same word. She hesitated for just a second, then said, "C-O-M-P-A-N- Y."

She left as quickly as she came, and I sat back down, humiliated. Not just for being wrong, but for having my younger sister called in to correct me in front of everyone. That's what stung most. I shrank back, exposed and a little angry—not at her, but at the situation. I couldn't understand why Mr. Wilson had done that.

But he wasn't mocking me. He didn't laugh or make a joke. After a long pause, he said something that stuck with me: "People around us, even those younger or quieter, can teach us important things. It's not about knowing everything, but being open to learning."

It took me a long time to fully understand the lesson, but that day taught me a kind of humility that's stayed with me ever since. Sometimes, growth doesn't come from winning but from getting it wrong and learning to accept it.

That truth became clearer as I found comfort in English class. I was still shy, but my talent with words became a refuge. Despite the teasing and bullying, I had something steady to hold onto. Spelling class became a place where I shone, a space that grounded me—even when the world outside felt uncertain. Each small victory reminded me I was capable—and, like in the spelling bee, ready to face challenges head-on.

After that day in class, I started winning the weekly spelling bees. It became a small but steady routine. I'd stand at the front of the room, nervous but focused, spelling each word with careful precision.

My wins got some light claps from classmates, but behind the smiles, I caught their side-eyes.

Recess told a different story. Some kids started mocking me for always coming out on top. I kept quiet, stuck to myself. Somehow, that seemed to bother them more. The jokes turned sharp, the laughter edged with something meaner.

And one day after school, all that tension—the stares, the side comments, the fake claps—finally snapped.

Joey, the loudest one in the bunch, always quick with a slick comment, stepped forward at recess. His chest puffed out, voice slicing through the chatter as he called me out in front of everyone.

Charged-up kids hungry for a show quickly formed a tight circle. My stomach flipped, but I didn't move. I didn't speak. I just stared at him, heart pounding like a drum in my ears, trying not to let the fear show.

Joey didn't wait. He rushed me with a wild swing—teeth clenched, all anger and fire—like he'd been holding it in too long. I ducked, felt the wind of his punch graze my head, and came up swinging. My fist connected with the side of his jaw, hard enough to make him stumble, but he didn't go down. He came back fast—sloppy, but fierce—and landed a shot to my shoulder.

Pain flared, but I ignored it, stepping in and throwing punch after punch, fists fueled by weeks of whispers and sideways glances.

He tried to grab me, but I slipped free and hit him again—this time, right in the nose. Blood sprayed—bright red, sudden—and the crowd gasped, then cheered even louder. He dropped to one knee, dazed, trying to wipe the blood away with his sleeve. I didn't stop. I shoved him hard, and he hit the ground with a dull thud.

Before anyone could pull me back or break it up, I kicked him— once in the ribs, then again, harder. His body folded in on itself, a sharp grunt escaping his mouth as he rolled over, trying to cover up.

The cheering shifted. It wasn't excitement anymore; it turned into something darker, something mean. A few kids started laughing; others just stared, unsure of what they'd just witnessed. And as Joey lay there groaning, holding his side, a voice broke through from the back: "Alvin is White."

Suddenly, the crowd turned. Just like that, I was no longer the underdog standing his ground; I was the target.

I knew something bad was about to happen. I ran—down Dale, onto Warren—legs burning, breath short, the chants chasing me.

At home, I slammed the door and leaned into it, chest heaving. I peeked through the window. One of them stood across the street, still yelling, trying to pull others in.

I sat with it, shaken, angry, and unsure why doing well had turned into something to hate me for.

Later, my sister checked in, asking what was going on. I shrugged, gave her nothing. She let it be, but her eyes stayed on me.

The next day, school moved on. Kids filled the halls like nothing had happened. But I hadn't moved on. I was still carrying it. When one of the boys who'd chased me walked by and smiled like we were friends, it hit me—what hurt me didn't even register for them. It had passed for everyone but me.

CHAPTER 58

A COWBOY'S CHRISTMAS, PAID IN LOVE

The winter wind bit into my skin as I waited at the corner of Humboldt Avenue for the bus to Dudley. It was December 20, 1957—just days before Christmas—but something about this year felt off. Money was tight, and gifts weren't a priority. Momma had already figured out something for Gladys and Gloria, but I didn't expect much for myself.

From the hallway, I could hear faint voices drifting in from the kitchen—Momma and Juanita, talking low. Most of the words slipped past me, but one question caught my ear: "Is there anything he wants for Christmas?" A flicker of hope stirred, even if I didn't dare believe it would lead to anything.

Momma's reply came with a tired edge. She spoke of tough times, then mentioned a toy I'd brought up weeks earlier—a gun and holster set. I had long since let go of that wish, knowing toys came last in our house.

Then Juanita said something that made me freeze. She offered to buy it. My breath caught mid-step as I crept closer to the kitchen, heart thudding, afraid I'd misheard. Momma blinked, surprised. "You sure?"

Looking at me, Juanita stood tall. "I got a job now. I want to do this for him."

Excitement surged through me, but I tried to play it cool as she shared the plan: Meet her at Robell's after work on Friday…

I didn't care about the cold or the wait. The gun set was going to be mine. I thanked her, doing my best to sound casual, but I couldn't hide the thrill in my voice. Juanita grinned and called me her little cowboy.

I couldn't stop thinking about it. In my mind, I was already riding through the Wild West with my horse, Silver, and my partner, Tonto. I imagined the weight of the holsters on my hips, the feel of the plastic grips in my hands. I felt invincible.

Friday finally came. Momma gave me a quarter for the bus, and I headed to Dudley, heart pounding. The cold stung my face, but the excitement kept me warm. Shoppers bustled past with arms full of bags. A man dressed as Santa stood by the entrance, ringing a bell with one hand and holding a red donation bucket with the other.

And then I saw her. Juanita walked toward me, her smile cutting through the cold like sunlight breaking through clouds. She wore a black winter coat, gloves, and a brown-and-white scarf snug around her neck. Her eyes sparkled as she leaned in and wrapped her arms around me. I pointed to the gun and holster set displayed behind the glass. She gave a quick nod, and we stepped inside.

Warmth wrapped around us the moment we stepped through the door. Christmas music floated through the store—soft, cheerful, familiar. The air smelled of buttered popcorn and peppermint.

Juanita took my hand. A sales clerk led us to the counter, reached below the register, and placed the toy set on top. Then she tucked it into a paper bag.

My hands closed around it, the weight in my arms somehow heavier with meaning.

I looked down, then back up at Juanita, trying to find the right words. "Thank you. You don't even know how much this means."

She gave my shoulder a light squeeze. "I think I do."

She smiled again and told me to go on my adventure.

As we stepped outside, I couldn't help it—I shouted with excitement, already imagining myself riding off into the sunset, fearless and free.

Juanita laughed and shook her head as we caught the bus home. The thrill still buzzed inside me, but this Christmas was about more than just a gift. What mattered most—what stayed with me— was how Juanita stepped up for me, right when I needed it. Momma had made sure Gladys and Gloria would have something to open on Christmas Day, but this moment with Juanita was something I'd never forget.

CHAPTER 59

WHERE HOPE MET THE EDGE OF A NEW BEGINNING

After World War II, job opportunities in cities like Boston brought hope for a better life. Many Black Americans, including my family, moved north to escape the oppression and limitations of the South, seeking freedom and a fresh start.

In Boston, discriminatory practices confined Black families to neighborhoods such as Roxbury, the South End, and parts of Dorchester. Still, the city offered possibilities. My family was part of this migration, and life here held more promise than the small town of Wintersville, where we came from.

On an April day in 1958, Momma came home holding a letter, her face brighter than I'd seen in a while. It was from Melvin. He was graduating from high school in June and planned to move to Boston afterward. The thought of him coming felt like a blessing, but the reality of our cramped apartment stirred doubts.

Juanita asked where he'd stay. Momma suggested he could live with TJ, our cousin, and his wife, Eula Bess. Juanita hesitated, unsure how Eula Bess would take it, but Momma was confident that the family would step in.

Relief washed over her, knowing Melvin had a chance to build a life in Boston. Yet, beneath that relief, a quiet ache lingered. She had always dreamed of guiding him into manhood, but distance and circumstance kept them apart, and he was now grown. She would finally have him close, but the lost years hung heavy. She hadn't shaped his early life or stood beside him through those critical moments.

Still, she was ready now to offer safety beyond the reach of Southern threats, to help him build something new, to stand with him as he stepped into his future.

As she hummed while starting supper, a quiet sense of possibility filled the room. Boston wasn't perfect, but it offered Melvin a chance—freedom from fear, room to grow. Momma hadn't raised him, but she would be there now, ready to help him shape what came next.

CHAPTER 60

WHEN EVERYONE WAS HOME

On a June day in 1958, Melvin arrived from Georgia with a presence you couldn't ignore. The moment he walked through the door, his height and booming voice filled the space. He jumped right into stories about his girlfriend back in Georgia, Mildred, proudly flashing her photo to anyone willing to look.

Momma said she was pretty, but Juanita snatched the picture with a grin and said Mildred needed some lipstick. Momma told her to quit joking, and the room filled with laughter. Melvin just grinned, took the photo back, and slid it into his pocket.

Then he started telling us about his long bus ride to Boston. He'd chosen the cheaper Trailways bus over the more popular Greyhound, hoping to save a little money. Turned out to be a mistake. The bus was old, with torn seats and a mix of passengers he called "colorful."

He painted the picture—chickens in crates, strange food passed around, and one man snoring like he was preaching in his sleep. By the time he arrived in Boston, two days late, he swore off Trailways for good.

We laughed at the story, but it came with a quiet lesson—cheapest isn't always best. Still, Melvin had a way of turning every misstep into something worth remembering.

Later, he brought up the NFL Championship game. Sports weren't really my thing, but I sat beside him anyway. His excitement lit up the room, and being near him mattered more than whatever was playing on the screen.

On a day in July 1958, the morning buzzed with the familiar rhythm of family activity. The scent of home-cooked food filled the air—baked ham, potato salad, collard greens, and sweet potato pies. Sunday gatherings like this brought out the best in Momma. She lit up when her table was full and her children were close.

One by one, the family arrived, filling the house with voices and laughter. Melvin was the first, eager to experience his first Sunday dinner in Boston. He spoke with excitement about his new life, sharing stories of his plans while everyone else caught up, adding their own memories to the mix. The room buzzed with chatter and joy. Yet beneath it all, an unspoken sense of change lingered—quiet but unmistakable. Ruby Nelle, always the calming presence at their gatherings, didn't come. Her absence was noticeable, though no one mentioned it aloud.

As the day went on, conversation moved between nostalgia and the present. Old memories surfaced—times when life felt simpler, like during power outages when they'd sit together in the dark telling ghost stories. Those stories now floated through the room, a comforting echo of the past.

Momma, sitting at the head of the table, took it all in with quiet pride. Her children were gathered around her, the house alive with their presence. But something in her eyes lingered—a flicker of sadness, a recognition that time was slipping away. Her children were grown now, leading lives of their own. The house, once full of their constant noise and motion, grew quieter with each passing year.

As evening settled in, the house began to empty. One by one, people said their goodbyes and drifted out the door. The laughter that had filled the rooms slowly faded, leaving behind the clinking of dishes and the quiet hum of leftover conversation. Dinner had wrapped up, the football game on the television had ended, and the earlier energy was now giving way to stillness.

Benny, a friend of Melvin's who had once introduced him to Juanita, stood near the door with his hands tucked into his jacket pockets. He was shorter than Melvin but carried himself with the relaxed confidence of someone who felt at ease no matter where he stood. He glanced at the table, where voices still lingered, but his posture made it clear—he was ready to go.

Juanita, smiling and unbothered, moved with the lightness of someone excited for the night ahead. She leaned over, kissed Momma, and reached for her jacket, slipping it on quickly as she followed Benny out. He held the door open for her, and without much pause, they were gone. The sound of the door closing left a stillness behind, one that felt heavier than expected.

The house grew quieter with their departure. The momentum of the day slowed. Johnnie pushed back from the table, stood, and, without saying much, headed toward the door. His movements were calm but purposeful, a silent signal that he had somewhere to be. Before anyone could respond, he stepped out, leaving only the soft thud of the door behind him.

Now, only Momma, Gladys, Gloria, and I remained. The warmth of the day lingered faintly in the air, but the house had clearly shifted. The noise was gone. The space, once buzzing with voices and movement, now held a calm that came with endings—soft, steady, and sure.

Sundays meant everything to Momma. These gatherings were the heartbeat of the house—the laughter, the food, the stories passed around the table. She lived for these moments. But once Juanita, Melvin, and Johnnie were gone, the atmosphere shifted. The empty chairs didn't tell the whole story—it was the loss of their energy. The house, once vibrant, grew dim. A hush settled deep into the walls, and a quiet longing took hold in my chest.

Even as the scent of Momma's cooking lingered in the air, I found myself wishing for more time—more moments like this, when noise and love filled the rooms. But as the silence deepened, reality settled in: nothing stays the same.

For a moment, I saw that quiet ache in Momma's eyes, softened by a flicker of hope. The family had scattered, but we all understood the rhythm. Another Sunday would come, bringing laughter, food, and warmth back into the house. It might not be the same, but it would still be ours—a gathering rooted in love and togetherness. That thought offered a quiet comfort, knowing the tradition would hold, and no matter what changed, we'd find our way back to each other.

CHAPTER 61

WHERE I FIRST FOUND THE GAME

On a Saturday in July 1958, Melvin came over and told me he had an interview with Biltright at 2:30, so he couldn't stay. I nodded, though I wasn't sure what he meant. Baseball wasn't my thing yet, but Melvin sounded confident, so I decided to give it a try.

I sat down in front of the black-and-white TV, fiddling with the antenna until the picture cleared. The Red Sox were playing the White Sox. At first, nothing made much sense. The players were just blurry shapes on the screen, and it was hard to tell who was who. Still, I stayed focused, keeping my attention fixed on the game.

Gladys stood in the doorway, arms crossed, asking why I was watching the game instead of something else. I explained Melvin's suggestion. Gloria walked in, teasing me about suddenly liking baseball. I brushed them off, insisting I was trying to learn.

As the game continued, my attention sharpened. The announcer's voice guided the action—pitch by pitch, hit by hit—and the rhythm of the game started to make sense. I still didn't know the players or all the rules, but the flow began to click.

Still, something unsettled me. There were no Black players on the Red Sox roster, a fact that sat heavily. My connection to the game wavered when no one on the field looked like me. It stirred quiet doubts about whether I belonged in a world that seemed to overlook people like us.

About an hour later, Gladys returned and asked if I was still watching the game.

I shot her an incredulous look, as if the answer should've been obvious. She'd already interrupted once, and now she was back with the same question. Really, she wanted to watch *American Bandstand,* but turning off the game wasn't an option.

She rolled her eyes, but I held my ground. Baseball was still new to me, but something about it was starting to stick.

That night, I sat in my room, pretending to call the plays in an imaginary game. I narrated every pitch and hit like I was part of something big. The house was quiet. Gloria and Gladys were asleep, and Momma was on the phone, speaking softly.

But my noise didn't go unnoticed. Gladys complained about the racket, and Momma came in to tell me to quiet down. I argued, but she stood firm, saying I needed to keep it down so I wouldn't disturb everyone else. I agreed with a quiet grumble, muttering under my breath that they didn't understand how important the game was to me. But when Momma smiled and reminded me to keep dreaming, some of the weight lifted.

Even with the interruptions, baseball became my escape. It offered a glimpse of something bigger, something I might one day be part of, even if I didn't fully understand it yet. I was still figuring out where I fit in the world, but in that moment, the game gave me something real to hold onto.

CHAPTER 62

WHAT LITTLE BROTHERS NEVER SAY

On the afternoon of August 3, 1958, the sun shone brightly as we gathered in the living room of our house on St. James Street, not far from the church. Momma's cake cooled on the counter, filling the air with its sweet aroma, while I sat on the floor flipping through a *Sports Illustrated* magazine. Juanita and Benny walked in, both looking like they had something important to share.

Juanita held out her hand, showing off an engagement ring, a diamond that caught the sunlight streaming through the window. Momma paused, her hands still on the iron, and leaned in to take a closer look. She seemed unsure, asking Juanita if she was certain about her decision, reminding her that she'd once talked about going to college. Juanita reassured her, saying she could still go later. She was ready for marriage because Benny loved her, and she loved Benny.

Benny stood nearby, his arm draped around Juanita like he was proud to show her off. Inside, I fumed. I had never liked Benny. Every time he came around, he'd pinch and twist my arm until it turned red. I hated it.

Juanita must've sensed my silence because she came over and showed me the ring, waiting for a reaction. I shrugged, unsure how to respond. She asked if I was happy for her.

Guilt tugged at me. Juanita always looked out for me when Momma was busy with Gloria or Ruby Nelle had other things to do. I told her I was happy for her, though I wasn't sure I meant it.

Her face lit up. She kissed the top of my head, then returned to Benny, already talking about wedding plans—Nellie as her maid of honor, Gloria as the flower girl. Her voice bubbled with excitement as she mentioned calling Daddy in Ohio to ask if he'd come give her away at the wedding. But Momma reminded us it had been three years since anyone had heard from him.

Still, Juanita's mood stayed bright. Nothing could dull her excitement. I sat quietly, conflicted. I didn't like Benny, but I didn't want to ruin Juanita's joy. She deserved happiness, even if I doubted the man she chose.

CHAPTER 63

FALCONS RISING FROM WARREN STREET

A warm afternoon settled over Dale Street, a busy area where most of my friends lived during a day in September 1958. We were deep into a lively game of dodgeball—balls flying, laughter echoing through the neighborhood—when a young white man approached with a surprising offer.

He was tall, his hair tousled like he'd just finished running. A snug T-shirt clung to his lean frame, and faded jeans, their cuffs rolled above worn sneakers, hung comfortably on his legs. He stood with ease, hands at his sides, a friendly smile on his face.

He introduced himself as Neil Coe, a staff member at the Young Men's Christian Association on Warren Street. He told us they were starting a youth group and asked if we'd be interested in joining. The idea sounded promising. Neil explained the group would meet every Wednesday evening at the Elliott Church, right on the corner of Dale and Warren.

Marshall Lewis, one of my friends known for his basketball skills at nearby Lewis Jr. High, quickly spoke up. His mustache and early facial hair made him look older than the rest of us, and his confidence always stood out. His enthusiasm caught on, and soon we were all convinced this could be something fun and worthwhile.

Neil handed out consent forms to take home to our parents. He asked that they be signed and returned by Wednesday so the group could officially begin and officers could be elected.

That evening marked the start of our involvement with the youth group.

At home, I handed the form to my mother. She read it carefully, her expression shifting—pride mingling with a trace of concern. The pride came from recognizing the Young Men's Christian Association as a good opportunity. The concern took longer to place.

Her expression softened into a smile as she finished reading. Then she asked if there was a similar group for girls, wondering if my sisters could join the YWCA. Her desire for fairness was clear.

I explained that the Young Women's Christian Association downtown required a train ride. She considered this, torn between wanting her daughters to have the same chances and worrying about their safety. After a pause, she said she'd think about finding something for them through the church instead.

Standing there, I understood my mother's determination to secure equally valuable opportunities for all her children. She signed the form for me, already turning her thoughts toward finding the right paths for each of us. This moment wasn't just about joining a youth group; it reflected her deep care and unwavering commitment to fairness and the future success of every one of us.

We gathered outside Elliott Church, buzzing with excitement for our first youth group meeting. The anticipation was thick in the air. Everyone seemed eager to get started.

Inside, Neil led us to a small room across the hall from the basketball court. He explained this would be our regular meeting spot, and occasionally, we'd use it for basketball games. Every couple of weeks, we'd play friendly matches against other YMCA teams. Though the games could get competitive, the focus was always on community and teamwork, not on winning championships.

Once everyone had settled in, Neil officially kicked off the meeting. He said we'd start with some business, then play basketball until 6:00. He introduced us to parliamentary procedure, a way to keep meetings organized and decision-making fair. Today, he said, we'd be electing officers for the group.

The mention of elections stirred a mix of excitement and nervousness in me. I considered nominating myself and imagined what that might feel like, but the weight of responsibility felt too heavy. For now, I decided just to observe.

As the nominations began, Marshall was chosen for president. With his confidence and natural charisma, he was the obvious choice. He stood tall as others voiced their support, and before long, he was elected our leader. The group then chose Curt Clemmons as vice president, Bob Marion as secretary, and Jerome Hart as treasurer. Watching it all unfold filled me with pride for my new friends.

The meeting continued with a few lighthearted moments, like when Marshall cracked a joke about the flickering lights, making a few of us laugh, or when Bob knocked over a stack of papers and scrambled to pick them up while everyone chuckled. Between the serious parts, there was easygoing teasing and friendly chatter. It made the room feel relaxed and familiar—a place where we could just be ourselves, away from the watchful eyes of adults.

Marshall, who always seemed to command the room's attention, leaned back in his chair— relaxed, yet fully tuned in. After a brief pause, he spoke up, proposing a name for the group. He wanted something strong and meaningful. The room went quiet as he suggested "Falcons"—a symbol of speed, intelligence, and control. Everyone agreed. From that moment on, we were the Falcons.

Neil then announced a Saturday morning swimming event at the Charlestown YMCA—a chance to swim for fun, take lessons, or compete in relay races. A wave of excitement moved through the room. Marshall, stepping into his new role, made sure everyone understood the plan: meet early at the YMCA office on Warren Street, then head to Charlestown together. It was something we could all look forward to.

But then the mood shifted. Neil brought up the swimming rule. He explained that everyone would swim without swimsuits, a long-standing YMCA practice. Silence swept over the group. A few laughed nervously; others exchanged uneasy glances. The idea felt strange—unsettling, even. Still, Neil clarified that the policy applied to all participants. If we wanted to be involved, we'd have to go along with it.

Despite the initial shock, the meeting carried on. Neil lightened the mood by bringing in a box of donuts and bottles of Coca-Cola. The energy shifted immediately—everyone perked up, grabbed snacks, and began chatting again. Laughter filled the room, and the tension slowly melted away. We shared the treats, joked around, and simply enjoyed the moment.

By the end of the meeting, we had a name, permission slips, a plan for the swim event, and a new sense of unity. We weren't just a group of kids anymore; we were becoming a team.

Afterward, we split into teams and headed to the basketball court for a few friendly scrimmages. The matchups were fair, and we played hard. The rhythm of sneakers on wood blended with bursts of laughter. There was a quiet joy in how we moved together—a natural ease that made this group feel different. With each pass and shout, something started to settle in me, like I'd found a place where I truly belonged.

I walked out of the building with a quiet confidence, as if I were stepping into something larger than myself. No title, no official role—just a sense that maybe, finally, I had a place here.

As I made my way home, details from the meeting swirled through my mind. I liked the idea of swimming lessons, but the no-trunks rule lingered, puzzling and out of place. By the time I

reached the house, I'd decided to ask Momma for permission—just not about that part. I wasn't ready to bring it up.

When I got inside, she was folding laundry in the living room. I took a breath and stepped closer.

I took a breath and mentioned the church was offering free swim lessons at the Charlestown YMCA on Saturday mornings. I kept my tone light, not wanting it to seem like a big deal. She paused, considered it, then gave a simple nod. If the church was involved, she saw no harm—just reminded me to behave.

I felt relieved. No follow-up questions, no long talk. I thought about bringing up the no-trunks policy but let it go. I wasn't sure how to explain something that odd, and I wasn't ready for the look she might give.

Later that night, lying in bed, the no-trunks rule lingered. Not just the rule itself, but how no one seemed to think it was strange. Back then, I didn't have the words for what felt off. Now I know—it was all about context. And the context was never really explained.

The morning of the swim event arrived, and we gathered at the YMCA office on Warren Street. The air was cool, and we buzzed with a mix of excitement and nerves. Neil stood nearby, offering a few last-minute instructions before we set off. We walked to Dudley Station, chatting along the way.

At the platform, the wait was brief before our train pulled in. We found seats quickly, talking and laughing as the ride carried us toward Charlestown. With every stop, anticipation built.

The best part came when the train pulled up right in front of the YMCA—no bus transfers or long walks, just a few steps, and we were there, facing the tall brick building. A knot tightened in my stomach as I stepped off.

Inside, the pool dominated the space, and my nerves spiked again. We shuffled into the dressing room, quiet under the hum of fluorescent lights. The air was thick with chlorine, damp cotton, and tile. I picked a corner and changed quickly, keeping my eyes down. There was an unspoken tension in the room—each of us focused on getting through it without being noticed.

That morning marked my first real step into swimming. Curiosity pushed against discomfort. After changing, we headed to the pool. The wide blue surface stretched out before us as Marshall climbed the diving board, moved with calm purpose, and dove in. Before slipping under, he turned and called for us to join him.

I lingered at the edge, easing down the steps into the shallow end. It felt strange at first— standing there in my "Birthday Suit." But the moment that cold water hit me, sending a shock through my system, in a minute or two, my body temperature started to adjust, and the unease began to fade.

The water was a kind of equalizer. Once submerged, it didn't matter anymore. Step by step, I adjusted. Each movement grew smoother, less stiff.

Before long, I was floating, kicking, paddling—just enough to stay above water. Nothing fancy, just a beginning. I focused on moving my arms and legs, doing my best to mimic the freestyle stroke Neil was demonstrating.

The lessons were harder than I expected. Water got up my nose, and more than once, I had to stop to cough and catch my breath. Still, I was proud of the small progress I made—learning to float, kicking my legs, and making it halfway across the pool without clinging to the edge. By the end of the session, my awkwardness had mostly been replaced by a quiet sense of accomplishment.

As we toweled off, I found myself laughing with the others about how nervous we'd all been. "Man, I thought this was gonna be way worse," Darrell said, shaking his head. I nodded, feeling the same. It wasn't as bad as I'd imagined.

Looking back, the no-trunks policy felt strange at first, but it was just another rule everyone accepted without question. What once felt intimidating eventually faded into routine. It was a reminder that sometimes the things we worry about the most lose their power once we face them.

The following Wednesday, in October 1958, the fun continued. We met at the YMCA and set out on a field trip to the Boston Navy Yard, about forty minutes away. Permission slips had been signed earlier in the week, and excitement filled the air as we boarded the bus. Chatter filled the aisles as we rolled through the streets, all of us eager to catch a glimpse of the historic landmark.

When the bus pulled up to the Navy Yard, we were greeted by the imposing sight of the USS Constitution—Old Ironsides—rising tall and proud. The retired Navy ship stood as a symbol of history, its decks etched with stories of independence and triumph.

Our guide, a middle-aged man with a weathered voice and enthu- siastic manner, wore a navy- blue blazer with a gold anchor pin, a white shirt, a striped tie, and khaki pants. Polished brown shoes and a captain's hat completed the look. He welcomed us to the Navy Yard and the USS Constitution, and we gathered around as he launched into tales of the ship's past. He spoke of battles fought, storms en- dured, and victories won, painting a vivid picture of resilience and freedom.

After touring the ship, we made our way to the Navy Yard's dining hall, where rows of tables were already set for lunch. The buzz of conversation grew louder as we found our seats. Once everyone had settled, our guide stood at the front of the room and announced the meal: traditional New England meatloaf, mashed potatoes with gra- vy, string beans, and blueberry pie for dessert. The group responded with excited murmurs and a round of polite applause.

Staff members in white aprons brought out trays of food, serving each table one by one. As the plates arrived, the room quieted and attention shifted to the meal. When the blueberry pie was served, a cheer went up. Everyone had clearly been waiting for the sweet finish.

Before we ate, Neil stood at the head of the group and asked for a moment of grace. He led a brief prayer of gratitude for the experi- ence, the food, and the people who made it all possible.

After lunch, we boarded the bus for the ride back to the YMCA. The return trip was quiet, the hum of the engine and gentle sway- ing of the bus lulling most of the group to sleep. A few of us stayed awake, staring out the windows, lost in thought. It had been a good day, and as I sat in silence, a strong sense of belonging settled over me.

CHAPTER 64

SMOKE, DICE, AND MARY'S SMILE

While I was having wholesome experiences with the Falcons and at the YMCA, my brother, Johnnie, was living a very different life. I didn't learn about it until much later from Mary, who was his girlfriend at the time and later became his wife.

Mary told me stories about Johnnie from those days, including one vivid moment that took place in the hallway of a tenement building on Washington Street and Massachusetts Avenue.

Golden light streamed through a narrow hallway window, casting warm tones on the scuffed walls and bare floors. Johnnie stood there with his two new friends, twin brothers Bobby and Billy, their laughter echoing off the close walls.

Johnnie had fallen in with a different crowd—one where alcohol and marijuana had started casting shadows over his once-promising path.

Bobby pulled a joint from his pocket and lit it with practiced ease. He held it out to Johnnie, who hesitated, his brow furrowed as he weighed the choice. "I'm not sure about this."

The hallway stank of stale smoke and faint grease from Miss Ethel's fried chicken. Overhead, a buzzing bulb flickered, casting jittery shadows across the peeling wallpaper. Bobby leaned against the wall, spinning the joint between his fingers. Billy clutched a brown paper bag with a half-empty bottle of Ripple, the cap already loose.

Johnnie crouched beside a wooden crate they used as a makeshift dice table, his fingertips brushing the smooth plastic cubes. He'd been smoking cigarettes for a couple of months— bumming off Billy, buying his own when he could—but the joint in Bobby's hand felt like more than just the next step. It felt like a decision.

"Come on, Garfield," Bobby said, grinning as he used Johnnie's middle name. "Little smoke won't kill you. Stop actin' like a jive turkey. Just take it."

Billy held the bottle toward him. "Wash it down with this. Might help you breathe easier." Johnnie's hand hovered, then pulled back. He didn't say no—just shifted his gaze to the dice in Bobby's other hand.

Bobby caught the dodge and tilted his head. "Aight. You gon' stop playin' scared and hit this, or what?"

Johnnie stayed crouched, his fingers twitching against his knees. The earthy bite of the smoke hung heavy in the air, mixing with the musty hallway. It wasn't inviting, but it wasn't unfamiliar either.

"I don't know, man. Ain't like I never smoked before, but this..." He let the thought trail off.

Billy took a long pull from the bottle. "Boy, please. You smoke them squares like it's your job. This ain't no different. Might even give you better rolls."

Bobby exhaled slowly, a lazy stream of smoke curling past his lips. "Yeah. You always stressin' about school, trade class, whatever. Loosen up. Ain't nobody here gonna snitch."

Johnnie reached for the dice, trying to shift the focus. "Let's just roll."

Bobby didn't move. He held the joint a little closer. "You ain't gettin' out that easy. Your time, Garfield."

Johnnie looked from Bobby to Billy, who gave a slight nod, that same crooked smirk on his face. His chest tightened—curiosity wrestling with caution. He remembered his first cigarette, how wrong it felt at first. Now, it was like lacing up sneakers.

He took the joint, holding it like it might say something first. His eyes flicked back to Bobby, waiting for a signal.

Bobby's grin widened. "Just don't choke, man. We don't need you coughin' up your lungs."

Johnnie brought it to his lips. The burn hit fast and deep, sharper than he expected. He doubled over, coughing hard, shoulders shaking.

Billy whistled and leaned back. "There it is."

Johnnie waved the smoke from his face, eyes watery as he tried to recover. He straightened up and picked up the dice again, his hands still trembling slightly. "Alright. Now we roll."

A soft, confident voice cut through the chatter. "Crap master, huh? Let's see if you are as smooth in conversation as you are with them dice."

Johnnie turned, and there was Mary, a 15-year-old girl, standing a few steps away. She clutched a small bag from the corner store, shifting her weight like she wasn't sure whether to step closer. Her smile, though hesitant, carried a quiet warmth that lit up the dim, worn hallway.

Johnnie froze for a second, caught off guard by her presence, then offered a small grin of his own.

"Hey there," he said, his voice softer than it had been all day.

Mary lifted her eyes to meet his, her smile growing just a little but still shy. "Hey." She gripped the bag tightly, as if it gave her courage. Then, after a pause: "So... you the one they call Garfield?" Her voice was light and curious, like she wasn't quite sure how to ask but needed to know.

The name "Garfield" had been buzzing around the neighborhood. In a tight-knit place like theirs, word traveled fast, especially about Johnnie, who was making a name for himself as a sharpshooter in dice games.

"Well, look at you." Johnnie pushed himself up. "You know my middle name, but I don't even know your first. What's yours?"

"Mary." She stepped closer. "And you must be Garfield. Nice to meet you."

A chuckle escaped Johnnie as he brushed dust from his hands. "Pleasure's all mine."

Mary's eyes flicked to the dice scattered on the crate. "So, you really that good, or they just lettin' you win?"

Billy cracked up. "Letting him win? Nah, he been cleanin' us out all day!"

Johnnie's grin widened as he slipped the dice into his pocket. "You can watch me play anytime, Mary. Might even teach you a thing or two."

Leaning back against the wall, he rolled the dice in his hand, flashing her a casual grin. "So, Mary," he tilted his head, "you ever been to the Rivoli? They showin' that new flick, *Lilies of the Field*, this weekend."

Mary blinked, caught off guard by the shift in topic. "Yes, I've been there before," she said softly. "I heard about that movie with Sidney Poitier."

Johnnie smiled, tucking the dice away. "Well, how 'bout this— Saturday, you and me go see it?

My treat. Gotta spend these winnings on somethin' good." Mary hesitated, her shy smile returning. "You sure about that?"

"Course I'm sure." Johnnie's confidence was as smooth as ever. "What's the point of winnin' if I can't take a pretty girl to the movies?"

Mary glanced down at her bag, then back at him. "Alright, Garfield. Saturday it is."

Johnnie nodded, a spark of satisfaction in his eyes. "Seven o'clock. Don't make me wait now." "I won't," she said, already turning to leave, her smile lingering as she disappeared down the hallway.

As her footsteps faded, Bobby leaned in, grinning. "Man, Garfield, you got a smooth rap. Pullin' all kinds of luck with the ladies and shootin' crap good tonight."

Johnnie shrugged, playing it cool, though the pride in his expression gave him away. "It's strategy, fellas. Same as the dice."

Mary nodded to herself, her smile still lingering. "Maybe." She glanced back one last time before heading down the hallway.

CHAPTER 65

COACH WIMBERLY TAUGHT US MORE—AND WE LISTENED

On the following Wednesday, we gathered in the Elliott Church gym, unsure of what to expect. Some guys joked and shoved each other, while others bounced basketballs. The noise cut instantly when Mr. Wimberly walked in. He didn't say much, but his presence alone commanded attention.

He called us into a circle around him. His navy-blue tracksuit looked sharp, and the whistle around his neck made it clear that he meant business.

He introduced himself as Coach Wimberly and told us that if we were part of the Y, we were part of the team. There wouldn't be try-outs, but that didn't mean we wouldn't work hard. We were going to sweat, push ourselves, and have fun—but most of all, we'd do it together.

Coach emphasized that basketball wasn't just about the game. His message focused on discipline, respect, and showing up for each other. Quitting, he said, wasn't an option—on the court or off.

He named Marshall team captain and Jerome assistant captain, asking them to lead by example. Both stepped up, clearly ready for the challenge.

Coach told us we weren't running drills that day. Instead, we'd scrimmage. Marshall and Jerome started calling out names. My stomach tightened with every pick. I didn't want to be the last one left standing.

Finally, Marshall pointed at me and called me over. Relief flooded through me, and Marcus, already on the team, reached out for a quick handshake.

The scrimmage got underway. It had its rough patches, but everyone hustled. Coach Wimberly stood on the sidelines, arms folded, offering the occasional tip. Mostly, he stayed quiet, letting us figure things out for ourselves.

After the game, he brought us in and clapped his hands once. The room stilled. He said the energy was strong, and while we had plenty to work on, the effort stood out. If we kept showing up like that, the season had real promise.

Just like that, the team began to take shape. No full practice yet, but under Coach Wimberly's lead, something solid was already

The following Wednesday, the gym echoed with the usual sounds of basketballs bouncing and sneakers squeaking on the polished floor. We gathered in a loose circle near the sideline, laughing and teasing each other as Mr. Wimberly called us to Coach Wimberly clapped his hands, loud and sharp, then shouted, "Aight, fellas, bring it in."

We hustled toward him, sneakers chirping on the floor, sweat still clinging to our necks. He stood tall and broad-shouldered, always wearing that same whistle and a quiet authority that made you want to stand up straighter. He didn't have to yell to earn respect. You could just tell he'd been through some things, and he carried that weight with purpose.

"Y'all the Falcons now," he said once we'd formed a crooked half-circle around him. "And that name means somethin'. Means we work hard. Means we respect each other. Means we show up—on this court and in life."

Some of us nodded; a few grinned. I remember trying to wipe the smile off my own face, not wanting to seem too eager.

Coach's eyes moved from face to face. "This ain't just about basketball. This is about how you carry yourself when nobody's lookin'."

He pointed toward the gym doors and said, "Out there, the world might not hand you the respect you deserve. But in here, we give it to each other. That's how we start."

A low rumble of "Yes, Coach" rolled through the group, but Marshall—never one to sit back— raised his voice a notch. "We got you, Coach."

Coach cracked a half-smile. "That's why you're captain."

Marshall stood a little taller, trying to play it cool. "I got you, Coach." Jerome nodded once. "Alright then. Let's keep each other sharp."

Coach turned to him without missing a beat. "That's fine, 'cause you're assistant captain. Help keep this team together."

Jerome gave a quick salute, his grin more relaxed than serious. "Yessir, Coach."

Laughter rolled through the gym—real laughter, not the kind you fake to be polite. For the first time in a long while, I wasn't just standing on the edge of something; I was in it. That rundown gym, with its scuffed floors and flickering lights, became our place. Coach's voice echoing off the walls, sneakers squeaking, elbows bumping— none of it was just about drills or plays. We were learning how to carry ourselves in a world that wasn't exactly built with us in mind. And for those few hours, we weren't just getting by; we belonged.

Across the room, Neil leaned against the wall, observing with a calm gaze. Neil was White, and in a time when race sat at the center of every conversation, he stood out. But he never acted like he didn't belong. Instead, he listened, supported, and showed up for us. That counted for something.

As practice ended, Mr. Wimberly clapped his hands. "Alright, good work today, fellas. Go get cleaned up. And remember—being on this team means something. Carry yourself like you mean it, both on and off the court."

I nodded, grabbed a stray basketball, and wiped the sweat from my face. Walking off the court, I caught Neil's small nod of approval. Having both Neil and Mr. Wimberly in our corner felt rare—one quiet, the other fierce. In a world that often stacked the odds against us, here stood a team. Not just on the court, but in life.

Wednesdays couldn't come fast enough. It wasn't just about the meeting at Eliot Church—it was what came after. That's when we hit the court. The squeak of sneakers, the bounce of the ball, and Coach Wimberly's booming voice filled the gym—those were the moments we lived for.

This particular Wednesday, Coach Wimberly walked in with a big box and a grin that said he could hardly wait to share the surprise. He dropped the box in the middle of the court with a loud thud.

"Alright, fellas, listen up!" he shouted, clapping his hands. "Line up. I got somethin' for y'all."

We hurried into line, craning our necks to see inside the box. Coach reached in and pulled out a bright red jersey, holding it high. White letters stretched across the chest—"S.C.A.A."

"Marshall, you're up first," he said, pulling out a jersey.

Marshall jogged over, his excitement obvious. Coach tossed him the number 17 jersey. "Same number as Havlicek." Marshall grinned and held it up with pride. One by one, Coach called out our names, and we stepped forward to claim our jerseys.

When my name came, I walked up trying to play it cool, though my heart was pounding. Coach handed me the jersey. I ran my fingers over the smooth fabric. Bold white letters stood out against the red, and the number 24 was printed on the back—Sam Jones's number.

A flicker of disappointment hit when I noticed "Falcons" wasn't anywhere on the jersey. A glance around showed that the others felt it too. But no one said a word. Maybe we all understood this wasn't about the name. It was about what the jersey stood for.

Marshall pulled his on right there, flexing his arms. "Man, we look good, don't we?" he said, spinning like he was on stage.

"Yeah, we do," Jerome said, slapping him on the back. "S.C.A.A. or not, ain't nobody stoppin' the Falcons."

Coach Wimberly stepped forward, his voice steady and strong. "Y'all listen up. It ain't about what's written on this jersey. It's about what you do when you wear it. This jersey stands for our team, our hard work, and the pride of bein' part of somethin' bigger than you.

"When you put this on, you're representin' this team, this community, and everything we've worked for. It ain't the name that matters—it's the heart you bring to the court. Got it?"

"Yes, Coach!" we shouted in unison.

I looked down at the jersey in my hands, pride swelling in my chest. This wasn't just a uniform; it was a symbol. Whether it said Falcons or S.C.A.A., it didn't matter. What mattered was that we'd wear it together.

As practice wound down, we lingered on the court, shooting hoops and laughing. Jerome sank a bank shot and threw his arms up. "Man, they ain't ready for us!"

Marshall laughed. "Talk big now, but don't be the first one outta breath on game day!"

I laughed along with the others, tucking my jersey under my arm as we headed out. I couldn't wait to wear it in a real game—to show the city who the Falcons were, name or no name.

The Falcons were soaring above the competition, making a name for ourselves as the best YMCA team in Boston. Our victories echoed through the streets of Roxbury. We had a starting five that couldn't be touched: Marshall Lewis, Curt Clemens, Bob Marion, Milton Warnham, and Jerome Hart. Roscoe Thomas, Jake Baker, and I held down the bench, waiting for our chance when the game turned into a blowout.

Coach Wimberly paced the sidelines during games, his voice booming over the crowd. "Move the ball, Jerome! Don't hog it!" He clapped his hands as Jerome nodded, his face focused, and dished the ball to Curt, whose jumper was so smooth it felt like poetry.

Even though I spent most games on the bench, I didn't mind. It was a thrill just to travel across the city in our maroon jerseys, knowing we were part of something bigger. I'd sit there clapping and hollering, as loud as anyone on the court.

"Alvin, you up!"

We were up by 30, and it was time to clear the bench. My heart raced as I peeled off my warm- up.

I jogged onto the court, and Milton clapped me on the back as we switched out. "Go 'head, Alvin! Show 'em what you got!"

The ball hit my hands after a few passes, and adrenaline surged through me. I drove to the basket, laying it up past the outstretched hand of a defender. The crowd erupted, and my teammates jumped to their feet, cheering me on.

"Look at my boy!" I heard Jerome shout.

After the game, as we huddled in the locker room, Coach stood in the center. "Y'all played good tonight," he said, voice steady but full of pride. "It ain't just about winnin'. It's about playin' together, liftin' each other up. That's how we keep this team strong."

Marshall nodded, slinging an arm around Curt. "Man, we got somethin' special here. Ain't no other team got a bond like ours."

He wasn't wrong. The camaraderie we built wasn't just about basketball; it was about belonging, about being part of something that mattered. The Falcons weren't just a team; they were family. Every pass, every cheer, every moment on and off the court deepened that brotherhood—a bond I knew I'd carry with me long after the season ended.

CHAPTER 66

FISHNETS AND FAITH
BENEATH A DYING FLAME

After those weeks of fun—swimming, touring Old Ironsides, and our Wednesday basketball practices, where we were still finding our rhythm as a team—the pace of life shifted. The excitement of the upcoming wedding filled the air, bringing a different kind of energy. It was a beautiful occasion, one of those rare bright moments in our family's often complicated life.

Gloria, the flower girl, took her role as seriously as she could—in her own way. Later, she confessed with a mischievous smile that she hadn't scattered the flowers as expected. They were too pretty to give up. Instead, she tossed just the petals and kept the blooms for herself, like little treasures.

My brother, Melvin, stood beside Benny as best man, a role that suited him perfectly. I still have the photo of him standing tall next to Benny, Juanita, and the rest of the wedding party. Juanita looked radiant in her white gown, her smile glowing with happiness and love.

The most unexpected moment came when my father arrived from Wintersville, bringing Newton and Amos with him. Three years had passed since we last saw him, and his presence stirred emotions I hadn't prepared for.

I wanted to be glad he was there, but something inside tightened. Questions I'd tucked away came rushing back—why hadn't he come with us to Boston? What made him stay behind?

When they visited the house, the air felt heavy with unspoken words. My father seemed out of place in our new life, and my mother carried herself differently around him. She wore a deep blue dress that fit her simply and stylishly, paired with black fishnet stockings that added a touch of flair.

Despite her composed appearance, disappointment flickered in her eyes. At one point, she asked where he planned to stay during his visit. His answer landed like a blow: he would be staying with his brother, Willie B.

Her face stayed calm, but those words landed hard. Though still married after three years of separation, she had held onto hope for reconciliation. A few months earlier, divorce papers had arrived in the mail, but she refused to sign them.

Instead, she returned them unsigned, clinging to the vows they once exchanged—vows she still believed in, even as he seemed to have lost faith long ago.

Later, Gladys told me our father had admitted to Momma that they could never live as man and wife again. Hearing that felt like a blow to the kidney. I knew how much hope she had carried, how tightly she'd held onto the belief that things could still get better.

Meanwhile, my brother Johnnie—stationed at Fort Campbell, Kentucky—missed the wedding because duty came first. His absence was felt, but we all respected his path of service.

At the wedding, there was no room for confrontation or sorrow. The day belonged to Juanita, as it should, and Momma carried herself with the quiet dignity she always showed in life's hardest moments.

For me, the day was bittersweet—a celebration for Juanita and Benny, a joyful occasion for the family, but also a reminder of how fractured things had become. The bonds that once held us together now felt stretched thin, ready to snap at any moment.

On March 27, 1959, Benny and Juanita gave Momma her first grandchild, Anita Marie Wilson. She was such a beautiful baby that when she turned one, they took her to a photographer for a portrait. Dressed in a white gown Momma had bought for her, with a blue ribbon in her hair, Anita charmed the photographer so completely that he made an extra print to display in his shop window.

I don't remember how long that picture stayed up, but every time I passed the shop, there she was—my niece, displayed with pride. The shop stood right next to the barbershop that had once refused to cut my hair. Today, those buildings along Warren Street are gone, replaced by the Roxbury Boys and Girls Club.

Ruby Nelle had three children, and Momma loved each of them, but little Nita was different. She was Momma's first grandchild from her own bloodline.

Momma treated Nita like a precious jewel. Every time Benny and Juanita dropped her off, Momma would scoop her up and hold her close. She'd hum little songs while Nita cooed and reached for her face, Momma's smile stretching wide, like she'd just won something rare and wonderful.

She carried Nita everywhere—even to church. At the front, Elder Young would often pause his sermon just to smile at Nita and praise her presence. Momma would gently pat her back, her joy shining without hesitation.

Almost every weekend, Momma bought Nita a new outfit—tiny dresses, bonnets, shiny shoes. Whatever she found, Nita had it.

The happiness on Momma's face hadn't shown so brightly in years—not since the day she met me and Johnnie at the bus station when we came from Wintersville. Having Nita around brought her back to life. She laughed more. She smiled more.

This was part of Momma's vision when she chose to leave Wintersville. She had hoped for something brighter, and in those moments with Nita, that hope felt real. When Momma held her, laughing and smiling, she truly believed she'd made the right choice.

CHAPTER 67

THE PATH WAS COLD, BUT GOD WAS WATCHING

The wind howled down St. James Street that bitter winter evening in December 1960, biting at exposed skin and seeping through even the thickest layers. The smell of kerosene lingered in the air, a constant reminder of how we kept warm against the chill. The family home stood firm against the elements, offering warmth and shelter inside. Momma paced near the stove with concern etched across her face.

She needed me to go to the gas station and fill the two ten-gallon kerosene tanks. I nodded, the weight of responsibility settling on my shoulders. I layered on clothes and stepped outside, the cold cutting through me and stealing my breath. Each step through the snow was heavy, but I kept moving toward the gas station.

As I passed the YMCA, I saw Mr. Wimberly watching me from the window. He was warm inside, his face lit by a desk lamp. He gave a small shake of his head—his look full of concern. I nodded in return, and for a moment, a sense of warmth spread through me—not from the weather, but from the silent understanding in his eyes.

The return trip was worse. The tanks were full now, and they grew heavier with every step. At the corner of Warren and St. James, I had to stop and rest, setting the tanks down to catch my breath before crossing the street. My fingers were numb and stiff, but I pushed forward. As I lifted the tanks again, one slipped from my grip, spilling kerosene all over my clothes. The sharp smell clung to me.

I caught sight of Momma's face framed in the window, her eyes filled with worry as they searched the dark street for me. The cold bit deep, and the two ten-gallon tanks felt like they were dragging me down with every step. When I finally reached the house—soaked in kerosene and aching from the weight—Momma didn't hesitate. She opened the door and pulled me inside.

Her sigh of relief was a balm to my frozen soul, and for a moment, the warmth of home washed over me, chasing away the biting cold and the burden I carried.

I didn't say much; my hands hurt too badly to speak. I removed my boots and headed for the bathroom, hoping to warm them under the sink.

The moment the warm water hit my frozen fingers, the pain was excruciating. Sharp needles pierced my skin, and I cried out, tears streaming down my face as the heat seared through the cold.

Momma appeared in the doorway, alarm in her eyes. She hurried to me, telling me to take off my kerosene-soaked clothes. She pointed to the laundry basket and ordered me to put them there. I pulled off my coat and gloves, wincing as the fabric tugged against my stiff fingers. The pain was unbearable. Momma grabbed a towel and gently rubbed my hands, murmuring how proud she was of me for taking care of the family.

That night, sitting by the kerosene heater with my hands wrapped in a warm towel, a quiet sense of accomplishment settled over me. I had braved the freezing night and done what needed to be done. I was still a boy, but in moments like that, the weight of responsibility sat heavy, like I was carrying the load of a man.

CHAPTER 68

WHEN THE HOUSE BURNED,
THE FAMILY DIDN'T

On a school day in January 1961, I sat at my desk in Ms. O'Hara's class, trying to focus, when the intercom crackled to life. A voice called my name, asking me to come to the office. The room went quiet, and all eyes turned toward me. My stomach dropped. What had I done?

I packed my books, hands trembling, and walked down the hall toward the principal's office. When I opened the door, Momma was standing there, her face tight with worry. She held Gloria in her arms—her eyes red, her cheeks damp with tears.

Momma told me the house had caught fire. The kerosene heater in her room had started it, and the flames spread too fast. There was nothing left. I stood frozen, struggling to process what she'd said.

She told me I'd be staying with Melvin for now, while she, Gloria, and Gladys would stay with Sister Owens. I was to check the apartment for anything salvageable before heading to Melvin's. She gave me a few dollars for food and reassured me we'd get through this. Gloria didn't want to stay with Sister Owens, but Momma calmed her gently.

I left the office, my mind spinning, and walked to the apartment. The building reeked of smoke, and the damage inside was clear. The furniture was gone—reduced to ash. Momma's room was unrecognizable, the bed and dresser destroyed. My room was in better shape, but everything smelled like smoke. I gathered what I could—my church clothes and shoes—and left, still reeling from the loss.

I walked down St. James Street, a shopping bag with my belongings in hand. The familiar sights of the neighborhood felt distant, as if everything had changed. At the bus stop, I waited for the Humboldt Avenue bus, my thoughts heavy.

When I got off at Charing Street, I crossed to Melvin's building. Mildred greeted me and let me in. The smell of dinner filled the air. Little Melvin and Sherry played on the floor, barely glancing at me as I sank onto the couch. Melvin came home soon after, and his face softened when he saw me. He gave me a tight hug and told me everything would be okay.

Dinner was quiet but comforting. Afterward, Melvin said I'd be sleeping on the couch until things got sorted out. For the first time that day, a calm settled over me. Somehow, everything would be alright.

A few days after I started settling into Melvin's couch, Momma showed up without warning. She told me I'd be staying with Juanita and Benny now. There was no explanation; she just told me to grab my things. I packed my bag and followed her out without asking questions.

We rode the Humboldt Ave bus in silence. Momma stared out the window, lost in thought. I sat beside her, clutching my bag, unsure why I was leaving Melvin's so soon.

Juanita's building on Crawford Street was a tall brownstone, part of a long row. She opened the door, wearing a worn bathrobe, her belly round with her second child. The apartment was cluttered with toys. She looked tired but told me I could always count on her.

Later, I found out Mildred had complained that I was wearing out Melvin's couch. Juanita shook her head and said Mildred ran the house, and Melvin just followed her lead.

Momma sat quietly, her gaze far away. After a while, she said she'd gone to the welfare office. Because of the fire, they were fast-tracking us for public housing. With her foot still injured and Daddy sending little money, she had no other choice.

Juanita didn't say much—just rubbed her belly and told me I'd be sleeping on the living room couch. I nodded. I'd already been moved around enough and didn't want to cause more trouble. I was tired but stayed quiet.

Momma was doing what she could. We were all just trying to make do. (Side note: Momma had injured her foot weeks ago and couldn't work. My dad had irregularly sent money, so she went to the welfare office looking for help.)

It was my third day out of school. I sat on the sagging couch, flipping through one of Juanita's old Sears catalogs. Little Nita, my two-year-old niece, came tearing through the room with a pair of scissors in her hand. My heart jumped. I leapt up and tried to stop her, but she darted away, laughing and weaving through the furniture.

Juanita was on the bed, phone tucked to her ear, unaware of the chaos behind her. I chased Nita around the room, but she was quick. Just as I cornered her near the open doorway, she flung the scissors into the air.

Time seemed to slow. The scissors spun into the bedroom, rising and falling in a sharp arc, then landed point-first in Juanita's upper arm.

She screamed and twisted around, blood spreading across her nightgown. I froze, stunned. She clutched her belly with one hand, her face tight with pain. Then she pointed toward the bathroom, signaling for a towel.

I ran, grabbed a towel, and rushed it back. She pressed it to her arm.

Juanita's breathing steadied as the bleeding slowed. She met my eyes with a tired, knowing look and gave a small nod, as if to say she understood—I'd done what I could. Sometimes kids move too fast to stop.

I nodded, still shaken. The scissors could've hit her in the back. It could've been worse. Little Nita came over, whispered a soft "I'm sorry," and climbed into Juanita's lap. Juanita wrapped her in a gentle hug and reminded her not to throw things again.

Then she looked at me and asked me to clean up. I grabbed a rag and wiped up the blood, my hands trembling. The image of those scissors in the air stayed with me, but so did the sight of Juanita and her daughter, safe together. I was grateful.

CHAPTER 69

THE SCAR BENEATH HER EYE

The sun poured through the window of Juanita's living room that Friday morning, April 28, 1961, lighting up the old couch I'd been sleeping on. It was my first week back at school, and I was still trying to figure out what normal felt like.

I grabbed my books and headed out. From her bedroom, her soft goodbye drifted through the cracked door, reaching me like a quiet hug. I paused, uneasy without knowing why. Something in her voice stayed with me as I stepped outside—the sun too bright, the air too still.

By mid-morning, I was in class, staring out the window, lost in thought. Then the intercom buzzed. They called me to the office.

I walked down the hall with a sinking feeling. When I got there, Momma stood by the principal's desk, her face heavy with sorrow. Gloria came in right after me, smiling—until she saw Momma.

Momma said Juanita had gone to the hospital. The baby came early—a boy, Benny Wilson III.

But Juanita didn't survive. She was gone.

Gloria's books hit the floor. Her cries filled the room. I stood frozen. Juanita couldn't be gone.

She had always been there—for Momma, for Gloria, for me.

I was just 19 months old when Gloria was born. That's when Juanita, only seven herself, stepped in to care for me—the knee baby—while

Momma tended to the newborn. By the time I was three, a shard of glass came flying toward me. It missed but struck Juanita instead. Blood streamed down her face, but all she cared about was keeping me safe. The scar beneath her right eye stayed with her—proof of a love I didn't yet understand but always felt.

Momma said Benny was still at the hospital with the baby, and the kids would be staying with his mother. Then she looked at me, her voice quiet. If I stayed at Juanita's, I'd be alone. She asked if I wanted to stay somewhere else.

The thought of leaving felt like losing Juanita all over again. I shook my head. I couldn't do it.

I told her I'd stay. She pulled me into a hug and told me to let her know if it ever got too hard. We stepped outside into the sunlight, but the brightness didn't match the weight of the day.

Nothing did. I didn't know how we'd move forward without her—only that I wasn't ready to let her go.

That Saturday, at the funeral, Benny broke down—his shoulders trembling as grief overtook him. Friends and relatives gathered around, offering steady hands and quiet words. The family decided the service would be too upsetting for little Nita, so she and the baby stayed behind in the care of Benny's mother.

The choir was singing, but the sound seemed distant, like I was underwater. I sat still, staring at the white-covered casket. That was Juanita in there.

It didn't seem real. No more hearing her laugh in the kitchen. No more hugs. Just flowers everywhere, people crying, and a heavy weight pressing on my chest.

When they started rolling the casket out, something inside me cracked. It was as if they weren't just taking her—they were taking part of me too.

That's when I broke. The tears came hard, and I couldn't stop them. My shoulders shook, and for the first time, I didn't care who saw. She was gone—and I couldn't hold it in anymore.

Grief stayed with us long after the service ended. But life didn't pause—not for sorrow, not for loss. It kept moving, and so did we.

CHAPTER 70

THOSE EARLY DAYS ON ANNUNCIATION

The fire on St. James Street changed everything. We moved into a three-bedroom apartment on the third floor of 58 Annunciation Road, Apt. 366. Twelve orange-brick buildings—some seven stories, others just two—stood crowded together like a small city within the city. It was public housing, plain and simple, but to me, it marked a scary yet fresh start.

At least now we had heat. No more dragging kerosene cans up the stairs in the dead of winter just to keep warm. That alone made it feel like a step up.

Johnnie had come back from the Army by then. He already knew how the streets moved. School was never his thing, but he slid back into the neighborhood like he'd never left., I was different. I stayed close to the apartment, listening to Red Sox or Celtics games on my little transistor radio, or tossing paper balls into a cap like I was pitching at Fenway.

Johnnie understood the streets, and he understood me. He knew what they could do to a kid like me. From the jump, he told me not to get too comfortable outside, not around the basketball court, not on the corners. He didn't say it to scare me. He said it because he'd seen how fast the wrong choice could flip your whole life.

And I listened. His voice became a steady compass in my head, guiding me even when he wasn't around. I kept my distance from the crowds, sidestepped the traps, and stayed clear of the spots he warned me about.

The streets belonged to Johnnie. He walked them with a quiet authority, like he spoke their language. But he made it clear that they weren't meant for me. So I stayed on my path, holding tight to the wisdom he handed down, long before I understood just how much it would matter.

Johnnie's advice stuck with me, but I still craved friends my own age. At school, I had Tommy and Jose, who lived in Marcella—a quieter neighborhood with single-family homes and a few two- or three-story tenements. It was just a 20-minute walk from Annunciation Road, but it felt like a different world. Marcella Park offered space to breathe, and playing ball there brought a sense of safety that the courts in the projects never could. More than anything, I needed that sense of belonging.

I walked up Columbus Avenue toward Ziegler Street, headed for the park. I moved with purpose—focused and alert—keeping Johnnie's advice in mind: know where you're going, and don't linger.

The streets buzzed with noise—voices from crowded sidewalks, car horns blaring, the faint crash of bottles. Tall buildings loomed on either side, casting long shadows across the cracked pavement. Marcella Park pulled me in, promising a break from the tension outside.

Marcella Park stretched out like a communal backyard, surrounded by small homes and worn apartment buildings with rusted fire escapes and peeling paint. The baseball field in the center was beat up—hard-packed dirt, faded chalk, patchy grass—but it was still a place where kids chased dreams. On the other side, the basketball court stood ready. The blacktop was cracked, the rims bent, the backboards scarred, but it was alive. Fences rattled when the game got rough, and the sounds of the neighborhood—radios, voices, clanging pots—filled the air.

Tommy, Jose, and I met at the court. We jumped into our usual game of H.O.R.S.E. Tommy had the ball first, spinning it on his finger with swagger. He always brought the energy, turning every shot into a performance. Jose kept things grounded—quiet, focused, sharp with his comebacks. I moved in rhythm with both of them, matching shots, laughing off misses, and letting the game carry us.

We traded tricks and jokes. Tommy bragged about his side hustle at the Greyhound station, shining shoes for quick cash. He spoke with pride—about greasing palms, working his corner. It was his way of surviving, of making something out of nothing.

The game carried on as the sun sank lower, the court fading into shadow. The laughter stayed strong—shots, misses, trash talk, and that brief, perfect feeling that we were untouchable.

Tommy glanced at the sky and said it was getting late. I agreed. I wiped my face, grabbed my stuff, and jogged home down Columbus Avenue. The air had cooled, but the city was still awake—cars idling, distant laughter, a shadow slipping into an alley.

I crossed Columbus and made my way toward Ziegler. The buildings came into view, their windows glowing in the dark. At the base of the steps, I paused—legs tired, heart still racing from the game. I climbed the concrete stairs, each step echoing. Inside, the hallway was warm. Kitchen light spilled across the floor, and I could hear pots clanging and my mother's voice calling me in.

Before I could catch my breath, she handed me a list, saying she needed ingredients for dinner. I nodded and headed back out, list in hand.

As I approached the back door, I heard shouts and laughter from the neighborhood boys.

Johnnie's warning echoed: don't mix with them. I reached for the doorknob, but the crash of a bottle nearby made me hesitate. Instead, I turned away and took the longer route around the front of the building, stepping carefully over cracked sidewalks and past dimly lit windows. The faint hum of distant traffic blended with the rustle of leaves in the cool night breeze as I made my way along the quieter, less-traveled path.

Outside, the air felt cleaner. Streetlights glowed above me as I passed buildings with lit windows. I kept Johnnie's words close—stay clear, stay focused. It wasn't always easy, but tonight, I made the right choice.

The corner store buzzed with energy—kids begging for candy, neighbors chatting like they had all night. I moved through, picked up the groceries, and paid the clerk, who said little. I took the bag and stepped back into the evening, the last bit of sunlight stretching across the sidewalk.

Walking home, I thought about the game earlier—Marcella Park, Tommy, and Jose, and how, for a little while, we'd had a sense of freedom. The streets could be hard, but moments like that made them bearable. Those friendships and that time on the court were something to hold onto.

Morning light filtered through the kitchen window as I sat at the table, picking at my breakfast. Momma stood at the stove, stirring a pot of grits, her hum low and steady beneath the soft gospel music playing on the radio.

A knock at the door broke the quiet. Momma turned slightly. "Go see who that is."

I opened it to find a woman with a tired but friendly smile and an empty cup in her hand. She said she and her husband had just moved in next door with their two daughters, and they were out of sugar.

Before I could respond, Momma was already behind me, steady and sure, extending a quiet hospitality that needed no words.

The woman stepped into the kitchen, her gaze drifting across the room. With practiced ease, Momma reached for the sugar jar, filled the cup without pause, and passed it over with a gesture that spoke of understanding—the kind that comes from knowing what it means to need something and not be judged for it.

The woman nodded, some of the tension leaving her face. "It's good to know folks look out for each other here."

Momma smiled. "That's how we live in this building. Nobody's on their own."

After she left, Momma turned to me. "You always help where you can. Around here, people remember that."

Soon enough, their family became part of the flow of daily life. Gloria started watching their daughters from time to time, and they took their place in the weekly rotation—sweeping the stairs, mopping the hallway, doing what needed to be done. That was the unspoken agreement in our building: contribute, respect the space, and look out for one another. What started as a simple knock became something more—a quiet entry into a community where belonging was built, not declared.

CHAPTER 71

WHAT MOMMA GAVE ME THAT DAY

November 20, 1961—my 14th birthday. The air outside carried a crisp edge, and the sounds of kids playing in the street drifted up to our third-floor apartment. I sat on my bed, flipping through a worn-out *Sports Illustrated*.

Momma's voice called from the hallway, pulling me from my thoughts. She stepped into the room holding a small, wrapped box.

She handed it to me with a smile and wished me a happy birthday. I peeled back the paper to find a sleek transistor radio inside.

My face lit up—I hadn't expected a gift like that.

Momma explained it was for listening to Red Sox games, so I wouldn't have to miss a single one, no matter where I was.

I thanked her and pulled her into a hug, her cooking apron carrying the scent of onions and flour, the warmth of her love folded into the moment.

That night, I lay in bed with the radio on the nightstand. The announcer's voice crackled softly in the dark, recapping the day's games. For the first time, Fenway Park felt close enough to touch.

Over the next few years, that little radio stayed by my side. I'd fall asleep listening to every pitch, swing, and play. In my head, I was there in the stands—crowd roaring, caught in the magic. Anything could happen—a no-hitter, a comeback, a record-breaking home run. Each night carried a new possibility.

Rainy days felt like punishment. I'd sit by the window, watching raindrops trace crooked paths down the glass, no game coming through the speaker. The silence in those moments was heavy, like the whole season had slipped away.

Still, I always came back. Baseball was more than a pastime. It connected me to something bigger. Even in a city like Boston, with its tangled and painful history, the game gave me reason to believe in change.

CHAPTER 72

QUESTIONS FOR THE ABSENT FATHER

In June 1962, I sat on the couch after an episode of *Father Knows Best*, wondering why we were stuck in the projects while our dad had a big house back in Ohio. It didn't seem right—my two sisters and I, left behind like we didn't matter.

By that age, the questions ran deeper. One night, after watching *Father Knows Best*, I stayed on the couch, staring at the blank screen. The show's neat endings only made our silence louder. Something was missing, and no perfect TV family could hide it.

You'd think Gladys would've spoken up. But she loved Boston. A sophomore at Girls' High, she was thriving—sharp, independent, focused. She wasn't thinking about Ohio. She was into books with strong female leads, the debate team, public speaking, and music. Boston gave her everything she needed. She wasn't looking back.

Gloria was younger and more attached to Momma. She was active in our church youth group, always by Momma's side. Daddy wasn't part of that world. He wasn't around enough to be. Gloria didn't seem to mind. She'd been five when we left Ohio—too young to remember much. If she had Momma, she was fine.

But me? I couldn't let it go. Why were we in the projects while Daddy had a house in Ohio? It didn't make sense. Not for me, not for any of us.

Momma held us together—steady, present, strong. Gloria leaned on her without question. Gladys built her own lane and stayed in it.

But I needed more. I needed answers. I needed a man in the house—someone to teach me how to be one, to ease the weight I was starting to carry.

The counselors at the Y must've seen it. They watched me, knowing I carried questions I couldn't say out loud. *Can I count on anyone? Who's really looking out for me? Am I good enough? Do I deserve more?*

Those questions stayed in the back of my mind every day.

That night, I lay in bed listening to Momma pray in the next room. Her voice was soft, almost like a lullaby. It brought comfort, but not clarity. So I got up.

I stood in the doorway, watching Momma read her Bible. Her praying had stopped. She sat on the bed, back to me, the Bible open on her lap. The lamp lit the gray in her hair, her glasses resting low on her nose. I hesitated, but I had to ask.

"Momma, why can't we all live together? Why can't we be with Daddy, like a real family?"

She took off her glasses and turned to me, her face thoughtful, weighing her words.

"Alvin, go to the dresser and get me some stationery." Her voice was plain and firm. I gave her the paper. As I reached out to hand her the pen, she said something I'll never forget.

"I want you to write your father a letter. Ask him the questions you're askin' me."

I didn't expect that, but it was my chance to speak my mind. She handed me the paper. "Write it all down. I'll stamp it and mail it in the mornin'."

When I spoke, my voice dropped to a whisper. I asked her what had been on my mind for a long time—why we weren't together as a family, why something always seemed to be missing.

She lowered her Bible, removed her glasses, and turned toward me. Her movements were deliberate, filled with quiet understanding, like she'd long anticipated this moment. Without hesitation or emotion, she guided me to the drawer to get a pen and some stationery.

I obeyed, confused but hopeful, my mind processing the unexpected calm in her response. There was no lecture, no long explanation. Instead, she offered me something more powerful: a way to speak for myself, to direct my questions to the one person who could answer them.

I stood stunned for a moment, realizing the weight of what she'd given me. For the first time, I had permission—and encouragement—to reach out to my father. It wasn't just about writing a letter; it was about being seen, being heard, taking a step toward the man whose absence had shaped so much of my inner world.

I took the paper and went to my room. Outside of school, this was my first personal letter to anyone. But the words came easily, and I wrote down all the questions I had.

Heart pounding, thoughts racing, I sat at the kitchen table. The house was quiet and still. This wasn't for school, not for a grade; it was for me. The words flowed, uncensored and honest, breaking through years of confusion and silence.

June 15, 1962

122 Ellsworth Street

Wintersville, Ohio 43952

Dear Daddy,

Why can't we live together as a family? Why do you have a big house in Ohio while we're living in the projects? I want to understand why we're apart. Do you miss us the way we miss you?

Your son,
Alvin

CHAPTER 73

THE SUMMER I WENT LOOKING FOR MY FATHER

The following week, Momma stepped into my room with a Greyhound ticket in hand.

"Your father wants you to visit him," she said.

I didn't know what to expect when I wrote that letter, but now I have my answer. This wasn't just a trip; it was the start of something new. For the first time, I wasn't just asking questions; I was moving toward the truth, toward manhood, toward my own path.

I stared at the ticket, feeling a mix of excitement and nerves. This was it—my chance to ask him the questions that had been eating at me. I was eager for the trip, but anxious too. I wanted answers from my dad, but I knew they might not be what I hoped. The bus ride wasn't just travel; it was a turning point.

That Saturday morning, I packed a small bag. Momma and I took the city bus across town to the terminal. Before I boarded, she gave me a few final instructions: don't talk to strangers; don't leave the bus for any reason; and when you change buses in Cleveland, pay attention—know where to go and head straight there. Then she slipped a two-dollar bill into my hand, just in case.

It was my first time traveling alone. Momma had packed me a lunch with fried chicken and a slice of chocolate cake, but I was too keyed up to eat more than a bite. I couldn't stop thinking about what was ahead. Momma had held the family together, but I was missing a father figure— someone to help me make sense of my feelings and carry some of the weight I'd been holding for too long. She couldn't replace my dad, but she prepared me the best she could.

She'd packed lunch for me: fried chicken wrapped in foil, a slice of chocolate cake, and a bottle of grape soda. But once I boarded and found a seat by the window, I wasn't hungry. I was fourteen, riding solo for the first time, with a two-dollar bill in my pocket and a twelve-hour trip ahead.

When the Greyhound pulled away, I turned to the window and saw Momma standing where we'd said goodbye. She didn't wave. She just stood there, arms crossed like she was holding herself together. Her eyes followed the bus—steady and full—until we turned the corner and she was gone.

I kept watching, even after I couldn't see her. Maybe if I searched deep enough, her strength would hold onto me just a little while longer.

Boston slipped away mile by mile, the streets giving way to open fields, buildings dissolving into trees, and the city noise softening into the steady hum of the road. The sky stretched above in shades of burnt orange and pink—the kind of heat you could almost see. I didn't say much. I just sat back and watched it all disappear.

I didn't know what was waiting for me in Ohio. But I carried her with me—her prayers, her warnings, her quiet hope. And that was enough to keep me facing forward.

The ride pressed on, and I watched the traffic outside—cars, trucks, all kinds. The road stretched ahead, filled with sedans, big rigs, and the occasional dented pickup. Each one seemed to carry its own story—families on trips, truckers hauling loads, folks heading home. The hum of the tires mixed with the low murmur of voices, turning the ride into something close to a lullaby.

By 7:00 a.m., we pulled into the New York Greyhound station. The city was already in full swing—people rushing down sidewalks, coffee in hand, ready to start their day. Skyscrapers sparkled in the early light, and yellow cabs zipped through the streets like they had somewhere important to be. The air held a mix of fresh bagels, roasted coffee, and a hint of city life.

I'd been to the New York Greyhound station once before, when I was seven. Johnnie was with me then, showing me the ropes. Now I was fourteen and on my own, trying to keep my head up and not look lost in the crowd.

The terminal pulsed with movement—suits, suitcases, snapshots, small talk. Everyone seemed to have somewhere to be. Voices, footsteps, and overhead announcements blended into a steady rhythm, like the station had its own heartbeat. I felt like I'd stepped into a story already in progress, still figuring out my role.

The loudspeaker crackled. I gripped my ticket like it might fly away. I wouldn't call it fear, but something tightened in my chest—like I was holding my breath without realizing it.

People moved around me—some rushing, others drifting. Businessmen kept their heads down; tourists stared up. People who lived there moved like they owned the place. I wasn't one of them—not yet. But I was learning.

I shifted my suitcase and stepped into line at the gate. Travelers ahead adjusted coats, held their bags close, and stared forward with the same tired look I'd seen in Momma when the day had taken more than it gave.

At the front, I handed over my ticket. The driver tore the stub, gave it back, took my bag, and waved me on.

I stepped into air tinged with old upholstery and faint cigarette smoke. The seats were worn, but clean enough. I slid into a spot near the window and took one last look at the bustling station.

The engine roared to life, and the bus shuddered as it pulled away. Through the window, I caught glimpses of New York fading—its towering buildings, its endless noise, its energy. As the city gave way to open highways, nerves and anticipation stirred inside me.

The city faded behind me, and the streets and buildings gave way to fields and the occasional farmhouse. The sun began to set, casting everything in a warm, golden light. The sky shifted to shades of orange and pink. I felt a mix of nerves and hope, wondering what I'd find at the end of this ride—maybe the answers I'd been waiting for would come.

By the time the Greyhound pulled into Cleveland, an early morning chill met me as I stepped off.

The station buzzed with clattering luggage and low voices. The smell of fried food mixed with diesel fumes gave the place a worn but restless feel.

I stepped into thick, muggy air that hit like a wet towel. Even in the early morning, the heat wrapped around me like a second skin. Inside, it was no better—stale air clung to the walls; fans rattled in the corners, doing nothing. Sweat gathered at the back of my neck as I moved through the crowd, suitcase in hand, trying not to look lost. The heat carried every scent—grease, fuel, bodies. The place pulsed with motion and quiet urgency, everyone heading somewhere.

The overhead speakers crackled, announcing arrivals and departures in a flat, robotic voice. I glanced at the schedule board, searching for my next bus to Steubenville.

With 40 minutes to wait, I found a quiet corner to sit, clutching my small suitcase and ticket. Hunger crept in, so I reached into my bag and started eating the chocolate cake, telling myself I'd save the chicken for later. Around me, travelers of all kinds—families, couples, and lone figures like me—waited with faces that ranged from tired to hopeful.

When they called my bus, I joined the line forming at Gate 7. The driver, a broad-shouldered man with a stern yet kind expression, took my bag and handed me my ticket with a quick nod. I climbed aboard and chose a seat near the window.

As we left Cleveland, the city gave way to an open road. I leaned against the window, watching it all blur past.

This stretch of the trip moved just as fast as before—same energy, same motion. Voices buzzed, bags shifted, and the wheels kept time. I stayed quiet, focused on what lay ahead.

Wintersville wasn't just a stop. It was where I'd face the truth—where my dad's world might begin to come into view. I was chasing answers, trying to make sense of his absence, hoping to connect. It wasn't just geography; it was a step closer to who I was becoming.

I changed buses in Cleveland, then again to Steubenville, my heart pounding with anticipation of what lay ahead.

By the time we pulled into the small Steubenville station, I was wide awake, my heart racing with excitement. The journey had been long, but the thought of seeing my dad made every mile worth it.

CHAPTER 74

I WAS 14 AND LEFT TO FIGURE IT OUT ON MY OWN

Around 9:00 AM that Saturday, we arrived in Steubenville.

As I stepped off the bus, I spotted my dad in the distance. He looked sharp in a brown suit, complete with a matching tie and hat. His dark brown Stacey Adams shoes gleamed in the morning sun. In that moment, I realized how much I was like him. (Now, looking back, I see how his impeccable style influenced my own love for fashion.)

As he got closer, he greeted me with a warm hug, his distinctive laugh echoing—a sound that was both teasing and comforting, the kind only Daddy could pull off.

"There's my baby boy!" he exclaimed, a big smile spreading across his face, his gold-framed eyeglasses catching the light.

The city around us bustled with life, but all I could focus on was the joy of being with him again.

We boarded the number twenty-two bus for the short, fifteen-minute ride to Wintersville. This bus—unlike the sleek ones I'd taken in Boston, New York, or Cleveland—had clearly seen better days. Every bump in the road sent a jolt through the cabin, causing heads to bobble in a clumsy, almost comical rhythm.

It was a stark contrast to the other buses I'd ridden on this journey. Those had been modern and efficient—built for speed and comfort.

This one, however, felt like it had weathered decades of use, with worn upholstery, rattling windows, and an engine that groaned with every uphill climb. Each bump sent a ripple through the cabin, making passengers sway in their seats like unsteady dancers. It wasn't sleek or smooth, but it carried a certain charm—a sense that it belonged here, on these rural roads, connecting small towns like Steubenville, Wintersville, and Cadiz.

The slower pace of this bus mirrored the rhythm of this leg of the journey. Unlike the hurried energy of the bigger cities, this ride seemed to insist on patience—even reflection. As I sat beside Daddy, I watched the countryside drift slowly past the smudged windows. The imperfections of the bus only added to its character, and I found myself settling into its unhurried pace, feeling more grounded as we approached home.

He filled the gaps with stories about my old pals, Pee-Wee and Clarence—names that tugged at childhood memories. "Pee-Wee says he's hoping to try out for the freshman football team this year," Daddy remarked, his gaze drifting to the passing scenery. His tone was casual, but I caught a hint of pride in his voice, as if talking about the boys I once knew brought him some small joy. I nodded, trying to match his light tone, but my thoughts lingered on the letter and the unspoken questions riding with us on that bus.

"That's great," I replied, keeping my voice easy.

I knew what he was doing—steering clear of the letter—but I let it slide. Daddy's way of navigating delicate subjects was an art form, one I'd come to understand over time.

The ride went by quickly, the conversation shifting to lighter topics.

As the bus pulled up to our stop at the top of Lane 2, I felt a mix of anticipation and relief.

Daddy's presence always had a way of making everything seem okay, even when it wasn't.

I stepped off the bus and took a deep breath. We waited for it to pull away before crossing the two-lane highway, checking both directions for traffic. The air carried the fresh, clean scent of the countryside, mingled with the faint but sharp tang of oil. The unpaved road leading past our house had been treated with oil to keep the dust down—a practical solution for rural living.

"This is it," Daddy said, gesturing toward the lane with a slight smile.

I nodded, savoring the mix of smells and the familiarity of home. The newly oiled road shimmered under the morning sun, and the quiet beyond the bus stop stood in sharp contrast to the rumble of the journey.

"You ready?" he asked, grabbing my bag.

I gave him a small smile. "Yeah, I'm ready."

Together, we started down the lane, the oil-tanned dust crunching gently beneath our shoes. The countryside stretched wide around us, and the rhythm of our steps felt like a homecoming in itself. The old trailer was gone, leaving a patch of overgrown weeds in its place. But the shack that my mom and dad had once made into a home still stood. Its sagging roof and peeling paint whispered of time's slow decay.

As we moved closer, loud barking erupted. My head snapped toward the noise, where a massive dog strained against its chain, tied to an old tree.

"Shut up, Bull!" Dad waved a hand at the dog, who wagged his tail as we approached. "You'll get a chance to feed him in a minute."

The dog's tail thumped against the ground as we passed, and I couldn't help but feel amused. This was so different from the projects in Boston I'd left behind.

A small man with gray hair stood smoking near the doorway, his thin frame almost blending into the shadows. "Who's that?" I asked, nodding toward him.

My dad glanced over, his lips curling into a faint smile. "That's Mr. Curley. When they let him out of the crazy house in Cambridge, he didn't have any family or anywhere to go, so I let him stay here."

He paused, then added in a firm tone, "But I don't let him smoke inside the house."

"Curley, this is my son," he said, a hint of pride in his voice. "He's come down for a visit."

Mr. Curley nodded, the cigarette resting between his lips. "Nice to meet ya, kid," he said gruffly, his eyes flicking over me before drifting back to some distant point on the horizon.

"Good to meet you, too," I said.

Something about him—the way he stood, his hunched shoulders, the slight tremor in his hand, his brief "Hello," and that far-off stare—felt a little off.

Inside, the house carried a faint scent of wood polish mixed with the earthy aroma of the outdoors—a sharp contrast to the acrid smoke that clung to Mr. Curley outside. Dad led me to a small room with a bed made just so and a worn dresser.

"Make yourself at home," he said, patting me on the back. His voice held a warmth that felt both reassuring and unfamiliar.

The gesture felt unfamiliar—not because it was unwelcome, but because it wasn't something he did often. My dad had always been more practical than affectionate; his emotions were rarely expressed through touch. That simple pat carried a warmth I wasn't used to, leaving me unsure how to react. It was both comforting and strangely foreign, like being invited into a part of him I'd never seen before.

I unpacked quickly, eager to follow him into the kitchen. He opened the pantry, revealing shelves packed with cans. "Everything you need to eat is here," he said, his voice tinged with pride.

The fridge told the same story—two bottles of RC Cola, eggs, milk, bologna, and cheese. In the freezer, stacks of frozen TV dinners stood like sentinels. I'd never seen so much food in one place. Back in Boston, we always had enough, but this felt like more than enough. This felt like comfort.

After filling two bowls—one with dog food, the other with water—Dad handed one to me. Together, we carried them out to Bull, whose tail wagged furiously at the sight of us.

"I've never taken care of an animal before," I said, watching Bull dig into his meal. Dad chuckled. "Well, there's a first time for everything. Just think of it as practice."

I told him about the time I caught a frog and named him Louie. "Brought him into the house in a jar. When Mamma found out, she made me let him go."

Dad's eyes crinkled. "Bull's a bit bigger than Louie the Frog, but he's just as friendly. You'll do fine."

The fresh country air filled my lungs. The earthy smell of grass and dirt grounded me in this unfamiliar place. I took a deep breath and thought, *This is going to be great.*

Later, I settled in with a soda and a bag of chips, flipping through channels until I landed on *Rin Tin Tin*. Dad said he was heading to the store for bread, leaving me alone in the living room. The clock read 2:00 p.m., and I sank into the couch, grateful for a moment of uninterrupted TV— something Mamma would never have allowed.

I flipped from *Rin Tin Tin* to *Wagon Train*, then to *The Mickey Mouse Club*. Hours slipped by, and the light outside slowly dimmed. I glanced at the clock—6:30 p.m.—and Dad still wasn't back.

A knot of anxiety started to form as the shadows stretched longer across the yard. *Maybe he ran into someone he knew,* I told myself, trying to stay calm.

But as the minutes dragged on, my chest tightened. I opened the front door and stared into the darkness, hoping to see his silhouette coming up the path. The road and driveway stayed empty.

To distract myself, I took Bull for a walk around the yard. The evening breeze rustled the trees, and lightning bugs blinked in and out of the tall grass. Bull's playful energy offered a bit of comfort, but the stillness of the countryside at night made me uneasy. Crickets chirped steadily, their rhythm a sharp contrast to the silence that waited inside.

What I didn't know then was that Dad hadn't just gone to the store. He'd gone to another house. Another life. A secret I wouldn't discover until much later.

For now, all I had was Bull and the TV, humming softly in the background, trying to fill the silence.

I sank into the couch, watching one game show blur into the next. When hunger crept in, I headed to the kitchen and pulled out a TV dinner—fried chicken, mashed potatoes, and string beans. I took it into the dining room, hesitated by the table, then sat down to eat.

The house was too quiet. Every so often, I glanced at the door, listening for footsteps. But there was nothing.

At 11:30, the TV cut to static. I turned it off and went to bed. The mattress was lumpy, the room cold. I pulled the thin blanket around me and stared at the ceiling. *He'll be back in the morning,* I whispered to myself.

But morning came, and he still wasn't home.

I turned on the TV again and watched *The Howdy Doody Show.* I ate Raisin Bran with milk, then sat back on the couch. The day passed slowly.

Later, I made another TV dinner—Salisbury steak this time. I drank RC Cola and ate chips while the television droned on. The hours crawled by. I thought about calling my brothers, Amos or Newton, but I didn't have their numbers.

By nightfall, the TV was still the only sound in the house. When the screen finally went blank again, I turned it off and sat there in the dark. My chest felt tight, and my hands wouldn't stop shaking.

"If he's not back in the morning," I whispered, "I'm calling the police."

I went to bed, but sleep never really came.

CHAPTER 75

A LOAF OF BREAD AND A VANISHING ACT

The next morning, I woke up around 9:00 a.m. Sunlight streamed through the thin curtains, casting pale beams across the floor. The house was silent—so quiet it made my uncertainty about Dad's absence feel even heavier. I sat up, rubbed the sleep from my eyes, and glanced at the phone on the nightstand. I started rehearsing the words in my head, preparing to make the call.

As if on cue, the shrill ring of the phone shattered the silence. I jumped to my feet, heart pounding. Was it Dad? I snatched up the receiver. "Hello?" I said, my voice shaking. "Hey, it's Newton," came a familiar voice, warm and steady. Relief flooded through me. "Where's Dae'dy? Is he okay?" I asked, the words tumbling out.

There was a pause. "He's fine," Newton said carefully. "He had to take care of something. Listen, I'm coming over with Ricky. We'll be there soon, okay? Just hang tight."

"Okay," I said, my voice steadier now. "Thanks, Newton."

I hung up the phone and let out a long breath. The tightness in my chest eased a little, replaced by anticipation. I moved to the window and peered out, waiting for any sign of Newton's car.

About an hour later, I heard the crunch of gravel under tires. I ran to the front door and threw it open, my heart racing again—this time with excitement. Newton stepped out of the car, his tall frame and broad shoulders unmistakable. He gave me a reassuring smile, his eyes full of quiet understanding. From the back seat, Ricky climbed out, his ten-year-old face lit up with a wide grin.

"Hey there, buddy," Newton called as he walked up the steps. His deep voice carried that calm, steady authority that always made me feel safe.

"Hey, Newton," I replied, my voice catching just a little.

Ricky bounded up the porch, buzzing with energy. "We're gonna have a lot of fun!" he exclaimed.

I forced a smile, trying to match their enthusiasm, but my eyes drifted to Bull, tied up in the yard. His tail wagged, and I noticed his food and water bowls were nearly empty.

"Hey, Ricky, can you help me with something first?" I asked. "Sure!" he said, eager to jump in.

We walked over to Bull, and I knelt to pat his head. "Let's grab his bowls and fill them up," I said. The metal bowls clinked together as we picked them up, the sound oddly heavy in the stillness.

Back in the kitchen, I filled the bowls while Ricky watched. "How long's he been out there like this?" he asked.

"Two days," I said, handing him one of the bowls.

We carried them back outside, and Bull dove into his food without hesitation.

I gave him one last pat before turning back to Newton, who stood waiting on the porch.

"Do you have a change of clothes?" he asked. "You're coming with us to Weirton. Daddy will see you later this week."

I nodded. A wave of mixed feelings washed over me. I was relieved and grateful Newton had come—but leaving the house, Dad's house, made his absence feel even heavier.

"Okay. I'll be right back," I said, and hurried inside. The floorboards creaked under my feet, grounding me in a fleeting sense of familiarity. This place was still my connection to Dad, even if he wasn't there.

I tossed some clothes and essentials into my suitcase, my thoughts racing. What would the next few days look like? I couldn't help but feel a flicker of excitement—being with Newton and Ricky felt like a break from the uncertainty that had hung over me.

Within minutes, I was back outside, suitcase in hand. Newton took it from me and placed it in the trunk, then opened the car door.

I climbed in, carrying the weight of unanswered questions—but also something I hadn't felt in days: hope.

Sliding into the back seat beside Ricky, he leaned in with a wide grin. "I got some cool new toys we can play with," he whispered, voice brimming with excitement.

I smiled, amused by his enthusiasm. At 13, I wasn't into toys anymore, but his energy was contagious. "Sounds fun," I said, deciding to go along with it.

Newton started the car. As we pulled out of the driveway, I glanced back at the house. Despite everything with Dad, there was comfort in knowing I was with family who cared.

The drive to Weirton was lively—Ricky chattered nonstop, and Newton's calm, steady presence anchored the ride. The miles slipped by. As we approached town, the Great Northern Steel Mill loomed ahead, its massive frame dominating the skyline.

Red dust coated the houses and cars, tinting everything with a rusty haze. "What's all that red dust?" I asked, staring out the window at the crimson-streaked streets and rooftops.

"That's graphite," Newton said. "Comes from the smoke at the mill. Gets everywhere."

I wrinkled my nose, trying to ignore the metallic taste settling on my tongue. "Doesn't it bother you?"

"You get used to it," he replied with a shrug.

Catching my eye in the rearview mirror, Newton flashed a sly smile. "Aight now, I know you a Red Sox fan, but you gotta admit—ain't nobody in baseball like Roberto Clemente."

I sat up, not about to let that slide. "Clemente? Yeah, he good, no doubt," I said, nodding. "But Carl Yastrzemski? Man, he the truth in Boston. You ever watch him play? He somethin' else."

Newton chuckled, shaking his head. "Yaz is good, I'll give you that. But Clemente? That arm, that bat, the way he play right field? Boy, ain't nobody out there like him."

I couldn't argue too much—Clemente was a legend. But still, I clung to my Sox pride as the car rolled deeper into town.

The air thickened with the graphite's metallic sting. It hung in my nostrils, sharp and bitter. As Newton's car pulled to a stop, three girls stood on the porch—Yvonne, thirteen; Patricia, twelve; and Lorraine, eleven—their eyes full of curiosity and the kind of famil-iarity that only family brings.

Even though we were about the same age, I was their uncle in name, and I intended to remind them of that.

Patricia smiled as I stepped out of the car. "Look how much you've grown since we last saw you before you went to Boston," she said, her tone light but teasing.

I nodded, smirking. "Yeah, I've grown. And don't forget to call me Uncle," I said, my voice carrying just enough authority to make the point.

Lorraine laughed, covering her mouth, but Yvonne stepped for-ward, arms crossed, chin raised. "Boy, I'm eight months older than you, and there ain't no way I'm callin' you Uncle," she said, tone sharp and unyielding.

Her words hit harder than I expected. A twinge of regret crept in. I thought back to the teasing remarks I'd made before heading to Boston—how I'd laughed when they lost their luggage and belong-ings on the trip from Jacksonville to Ohio, leaving them without clean clothes and their hair looking rough. The look on Yvonne's face said she hadn't forgotten.

Newton climbed out of the car, shaking his head at the spat. He took the suitcase from my hand.

"All right, y'all go on and help him get settled," he said, nodding toward Yvonne.

She huffed and stepped aside. "I ain't carryin' his bags." Patricia and Lorraine laughed behind her.

"It's fine," I said, brushing it off. "I got it."

Patricia offered a small smile as she walked inside with Lorraine. Yvonne lingered a second longer, gave me one last look, then turned and followed them.

The porch creaked under my feet as I stepped inside. I glanced around, feeling both the warmth of family and the sting of my past mistakes. Yvonne might not be ready to forget—but I told myself I'd find a way to make things right.

Newton clapped a hand on my shoulder, trying to lighten the mood as the tension hung in the air.

"Aight, y'all, let's get inside. Alvin, make yourself at home."

As we stepped into the house, the atmosphere felt heavy, thick with old memories and unresolved feelings. My thoughts drifted back to the day my mother left for Boston with my sisters, leaving me, Johnnie, and Dad behind. Not long after, Newton moved his family into the house. Those days had been full of change, adjustment, and a quiet tension that never fully went away.

I couldn't shake the feeling of Yvonne's animosity. It wasn't just about the teasing I'd done before leaving. It was deeper than that—rooted in those early days of living under one roof, navigating clashing personalities and shifting roles.

That evening, we gathered around the dinner table. The savory scent of meatloaf filled the air, masking the faint metallic trace of graphite that clung to everything. The conversation drifted between catching up and shared memories.

"Remember when we used to play in the yard?" Patricia asked, smiling.

"Yeah, those were good times," I said, glancing at Yvonne. She kept eating, eyes on her plate. "Glad you're here, Alvin," Lorraine added warmly. "It's nice having family around."

"Thanks, Lorraine. Glad to be here too."

That night, after the laughter and the stories had faded, I climbed into Ricky's bed. We lay head to foot in the dim room, the hum of a fan whispering in the corner. I wasn't ready to sleep just yet.

"Hey, Ricky," I said, wanting to keep the mood going. "Let me tell you about Camp Wokappa last summer."

His eyes lit up. "What happened there?" he asked, his voice full of curiosity.

"Every night before bed," I said, leaning back against the wall, "we had this chant. It went like this: Shah-hee, shah-high, shah-licka lacka, booma-raka, shish boom bah, Wokappa, Wokappa, Hoorah!"

Ricky sat up a little, grinning. "Shah-hee, shah-high…" He stumbled over the words but clearly loved it.

"Yeah, you got it! And it was loud, too. Everybody would shout it at the top of their lungs. The counselors acted mad, but deep down? I think they loved it."

Ricky laughed. "Sounds like fun. Did you do it every night?"

"Every single night. It was our way to end the day. Made you feel like you belonged, you know?"

He nodded, smile softening into something thoughtful. "That's cool. I'd wanna go to a camp like that someday."

"Maybe you will," I said, smiling. "And when you do, you can teach them the chant. Keep the Wokappa spirit alive."

For a moment, the room felt alive again—with the energy of summer nights and campfires, a world away from the here and now. Ricky yawned and flopped back onto his pillow, a content smile on his face.

"Goodnight, Alvin."

"Goodnight, Rick." I was ready for sleep myself.

The troubles of the past few days faded as I lay beside him. His steady breathing calmed me, and for a while, the worries about my dad slipped into the background.

I woke to the smell of bacon sizzling on the stove. Morning light streamed through the thin curtains, casting a soft glow across the room. Ricky was still asleep, a faint snore rising and falling with each breath.

I stretched, got up, and shuffled to the bathroom. The cold water on my face was refreshing, snapping me fully awake. When I returned, Ricky was sitting on the edge of the bed, rubbing sleep from his eyes.

"How'd you sleep last night?" he asked with a lazy smile. "Pretty good," I said, pulling a shirt from the chair.

From the kitchen came Yvonne's voice, loud and clear. "If y'all want to eat, you better come now!"

Ricky stretched and yawned, then disappeared into the bathroom. "Need to clean up first."

The smell of bacon guided me straight to the kitchen, where Yvonne stood at the stove, her back turned. She flipped strips of bacon with a practiced hand. The sizzle filled the room, blending with faint chatter from a radio on the counter.

"Cooked plenty of bacon and grits," she said over her shoulder. "But if y'all want eggs, you'll have to cook 'em yourselves."

I'd never fried eggs before, but now seemed as good a time as any to learn. When Ricky finished washing up, he came into the kitchen, opened the fridge, and pulled out four eggs. Then, with a grin, he handed them to me.

"How you like your eggs, fried or scrambled?" I asked, two eggs in each hand like a clumsy circus act waiting to happen.

"Scrambled," Ricky said. "And don't forget the cheese. Gotta have cheese." "Cheese?" I raised an eyebrow. "Ain't never had cheese in eggs."

Ricky grinned, pulling a package of cheese from the fridge. "Well, you about to have it today."

A rush of warmth filled the kitchen as we worked side by side, moving in sync like we'd done it a hundred times. Ricky felt like the little brother I never had, and together we figured out the rhythm of cooking. Butter melted and sizzled in the cast-iron pan.

"Here we go," I said, cracking the eggs into the pan. Ricky handed me two slices of cheese, which I tore up and tossed in without hesitation.

He leaned in, watching the eggs cook. "Don't forget the toast!" He grabbed a loaf of bread and slid a few slices into the oven.

From the dining room came a teasing voice. "Alvin, you sure you know what you doin' in there?"

"If this goes sideways, at least y'all got bacon to fall back on!" I called back, grinning. Laughter echoed through the kitchen.

The grits stayed warm, the bacon sat in a high pile on the plate, its scent rich and inviting. The eggs turned out fluffy, the cheese melting into a smooth, creamy surprise. Pride came easily in that moment.

After breakfast, Ricky's eyes lit up. "Let's walk to the Cove. Go swim at the Community Center."

The Cove was a two-mile stretch, but under the morning sun, the road felt more like an adventure than a hike. We strolled at an easy pace, the sky wide and cloudless above us.

Ricky, quick with a joke and full of wild stories, made even the smallest memory sound legendary. On that walk, he launched into a tale about Miss Margaret's cat.

"Did you hear? That old cat climbed the tallest tree in the field and wouldn't come down for a whole day!" His grin stretched wide, already laughing.

"Is that right?" I said, chuckling.

Ricky chuckled, building on the story as we walked. By the time he finished, the cat had caused such a stir that the fire department, the police, and even the National Guard had shown up.

"You must be kiddin' me." I shook my head slowly, grinning.

He laughed louder, the sound echoing down the busy street. We kept swapping stories, our words flowing with the breeze that carried us toward the Cove.

Then I started singing the Timilty Jr. High School cheer song:

Fight team and never give in, Give us your best on the field.

Fight while we cheer you to victory, Never falter, never yield.

Whether we win or we lose, Stand by the words of our banner. Knowledge is our sword, Character is our shield.

Never forget our motto, Fight with all your might, Victory's in sight for the James P. Timilty.

When approaching, use that coaching you were given. Stay out front and let your rival trail—Alma Mater hail! Rah, rah, fight, fight, fight!"

Laughter and banter echoed through the neighborhood, our voices carrying across porches and fences.

"Uncle Amos works as a mechanic's helper. The shop's on the way to the Community Center,"

Ricky said.

"Great. Been a while since I've seen my brother."

The clang of tools and the low hum of engines greeted us as we neared Rudy's Auto Shop. The air smelled of grease and red metallic dust from the Mill, warmed by the rising heat of the day. Amos was hunched over the hood of an old Chevy, his hands buried in the engine, a rag slung over his shoulder.

Ricky didn't wait for Amos to notice. "Uncle Amos!" he shouted, his voice cutting through the rhythm of the shop like it belonged there.

Amos looked up, blinking in our direction before a wide grin spread across his face. "Well, if it ain't my favorite nephew!"

Ricky jogged ahead, energy buzzing off him. Amos clapped a grease-stained hand on his shoulder, and the two launched into easy laughter and teasing, like no time had passed at all.

"Still think you can fix a car better'n me, huh?" Amos said with a smirk. Ricky grinned. "Give me them tools, and you'll see."

They laughed, moving like a well-rehearsed team. It was clear Ricky had grown up visiting Amos here, watching him work, handing him tools, soaking in his stories. Their bond was easy, built on years of shared time, while I lingered at the edges, an observer to their connection.

For a moment, I wondered what it would feel like to have that kind of relationship. Ricky was like the son Amos never had. And me? Just the half-brother who'd been gone too long.

"Amos," I called, stepping closer.

His gaze shifted to me, the grin fading for just a moment before recognition settled in.

"Well, I'll be damned." He squinted, like pulling a face from a distant memory. "Alvin! Damn, boy, ain't seen you in—what, six years?"

"Yeah, six years." My voice came out quieter than I'd expected.

Amos's grin returned, but it didn't carry the same warmth he'd given Ricky. He stepped forward and gave me a firm clap on the back—friendly but not quite familiar.

"Lookin' good. How tall now?"

"Five-nine," I said, trying to match his energy.

He nodded. "All grown up." His tone softened. "How's Momma, Gladys, and Gloria?" "They're doing fine. Momma's keepin' us in the church."

A small chuckle. "Good. Need to be in church. Keeps you outta trouble." A pause, then a quick once-over. "What grade now?"

"Going into ninth." I squared my shoulders with quiet pride.

A laugh, leaning back. "You know it, Amos. Ninth grade's where I start runnin' the show." For a moment, it felt almost normal. Ricky rifled through Amos's tools like he belonged there,

their conversation easy and unbroken. Still, the feeling stayed, standing just outside, looking in.

They stood by the old Chevy Amos was working on, talking and laughing like they had the world figured out between them. Off to the side, something pulled deep inside me—not jealousy, but a quiet longing. A yearning for that kind of closeness, the kind that grows from shared history. A rhythm already set. And me? Still trying to find the beat. I had mine, sure. But it felt different.

"Sometimes, it ain't 'bout what gets said or even what's done," one of Momma's old truths echoed. "It's 'bout the quiet way folks connect."

Watching Ricky and Amos, the feeling lingered—like standing just outside the door, waiting for someone to say, *Come on in. This is for you, too.*

As their chatter wound down, we made our way to the Community Center. The sun blazed above, our footsteps tapping against the sidewalk in a steady rhythm we all seemed to follow.

"Maan, you shoulda seen it," Ricky said, eyes lit up like sparks. "Back in fourth grade, I was king of the court. Couldn't nobody touch me at basketball!"

I chuckled, amused. "Is that right? The hoop master, huh?" A grin tugged at my lips.

Ricky's smile widened. "No doubt about it. Had moves left them boys in awe! Coach said I got the spirit of a champion. Maybe one day I'll make it big in the NBA."

I raised an eyebrow. "Back in fourth grade? What happened since?"

"Aw, man," he laughed, shrugging. "Still the king—summer just got me chillin', that's all."

We kept walking, Ricky's stories rolling smooth—slam dunks, buzzer-beaters, dreams of making it big. He barely stood five feet tall, but talked like a giant on the court. Honestly, there was something admirable about that kind of belief. Dreams were dreams, no matter the size.

The Community Center came into view, humming with life. Inside, the air smelled like rubber and old wood, the echo of bouncing balls filling the gym. Kids ran wild—shooting, shouting, laughing—a beautiful kind of chaos.

"Hittin' the pool first," Ricky said, voice bubbling with excitement. I blinked. "What? No ball first?"

"Nah," he grinned. "Let me cool off first. Then I'll show you how it's done." "Alright then," I said, shaking my head with a smile. "I'll be here waitin'."

Ricky jogged off toward the locker room, tossing a playful "See you in the gym!" over his shoulder. He vanished through the doors, and I stood there, pride and anticipation stirring in my chest. He had fire in him, no doubt. I couldn't wait to see if his game matched all that talk.

The gym buzzed around me, the sound of sneakers squeaking and balls hitting the hardwood rising like music. I stepped onto the court, eyes locked on the rim, ready for a rebound. One of the taller kids out there, with just enough reach to make it count.

When the ball bounced off the rim, I moved in like I'd done it a thousand times—smooth, calm, like a pro.

Leaping up, I snatched the ball and stood tall, mimicking the way Bill Russell used to stand on the court with the Celtics. It wasn't about showboating—just about moving like I belonged there.

In that moment, everything felt right. The game, the heat, the quiet promise of Ricky coming back for that challenge—it all felt like part of something bigger. And maybe, just maybe, this was what connection looked like. Nothing loud or flashy—just real and steady. Something shared in silence, in moments and time and history, without needing to say a word.

The tan leather basketball felt good in my hands—better than I remembered. Feet planted, stance firm—focused and ready. My mind flicked to Tommy Heinsohn, another Celtics great. I released a clean set shot—simple but solid. The ball sailed through the air like it had purpose, arching just right. When it swished through the net, I couldn't help but grin. It felt like a small victory, like the universe whispering, *Yeah, you got this.*

A fresh wave of confidence surged. I closed in on the rim, weaving through a half-dozen kids, elbows flared, feet scrambling for space.

Each one fought for position, eyes locked on the ball, waiting for the rebound.

I craved that rush again—that moment when everything clicks and the shot drops clean through the net. It pulled at me hard, that rush. The kind that tells you you're in the right place, doing the right thing.

That's when Ricky showed up, hustling onto the court like he had something to prove.

"Aight, aight, lemme see what y'all got!" he shouted, voice cracking just enough to show the moment mattered.

He was the smallest one out there—barely five feet and skinny as a rail. But, man, he had heart—the biggest I'd ever seen in a kid his size.

Ready stance, knees bent—Ricky and I locked in, both hungry for the rebound. The fire was real, but deep down, part of me was quietly rooting for him. Our eyes tracked the ball as it bounced off the rim. Ricky charged in, fearless as ever. I kept one eye on him, wondering, *Is this the one?*

He jumped like he was seven feet tall, even though he was the smallest kid on the court. *C'mon, Ricky,* I urged silently, chest tightening with anticipation. Rebounding wasn't easy for him, but you'd never know it from the way he played. Every ball was a lifeline, and he chased it like it was everything.

The ball came off the rim hard. Ricky lunged, but it slipped through his fingers. Someone else grabbed it, but he just shook it off.

"Aight, next one's mine!" he shouted, clapping his hands. The kid didn't quit, not for a second.

Then, like fate finally gave him a break, the ball rolled his way. A quick pause, sharp and clean, then he snatched it like it had always belonged to him. His face lit up, brighter than the sun, a small victory unfolding right there on the court.

"Go on, Ricky!" I yelled, louder than I meant to. He grinned, then launched the shot. It hit the backboard, danced on the rim, then dropped in.

"YEAH, BOY!" Ricky hollered, arms raised like he'd just won the championship.

"Aight, Ricky!" another kid called out. "Gettin' too good for the rest of us now, huh?"

Ricky laughed, wiping sweat from his brow. "Man, I'm just warmin' up. Y'all ain't ready!"

Oh, we ain't ready, huh? I thought, grinning. *Let's see if you get another one. Aight, Ricky— don't just talk about it. Be about it.*

I stood there, watching him hustle—every move full of fire, poured straight from the heart. On that court, Ricky was electric—a live wire in motion. Every step, every leap, every shout reminded me of what it meant to *love* the game.

In that moment, it all clicked. This wasn't just basketball. This was Ricky embracing life, one fearless shot at a time.

After a while, the heat in the gym started getting to me as we hustled for rebounds on the court. After about fifteen minutes of nonstop play, my stomach started rumbling. I turned to Ricky, wiping sweat from my tired face. "Hey man, hungry?"

Ricky didn't miss a beat. "Always," he shot back.

I slipped a hand into my pocket and felt the crinkle of a few worn bills. "Where we gonna eat? Got a few dollars."

Ricky paused, thinking. "Big Boy restaurant's 'bout a quarter mile down toward Steubenville."

The thought of walking another quarter mile in the blazing sun, drenched in sweat, didn't sound too smart. I shook my head. "Man, that's too far in this heat. I can hold out till we get to your house. What about you?"

Ricky nodded, wiping his brow. "Yeah, I can wait. Got fresh bread and bologna at home. Sandwiches'll do just fine once we get there."

"That sounds like a feast to me." A grin spread across my face as we started the walk back. The sharp scent of graphite from the mill mixed with the relentless summer sun overhead.

To take our minds off the heat, we laughed and swapped stories as we walked. Ricky grinned and launched into a tale about the time he tried to impress some neighborhood girls in his backyard.

"Man, let me tell you," he began, shaking his head. "Thought the next James Brown had arrived. The girls were sittin' on the porch watchin', so I started dancin', tryin' to show off like I was on stage at the Apollo. Then—bam! My foot slipped and I fell straight into the mud! Got it all over me—clothes and everything."

I burst out laughing. "Really thought James Brown was in the building, huh? Sounds like the mud had other plans!"

Ricky laughed too, joining in. "Man, I was so embarrassed. Mud everywhere, even on my head!" He shook his head, still laughing. "Reminds me of that time at the YMCA back in Boston.

Warm-ups before a big game—I was feelin' like the next Bill Russell."

I went for a layup, but the floor was slick. One foot slipped, and the next thing I knew, I was sliding across the court like a fish out of water. Laughter exploded from all sides—no one held back, not even me. No way to play that one off.

As we walked past Rudy's auto shop, locked up for the day, the heat pressed down harder. The five-and-dime next door was still open, so we grabbed a couple of bottles of Coke. That cold fizz was exactly what we needed.

By the time we reached Ricky's house, Yvonne and Lorraine were sitting on the porch, fanning themselves and cracking jokes.

"Here come those two lost souls!" Yvonne hollered when she spotted us.

We laughed as we climbed the steps. "Y'all stayin' cool?" Ricky asked, setting his Coke down.

"Tryin' to," Lorraine said, still fanning herself. "But y'all look like you been walkin' through a furnace."

"Sure feels like it." My stomach growled in agreement.

Patricia heard us and called out from the kitchen. "Y'all sit tight. Fixin' liver, onions, and rice. Better wash up before hittin' this table."

Inside, the smell of onions and liver filled the air, twisting my stomach with hunger.

"Ricky, hurry up in there!" I hollered as he went to wash up first.

"Hold on, James! Don't rush me," Ricky called back, using my middle name like he always did when he was annoyed.

"Man, I'm starvin'," I muttered, shifting from foot to foot, the aroma almost unbearable. Finally, Ricky stepped out, drying his hands. "Aight, your turn," he said with a smirk.

"'Bout time!" I grabbed the washcloth and headed for the sink. The thought of that hot meal waiting kept my feet moving.

As I waited, Patricia called from the kitchen, "Y'all better hurry up 'fore this food gets cold!"

When it was finally my turn, I scrubbed my hands quickly and made my way to the kitchen. Patricia had piled the plates high with steaming liver, onions, and rice. The smell wrapped the room in warmth and comfort. I fixed my plate, spooned the liver over the rice, and drowned it in warm gravy. Ricky was already halfway through his by the time I sat down.

Just as I was about to dig in, Ricky turned to me. "Don't you say grace 'fore you eat?"

I glanced over and shrugged. "Sometimes do, sometimes don't." But out of habit, I bowed my head and muttered the quick phrase Mama always taught me for moments like this: "Jesus wept." Then I went right in—the first bite hit my tongue like magic.

After I finished, I leaned back in my chair, patting my stomach. *Not quite like Momma's,* I thought. *Onions ain't done all the way—but she's still learnin'.*

Patricia noticed me grinning and laughed. "What you think? Not bad, huh?" "It was good," I said. The words hung in the air. "Ain't nobody complainin'."

After the meal, we sat around the table talking. Ricky and Lorraine chatted about elementary school, while Yvonne and Patricia were all hyped about starting Weir High.

"I'm wearin' them new high-tops the first day. Watch me," Yvonne grinned. "You gon' be fresh for real," Patricia added, laughing.

I stayed quiet, not bringing up my own school memories—or how Dad left me alone for those two days before Newton showed up. Instead, I kept it light. "Boston's been treatin' me good. Been spendin' time at the Roxbury YMCA, playin' on the basketball team."

Ricky's eyes lit up. "For real? Y'all good?"

I nodded, a flicker of pride beneath the surface. "Undefeated last season." "What's the most points you scored in a game?" Ricky asked.

There was a brief pause before I told the truth. "Rode the bench most of the time. Only got in when we was way ahead—which was every game." A chuckle slipped out. "Even if it was just the last two or three minutes, it felt good bein' out there, part of a winnin' team."

Ricky nodded. "Ain't nothin' wrong with that. Bein' part of a winnin' team? That's somethin'."

We laughed and swapped more stories late into the evening. It felt good being around family, but that feeling didn't last long.

Newton came home from work, his voice cutting through the warm, easy atmosphere.

"Dae'ddy's back in Wintersville. Takin' you there in the mornin'."

My heart sank. Time with the nieces and nephews had been so full that I'd let the thought of Dad fade into the background. Those two dreadful nights of being left behind had almost slipped from memory. But now, the thought of seeing him again stirred something uneasy in my stomach. I didn't know what to expect—only that one question kept circling my mind: *Why disappear after saying it was just a trip to buy a loaf of bread?* The thought lingered, heavier with each passing hour.

CHAPTER 76

ROUTE 22 AND THE FATHER WOUND

The next morning, bright and sunny, Ricky was already up and moving. His voice drifted through the house as he talked with Newton in the kitchen—every word just loud enough to catch. As I crawled out of bed, the soft clinking of dishes and easy laughter filled the air. My feet shuffled toward the bathroom; cool water splashed over my face, waking me up little by little.

By the time I made it to the kitchen, Newton was sitting at the table, eyes locked on the newspaper in front of him.

"Mornin'," he said, his tone light and full of energy, even as his gaze returned to the page. "Mornin'," I replied, sliding into a chair.

"Pirates beat the Dodgers last night," Newton announced, a hint of pride in his voice. "Clemente had three hits."

"Oh, OK." I nodded and reached for a cup. "How'd the Red Sox do?" A little hope crept into my voice, reaching for good news.

Newton scanned the sports page, then looked up with a sympathetic glance. "Red Sox lost to the Twins in the bottom of the ninth. Killebrew hit a three-run homer to end it."

I shook my head and sighed. "Man, that's tough. They were on a five-game winning streak, too."

Newton chuckled. "Don't matter anyway. Pirates gon' take it all—unless the Sox somehow make it to the World Series."

From the counter, Ricky chimed in with a mischievous grin. "Red Sox are sorry. They ain't never makin' it to no World Series."

I smirked and turned toward him. "Boy, please. Pigs gon' start flyin' before you say somethin' nice about the Sox."

Newton leaned back, laughter spilling from him. "Man, if pigs start flyin', we all better duck. Ricky might actually start rootin' for Boston, too."

Ricky grinned, but before I could fire back, he asked, "What kinda cereal you want? Cheerios or Corn Flakes?"

"Y'all got any shredded wheat?" I asked, a sly smile creeping in.

Ricky paused, then burst out laughing, shaking his head. "Man, that's cereal for White folks."

An eyebrow lifted, a grin flashed. "Oh, is that right? Well, if I see you eatin' Shredded Wheat, I'll be sure to let everyone know y'all must've hit the number."

Ricky snorted, grabbing the milk. "Ain't nobody too fancy. Just sayin'—I ain't eatin' no hay disguised as breakfast."

Newton laughed, folding the paper. "Boy, just pour the man some Cheerios and sit down. You talk too much first thing in the morning."

Yvonne's face lit up as she leaned over the table. "Yeah! Can we all go to Wintersville? We haven't seen Granddad in a while."

Newton looked up from his coffee, a small smile spreading across his face. "Yeah, y'all can come," he nodded. "Ricky and Alvin can sit in the back."

Ricky's head popped up from where he was pouring himself a second glass of orange juice.

"Man, that sounds good!" he said, grinning ear to ear.

Leaning back in the chair, my mind was already off and running— picturing the adventure ahead.

Shoot, we're gonna be ridin' in style, looking out the back window like kings.

Newton raised an eyebrow at us, his tone playful but firm. "Y'all better not start actin' up back there. This ain't no train. I ain't tryin' to hear no fussin'."

"Yes, sir," Ricky and I muttered in unison, trying not to laugh.

From the doorway, Lorraine and Patricia peeked into the kitchen, curiosity written all over their faces.

"We goin' somewhere?" Lorraine tilted her head.

"Yep!" Yvonne turned to her sisters, beaming. "Granddad said we can all go to Wintersville.

We're takin' the station wagon, and Ricky and Alvin get to sit in the way back!" Patricia clapped her hands. "Alright! Y'all better get ready, then."

Newton set his coffee down and stood up. "That's right. Everyone, hurry up. We'll be headin' out soon."

The kitchen burst into motion as everyone scrambled to get dressed and grab their things. The excitement was contagious, and the promise of those rear-facing seats felt like a special privilege.

As Patricia and Lorraine climbed into the middle seats, Ricky and I bolted for the back, racing like it was the final stretch of a track meet. Grins stretched wide as we slid into our throne-like spots.

Newton chuckled, catching our eyes in the rearview mirror. "Y'all behave back there, you hear?"

"Yes, sir!" we shouted, trying to sound serious—even though we were already plotting how to turn the back seat into our little kingdom.

"You'd better not start no mess back there. This is a treat, and I ain't tryin' to hear no fussin'," Yvonne warned.

With a rumble, the station wagon's engine came to life. Newton shifted into gear, and the car rolled down the driveway, echoing with laughter and playful banter.

As they cruised along the main road, Yvonne adjusted in her seat and glanced at her sisters.

"Granddad always tells the best stories," she said, her voice warm with anticipation.

Lorraine nodded eagerly. "Yeah, he sure does. Remember when we were little, and he told us Bull had puppies?"

Patricia leaned forward, laughing as she shook her head. "We spent half the day looking for those imaginary puppies!"

"And he just sat there watchin' us run around, laughing his head off," Yvonne said, her eyes sparkling at the memory.

The car erupted in laughter as the memory spread like wildfire. Even Newton cracked a smile as he steered onto the open road.

"Think he'll tell us a new one today?" Ricky asked, eyes wide with excitement. "Probably," Yvonne grinned. "He's always got somethin' up his sleeve."

Newton chuckled, glancing at them through the mirror. "Let's see if today gives him some new material," he said, turning onto the highway.

The yard was alive with motion. Dad stood by the small shack, tossing a worn tennis ball with aim as sharp as ever. Bull leapt and spun like he was still a pup, chasing after it with boundless energy. Lorraine rolled down the window and shouted, "Granddad!"

Dad turned, that carefree laugh spilling out of him—the kind that made you think he didn't have a worry in the world. The nieces and nephews poured out of the car, their laughter mixing with the sound of Bull dragging his chain across the yard. They rushed to Dad, tugging at his arms, pulling his attention in every direction.

Caught up in the whirlwind of their excitement, not a single glance was spared in my direction.

Watching him like that, my chest tightened. There was a need to confront him about the lie, about leaving under the pretense of getting bread. Those long, anxious nights still hung in the air, unanswered. Why couldn't we live together as a family? But I knew this wasn't the moment. *Not yet*, I thought. *But soon.*

Without a word, I turned and walked into the house, the weight of what needed saying pulling me down. I headed straight to my room, dropped off my bag, and caught a glimpse of Dad outside, talking to Newton.

A moment later, the door opened behind me as they came in.

Dad's voice was easy, light, like nothing had happened. "There you are." The words landed like time hadn't passed at all.

Like he hadn't left me wondering if he'd ever come back from the store.

I didn't turn. Didn't ask where he'd been. The urge to speak rose —but stayed buried. God knows I wanted to.

Still young enough to believe in heroes, I clung to the idea that he might still be one.

So I held it in. Stayed still—like silence was the price I had to pay to keep believing he was still the man I looked up to.

Even then, doubt had already started to settle in. Some wounds don't bleed. They echo in the silence they leave behind. Abandonment, distance, and broken promises don't always leave marks you can see— but they sink in deep and shape the way we come to see ourselves. That's the father wound.

Outside, I spotted Peewee in the yard talking to Ricky. His face lit up the moment he saw me.

His name on paper was Bill Carney, but folks had called him Peewee since he was a kid, when he was small and wiry. He was not so small anymore—standing nearly eye to eye at five-foot- nine. The same Peewee who once tied me to a tree during a game of Cowboys and Indians.

"Alvin!" he called.

I stepped forward, memories flashing—strapped to that tree, yelling, while Clarence and another boy ran off laughing. It used to sting. Now, it made me laugh. Time smooths things out.

"Heard you goin' out for football this year," he said with a grin. "Yeah," Peewee nodded. "Two-a-days start next week. I'm ready."

Not wanting to be left out, Ricky jumped in. "Where can we play some basketball?"

Peewee pointed over his shoulder. "Junior high court. Clarence got a ball. Could run two-on- two."

Before I could answer, a voice called from up the street.

"Alvin!"

I turned and saw Clarence—Peewee's old partner in crime—standing at the top of Second Lane, cupping his hands around his mouth like a human megaphone.

"You comin' or what?"

Peewee laughed. "Looks like the whole crew's ready. C'mon, Alvin. Let's see what kind of shot you got!"

I shook my head, smiling as we headed toward the court, laughter echoing down the block.

"Aight, y'all ready to play?" Clarence shouted, his voice slicing through the stillness. Peewee turned to him, eyes narrowing slightly like he was sizing him up. "Buster." The

nickname fit—Brown, like the old comic strip character, Buster Brown. "You ready to show 'em what us folks in Wintersville can do?"

Clarence didn't answer right away. He spun the ball once, twice, the motion smooth and steady.

His gaze flicked from Peewee to me, lingering a little too long.

"Man." The laugh came low and deliberate. "Been ready. Question is, y'all still got it?"

He tossed the ball into the air and caught it one-handed like it weighed nothing. The tension crackled—static before a storm. There was something in his laugh, something that felt like both a challenge and an olive branch.

I stepped forward, a small grin forming. "Let's find out."

The weight of old battles, old scars, didn't disappear. However, for the first time, it felt like maybe we could set it down. At least for a little while.

"Let's play." The words carried more than just the game.

I turned to Ricky. "Me and you against them. We gonna beat y'all like y'all stole somethin'."

Ricky laughed, puffing up his little chest—six feet of swagger packed into five-foot-one. "Sure will!"

Clarence snorted, tossing me the ball. "Man, I can check you and Ricky. Y'all don't stand a chance."

The banter kept goin' as we stood in the yard. I started bouncing the ball, looping it in smooth circles between my legs and behind my back, showing off just a little. Voices from Yvonne, Patricia, and Lorraine drifted in through the screen, floating out from the sun porch.

"Where y'all think y'all goin'?" Yvonne called, her voice playful but curious.

A pause, then a glance back. "'Bout to show Clarence and Peewee how it's done," I said, spinning the ball on my finger just to give 'em somethin' to watch.

They laughed, and I heard Patricia mutter something about "boys always actin' a fool," but it didn't matter.

"C'mon." Clarence gave me a nudge. "Let's get it goin'."

We headed up oil-treated First Lane, the air thick with sweat and the sound of playful chatter.

Clarence passed me the ball, and I let it bounce hard against the pavement, catchin' it clean with a flick of my wrist.

Behind us, the house faded into the background. The porch talk turned to an echo, and for a moment, the only thing that mattered was the game.

But as we walked, I turned to Peewee. "Where the pretty girls at in Wintersville?" I asked, half- joking.

Peewee let out a loud laugh, shaking his head. "Man, you gotta go to Steubenville or Smithfield for that. If you got a car, you can make it over there. But you only fourteen, so you stuck with the Boogie Bears here in Wintersville."

Clarence smirked, dribbling the ball lazily between his hands. "Man, don't even worry about it. Them Steubenville girls ain't checkin' for you anyway."

Peewee shot him a sharp look, eyebrows raised. "Oh, and they checkin' for you, Clarence?"

Clarence chuckled, the ball bouncing steadily. "Nah, but at least I know better than to waste my time with the Boogie Bears."

Peewee was hot now. "Ain't foolin' with these girls here—I got a girl in Steubenville. You ain't never had no pussy. Last time you got some ass was when your finger went through toilet paper."

Clarence didn't miss a beat. "Boy, stop lyin'. I know who you talkin' 'bout, and that girl in Steubenville don't even know your name. You just mad 'cause the Boogie Bears ain't checkin' for you neither."

Peewee crossed his arms, glancing at Clarence. "You know what, forget all that talk. Me and you, Clarence—we takin' them down. Let's see what these two think they got."

Clarence nodded, a sly grin spreading across his face. "Aight, bet. Ain't no way they takin' us. Peewee, you got boards, I got handles. They don't stand a chance."

Laughter slipped out as I tossed the ball up and caught it again with ease. "Oh, so now y'all wanna team up? Don't think that's gon' help. Ricky and me about to run the court."

Ricky stepped up, chest puffed out. "Yeah, y'all better team up. Otherwise, this gon' be too easy."

Clarence smirked, stepping into position. "We'll see about that, little man. Don't be cryin' when I cross you up."

Peewee clapped his hands, ready for the ball. "Y'all talkin' too much. Let's play."

As we approached the junior high school, the basketball court came into view. The backboard was worn, the net hung loose in places, but it was ours—the spot where we'd spent countless hours. The sun was high, casting sharp shadows across the asphalt.

Spots were claimed on the cracked pavement, the makeshift court coming alive with energy. Trash talk gave way to the rhythm of the game—passes, rebounds, quick moves, and fast breaks. Winning didn't matter, not really. For now, it was just us, lost in the game, trying to prove who had real skill.

Clarence bounced the ball and turned with a grin. "Alright, y'all ready to get schooled?"

Ever confident, Ricky shot back, "Boy, stop. You 'bout to see what Boston and Weirton is really about."

The game started fast, fueled by trash talk and laughter. The ball zipped from player to player, sneakers slapping against the pavement. Clarence dribbled down the court, trying to shake Ricky with a crossover, but Ricky stayed with him, quick on his feet. Clarence passed to Peewee, wide open near the foul line. Peewee took the shot—it hit the rim and bounced out.

I grabbed the rebound and tossed it to Ricky. "Fast break!" I yelled.

Ricky took off, darting down the court, then slowed just enough to pass me the ball. I caught it, went up for the layup, and barely got it off before Peewee came flying in, trying to block. The ball rolled around the rim, then dropped in.

"Two points, baby!" Ricky hollered, slapping me five.

The game rolled on—a blur of quick passes, missed shots, and trash talk flying faster than the ball itself. Sweat dripped down our faces, shirts stuck to our backs. At one point, Clarence called a timeout.

"Y'all got lucky on that last one," he said, breathing heavily.

Ricky grinned. "Lucky? Nah, that's skill, son. We ain't scared of no rematch." Clarence smirked but didn't reply, just bounced the ball as we caught our breath.

That's when I saw them: Patricia, Yvonne, and Lorraine, walking toward the court like they owned it. They strolled up in a line, arms linked, laughing about something we couldn't hear. Their sundresses swayed in the breeze, sunlight catching their hair.

The game stalled as we all glanced their way.

"Here we go," Ricky muttered, wiping his forehead.

"Y'all lookin' tired already," Yvonne called out, hands on her hips. "Ain't even played that long."

Ricky shot back, "Why don't y'all grab a ball and show us somethin', then?"

Yvonne laughed, shaking her head. "Nah, we here to watch y'all sweat. Go ahead. Don't mind us."

They took their spots on the sidelines, tossing jabs and laughing while we played. They weren't just spectators; they were part of the rhythm. Their voices mixed with the bounce of the ball, the scuff of sneakers on pavement, and the clang of the rim.

Ricky and I took the first game, but Peewee and Clarence came back swinging in the second. Between plays, Ricky pulled me aside, wiping sweat from his brow.

"Man, we can't let them take us down like this," he said, his voice low, urgent.

I nodded, catching my breath. "Not with your sisters watchin'. We gotta show 'em what the Harris boys can do. No excuses."

"Bet," Ricky said, energy flaring. "Let's do this."

The final game was different—no more jokes, no more lazy passes. The talking stopped, replaced by the locked-in silence of competition. Every move mattered now. The stakes climbed with each point, and Peewee wasn't letting anything go easy.

"Check ball," he said, passing it to me with a look like fire. It wasn't just a game anymore; it was a challenge.

I dribbled hard, cutting left, then right, hunting for an opening. Peewee stayed with me, step for step. I faked a pass to Ricky, spun behind the back, slipped past him—just barely. As I dished the ball off, Peewee sprang up, tipping it mid-air.

"Nice try!" Peewee shouted as he snatched the rebound and sprinted toward the foul line.

I took off after him, heart pounding, every muscle locked into the chase. He went for a layup, but I was right there. I leapt and swatted the ball away with everything I had.

"Not today!" I yelled, landing hard but steady, adrenaline surging through me.

The ball flew out of bounds, and we regrouped, the tension thick in the air. Ricky clapped me on the back. "That's what I'm talkin' about! Just like Russell!"

"Let's focus," I said, glancing his way. The chaos of the game, the girls' cheers, the heat—it all swirled around us. "We got this."

We pushed forward, giving it everything. Every dribble, every pass, every shot had to be earned. Peewee tried to drive past me again, but I held my ground. He pulled up for a jumper, but I was already in the air, blocking it clean.

The ball bounced straight to Ricky. "Fast break!" he yelled, taking off. I sprinted alongside him, caught his pass, and laid it in just in time.

"That's two!" I shouted, pride rushing through me as the girls cheered louder from the sidelines.

The game raged on—sweat, grit, and pure determination. With every point, the pressure built, but we played like nothing else mattered.

The sun beat down harder, but we didn't care. We were locked in, playing our hearts out. The score stayed tight, and both teams were pushing with everything they had. As the end neared, Clarence and Peewee threw everything at us—but we matched them, step for step.

With the score tied, we had possession. I dribbled down the court, scanning for a gap. Ricky cut to the basket. I saw the opening and hit him with a clean pass. He rose up for the shot.

The ball hung in the air, then dropped through the net.

"It's over!" Ricky shouted, grinning from ear to ear, bouncing with excitement. My nieces on the sidelines erupted in cheers. Ricky and I slapped hands, grinning widely. The win felt earned— fierce, exhausting, and real.

I turned to Peewee and Clarence. Peewee's face was twisted with frustration; Clarence didn't look much better.

"Y'all got lucky," Peewee muttered, eyes narrowed. "Ain't no way y'all beat us straight up."

Clarence crossed his arms, scowling. "Yeah, we had y'all most of the game. Y'all just got lucky."

I smirked. "Y'all just can't play."

Peewee stepped closer, his stance tense and aggressive. "Don't act all high and mighty, Alvin. We know how y'all play—cheap fouls and all."

Ricky bristled beside me, the joy on his face replaced with heat. "Cheap fouls? Man, y'all just couldn't handle real defense."

Clarence scoffed, his voice thick with sarcasm. "Right. Now y'all think you're so great, huh? Think you better than us?"

I shook my head, trying to cool things down. "It's just a game, Clarence. No need to get all heated. We can run it back another time."

Peewee's eyes flashed with defiance. "Yeah, and next time, we'll show you what's up. Y'all won't get lucky again."

Clarence added, "We'll see who's laughin' then."

The mood turned sour fast—the earlier camaraderie cracked and gone. Sensing the tension, Yvonne, Patricia, and Lorraine approached cautiously. Yvonne spoke first, voice calm but firm. "Come on, y'all. It's too hot for all this. Let's cool down and chill."

Patricia nodded. "Yeah, no reason to let a game get y'all twisted."

But Peewee and Clarence were already heading off, muttering as they walked. Peewee shot one last look over his shoulder, eyes full of fire. "Next time, Alvin. Next time."

They disappeared up Route 22, heading toward Silver Stream Knolls. Still, I felt good. Ricky was only ten and five-one, but he could ball. The game brought us closer.

I turned to him, still feeling the adrenaline, and tried to lift his spirits. "Don't worry about them," I said, trying to sound as sure as I felt. "We played our best—and we won fair and square."

The sun hung low over the court as we lingered, savoring the moment. My nieces buzzed with excitement, their laughter echoing like a victory song.

"Ricky," Patricia said, grinning, "you should've seen Peewee's face when you made that last shot!" She scrunched her face into a dramatic scowl, making the others laugh.

Ricky chuckled faintly but stayed quiet. I could see it—the way Peewee and Clarence's reactions weighed on him.

I nudged him with my elbow, keeping it light. "Come on, Ricky. Don't let them take this from us. We earned it."

He looked up, eyes uncertain. "Yeah, I get that. But you saw how they acted. You think it's just gonna stop here? Next time we play, they're gonna come even harder. They already think we cheated or somethin'."

I nodded, thinking it over. "I know. And I'm not saying it's gonna be easy. But that's exactly why we have to keep showing up—why we have to play again. If we beat them fair and square, maybe they'll finally get it. Maybe they'll see there's no cheating—that we're just better."

Ricky gave me a sidelong glance. "You really think that'll change anything? What if it just makes them madder?"

I sighed and kicked at a loose rock on the ground. "Maybe it will. But maybe it's not just about winning. It's about how we play—staying cool, being respectful, showing them it's just a game. We're not pros; we're just out here having fun."

Ricky hesitated, then let out a slow breath. "Alright, I hear you. But I'm tellin' you now—if Peewee pulls any of that mess again, I'm not just gonna let it slide."

I laughed and slapped him on the back. "Fair enough. But let's hope it doesn't come to that. For now, let's just enjoy this one."

Ricky's expression softened, but his smile was faint. "Yeah," he said quietly. "I just didn't think they'd take it like that."

We gathered our things, the weight of the moment still hanging between us. The sun sat high in the sky, casting long golden rays over the yard as we began the walk home. My nieces stayed close, their excited chatter about the game floating around us.

"They were mad 'cause Ricky hit the winning shot!" Patricia laughed, still riding the high of victory.

"That's how you do it!" Yvonne chimed in, raising her hands in an exaggerated jump shot.

As we walked down Route 22 toward the house, the heat lingered, but a breeze had picked up, finally offering some relief. Ricky and I were still buzzing from the win.

The conversation drifted from the game to what we might eat and drink once we got back.

Yvonne turned to Ricky. "Does Granddad still have his cabinet full of canned goods?" Ricky shook his head. "I dunno."

I jumped in. "Yeah, and he's got a fridge full of TV dinners," I said with a grin. "And plenty of tonic, too."

Yvonne gave me a puzzled look. "Tonic? You mean… hair tonic? That's the only tonic I know."

I laughed, shaking my head. "Nah—like RC Cola, Coca-Cola. Soda."

They all burst out laughing. Yvonne doubled over, holding her sides. "He's talkin' about soda!" I grinned, enjoying the moment. "That's what we call it in Boston—tonic."

"That's wild," Patricia said. "I've heard soda and pop, but tonic? That's a first for me!"

"Well, now you know," I said, still smiling. "Stick with me, and you'll learn all kinds of new things."

As the laughter faded, the warmth of the moment settled in, lightening the mood even more. The house wasn't far now, but the camaraderie we shared on the walk made the distance feel even shorter.

Ricky nudged me with a broad grin. "Man, Alvin, you gotta tell my sisters about your summer camp cheer," he said, laughing.

I grinned. "All right, lemme clear my throat and hit y'all with that Camp Wokappa chant one mo' time."

Launching into the cheer, I exaggerated every move—clapping, stomping, full of energy. My nieces giggled and clapped along, their laughter growing louder as I got more animated.

When I finished, Ricky was still chuckling, shaking his head. "That's crazy, man! But hold up— you got another one from that... uh, John Timothy school?"

I raised an eyebrow, smirking. "First off, it's James P. Timilty. And secondly, I got not one, but two cheers from there."

Yvonne raised her hand like she was in class, grinning. "Ooh, for real? Well, let's hear 'em!"

Clearing my throat again, I stepped into character—proud and theatrical. I delivered the first cheer with big gestures, stepping side to side and clapping in rhythm. My nieces laughed even harder, trying to keep up, though their timing was hilariously off.

"All right, all right, y'all ain't ready for the second one!" I said, hyping them up.

They cheered me on as I launched into the second cheer, adding even more flair—playful spins, dramatic stomps, anything to make them laugh. And they did, cracking up as they tried to follow my moves.

When I finished, I leaned back with a satisfied grin. "Now listen—I'mma work with y'all to memorize these cheers. Next time we play Peewee and Clarence, I want y'all to hit 'em with this from the sidelines."

Yvonne, catching my tone, smirked. "Oh, we got you, Alvin. We gon' cheer y'all on so good, Peewee and Clarence ain't gon' know what hit 'em!"

We spent the rest of the evening just like that, the air filled with laughter. It was one of those moments that felt like it could stretch on forever—the kind I look back on and realize: it's the simple times like this that mean the most.

CHAPTER 77

THAT SUMMER IN WINTERSVILLE

Back at the house, Dad and Newton were sitting on the porch—the place where conversations stretched out with the shadows cast by the setting sun. Dad was in a jovial mood, his laughter as infectious as it was comforting.

The grandchildren were everywhere, their laughter and shouts filling the air. He entertained them with stories and jokes, his face lighting up with each giggle and squeal.

I wasn't sure how to break that joyful mood to bring up something he didn't want to discuss.

I watched him from the doorway, feeling that familiar frustration—the ache of not knowing how to ask the questions swirling in my head about him and Mom.

Newton leaned back in one of those old-fashioned spring chairs, its creaks echoing under his weight. A quiet smile played on his lips as he listened to Dad. There was peace in their silence, a shared history that needed no words. Usually the quiet one, Newton seemed right at home in the moment. I envied his ease. If I had it, maybe I could ask what I needed to without shattering the mood.

My dad had a gift for storytelling, and one of his favorites was from his days "hoboing" as a youth. It always started the same way:

"Man, y'all don't know nothin' 'bout hard times 'til somebody snatch your shoes clean off your feet while you sleepin' on a train."

He'd lean back, shaking his head like he still couldn't believe it. "I was knocked out, ridin' that boxcar like I had a first-class ticket, thinkin' I was untouchable. Next thing I know, I wake up— and my shoes is gone. Straight gone! I'm sittin' there lookin' at my toes like, 'What kinda

triflin', no-good fool takes a man's shoes?' Left me barefoot, and I was real angry!"

We were laughing hard, but Dad wasn't done yet. "And let me tell you, that wasn't no quick ride. Naw, I had to sit there shoeless for two whole days, listenin' to that train clackin' on the tracks while my feet was freezin' up. You ever walk on steel barefoot?"

He'd pause for effect, looking each of us in the eye. "Now, here's the kicker—jumpin' off that train barefoot? Ha! That's a death wish right there. Them tracks don't play, and neither do them Railroad Bulls. You get caught, they ain't gon' pat you on the back and send you home. Nah, you goin' straight to jail for vagrancy."

"'So what you do, Daddy?'" Newton asked.

"What I do?" he'd say, grinning. "Man, I prayed, that's what I did—prayed that train slowed down somewhere with dirt softer than my pride! When I finally jumped, I hit that ground skippin' like my feet was on fire."

By that point, we'd be hollering, tears in our eyes. But Dad always had to drive it home.

"And let me tell y'all somethin'," he'd say, pointing his finger like he was preaching. "Since that day, I don't sleep with my shoes off. I don't care if I'm on a train, in a bed, or at the dinner table—my shoes stay on. You never know when you gon' need to run or jump, and I ain't tryna get caught slippin' again."

The punch line always cracked us up, but the real kicker was how Dad somehow managed to find a pair of shoes—too big, mismatched, but shoes nonetheless—left behind in some dusty town while looking for work.

"And that," he'd finish, "is why I never sleep with my shoes off. You never know when you'll need to run… or jump."

We laughed every time, but shoes never meant the same to me after that.

It was getting close to 3:00 p.m. Dad and Newton were getting ready for work, their movements full of practiced urgency, the rhythm of routine settled deep.

Yvonne, Patricia, and Lorraine were ready to head back to Weirton. Ricky had brought enough clothes to stay with me in Wintersville, and I was glad for the company.

As we were getting into Newton's car, Dad called out, "Hey y'all, get anything you want to eat out the fridge, but don't be leavin' this house 'til I get back, you hear me?"

Ricky and I nodded, catching the seriousness in his voice. We watched them climb into the car, the doors shutting with a certain finality. The engine roared to life, and with a wave, they were gone, leaving us to our own devices and the promise of a long, quiet afternoon.

After watching *Rin Tin Tin* on the small console TV, I headed to the fridge and asked Ricky what he wanted for dinner. I always went for the chicken dinner—peas, potatoes, and an apple pie dessert—while Ricky chose the meatloaf.

We settled at the dining room table. As we ate, Ricky, usually so carefree, turned suddenly serious. Out of nowhere, he said, "You know you got a little sister in Wheeling?"

I paused mid-bite, confused. "What you talkin' 'bout, Ricky?" "You got a little sister in Wheeling," he repeated, slower this time.

I still didn't get it. It felt like he was speaking another language. Not ready to deal with whatever that was, I changed the subject. "Hey, you wanna play basketball?" I was trying to lighten the mood.

Ricky's face lit up right away. "But we ain't got a ball!"

"Clarence got one. Maybe him and Peewee come by tomorrow."

And just like that, the talk about my little sister in Wheeling was over. It lingered in the back of my mind, but I wasn't ready to face it. Basketball I could handle. The rest would have to wait.

CHAPTER 78

IF YOU HEAR BARKIN', DON'T LOOK BACK

It was 1962. I was 14, about to turn 15, and getting ready to start high school. An idea came to me—what if I told my father I wanted to stay in Ohio and finish school down here? The air was fresh, and for the first time, I felt a kind of freedom I'd never known before. No more dodging kids in the projects. Just days filled with basketball, picking wild apples, strawberries, and blackberries.

The next day, Peewee came walking down the road. He stepped up to the screen door and tapped gently.

"Good morning, Elder Harris," he said.

Dad was talking with Mr. Curley. He turned to Peewee and smiled. "Good morning, little fella. I know you're looking for Alvin."

I was in the kitchen fixing a bowl of Raisin Bran, but I stepped out onto the porch when I heard them. Peewee motioned for me to come outside. We walked over by the mailbox.

"You and Ricky feel like picking some apples today?" he asked.

Mr. Snodgrass's yard was the biggest in town.

I nodded and said, "I remember that man—Mr. Snodgrass," as soon as Peewee mentioned his name.

He laid out the plan: we'd have to sneak under his chain-link fence and watch out for his big German shepherds that guarded the orchard.

A moment later, Ricky showed up at the screen door. He saw us talking and, curious as ever, joined right in. I filled him in on the plan.

"That sounds scary," Ricky said. "I'm afraid of dogs."

"Ricky, that's why we gotta be quiet," I told him. "Stick close and keep an eye out."

I thought to myself, *Here we are, planning to steal apples—with danger and everything. I just hope I can get a few.*

Peewee said he'd be back around two. I told him I'd see him then.

Meanwhile, Dad was up on a ladder installing a window on Mr. Curley's shack. He was singing as he worked:

"People, you know you can't do what you please, You can't run with sinners and do what they do, 'Cause all the people are lookin' at you."

Hammer in hand, calm settled over him. The mood felt too light to bring up anything serious.

Just then, Peewee came around the corner, keeping his voice low. "Yo, you ready to go pick them apples?"

I glanced at Dad, who was still singing away, then nodded. "Yeah, I'm ready. Let's get Ricky and head out."

We walked over to the porch where Ricky was sitting, looking uneasy. He fidgeted with his hands. "Man, I can't stop thinking 'bout them dogs. I ain't too sure 'bout this."

I patted him on the back. "Don't worry. We just gotta be quiet and stick together. We'll be in and out before they even know we there."

The orchard was quiet. Tall grass brushed against our legs as we moved quickly, stuffing apples into our bags. The thrill of sneaking them—of getting something for nothing—made each bite taste sweeter. I knew from experience these were the juiciest, most delicious apples I'd ever had. They were worth the risk.

I scanned the tree line. "Think we're good for now," I said, voice low but steady.

I grabbed the fence and pulled it high enough for Ricky, then Peewee, to scramble under the wire.

"You hear that?" Ricky whispered.

A faint bark echoed in the distance. I froze. The barking grew louder.

"Time to go," I said, urgency creeping into my voice.

Before we could move, a figure stepped onto the porch—Mr. Snodgrass. Middle-aged, graying hair, faded blue overalls. He leaned forward, eyes sharp and locked on us.

"You boys better get off my property before Shadow and Kaiser get to you!"

The barking turned frantic—closer now. Ricky didn't wait. Neither did we.

I reached the barbed wire fence first, yanking it up just enough for Ricky to slip through. "Go! Hurry!"

His paper bag snagged on the wire, tearing open. Apples spilled across the ground, rolling in every direction as he sprinted toward the road. By the time he reached the highway, only a half dozen remained in his arms.

Peewee was right behind him, clutching his bag tightly. Without a second thought, he dropped to the ground, slid under the fence, and scrambled to his feet just as the barking closed in.

I was halfway through when a deep growl rumbled just a few feet behind me. Shadow—big, black, and mean—was almost on me. I braced for the bite.

"HEEL, SHADOW!" Mr. Snodgrass barked.

The dog froze, snarling but obedient. Then, slowly, he backed off and trotted toward the house. Mr. Snodgrass didn't want his dogs to hurt us—just to scare us enough not to come sneaking into his yard for apples again.

Heart pounding, I turned and ran. We all bolted down Route 22 and didn't stop until we were safe in our yard. We collapsed onto the grass, breathless and wide-eyed.

Ricky's paper bag was torn—only about half a dozen apples remained by his side. A mix of relief and laughter lit up his face.

"Dang, that was close," Peewee said, wiping sweat from his forehead. "Yeah, but we got the apples," I said, holding up my bag with a grin.

Ricky, still a bit shaken, gave a weak smile. "Next time, let's just buy some apples from the store."

He and Peewee slapped hands in agreement.

"I sure ain't in the mood for bein' chased by no mean-ass dogs," Peewee muttered.

Then he turned to us, still munching on an apple. "Hey, y'all wanna play some ball later?" His eyes lit up. "Clarence went to Columbus, but Caesar said he'd play with us."

I nodded. I didn't know Caesar, but I was just glad to have a fourth player. "Yeah, sounds good. You got a ball?"

Peewee grinned. "Yeah, I got one—but it's more like a balloon-sized ball. It'll do, though." Ricky chuckled and shook his head. "A balloon-sized ball? Man, this oughta be interesting." Peewee shrugged. "Hey, it's better than nothin'. We can make it work."

I nodded, already picturing us chasing that oversized ball around the court. "Yeah, it'll be fun. Let's do it."

Ricky smiled, looking more relaxed now that our apple-picking adventure was over. "Alright, let's meet up after lunch then."

Peewee nodded. "Deal. I'll bring the ball, and we'll go get Caesar. Gonna be a good game."

As Peewee headed back up Ellsworth, I noticed his T-shirt was drenched in sweat. I figured it was from running so hard—maybe out of fear. Then I glanced down at my own shirt. It clung to my skin, soaked through. I hadn't even realized how much we'd been sweating until I saw him. We must've really been scared.

Ricky turned to me, eyeing the apples we'd gathered. "What are you gonna do with all these apples?" he asked, curiosity written all over his face.

I smiled, thinking about the plan I'd been mulling over. "I watched Gladys make applesauce once. I remember the recipe. Figured we'd try it out later."

Ricky's eyes lit up. "For real? I love me some homemade applesauce!"

Dad was upstairs asleep, so I quietly placed the apples on a chair in the kitchen. Ricky headed to the bathroom to wash up. I went to the fridge and pulled out a package of bologna and some cheese—my stomach was already growling.

When Ricky came back, I handed him the bag of Wonder Bread. "Here, make your sandwich." Ricky made a face. "You got any other kind of bread? I hate that stuff."

I shrugged. "That's the only kind I see." Then I headed to the bathroom to wash my hands. While I was gone, Ricky started rummaging through the kitchen, opening cabinets and drawers. "I found a loaf of rye bread!" he called out.

I rushed back in and quickly shushed him, glancing toward the stairs. "Be quiet, Rick! Dad's upstairs trying to sleep."

He lowered his voice, grinning sheepishly. "Sorry, I forgot. But hey, this bread looks way better."

When I came out of the bathroom, Ricky had already made his sandwich and poured himself a glass of Coca-Cola. I walked into the kitchen and saw him at the table, happily munching away.

"Hey, you couldn't wait for me?" I said as I reached for a glass. Ricky grinned, mouth full. "Sorry, man. I was hungry."

I opened the fridge and spotted the empty Coke bottle. "You drank all the soda? And left an empty bottle in the refrigerator?"

Ricky looked sheepish. "I was thirsty. There's still some orange juice left, though."

I sighed and grabbed the carton, pouring myself a glass. As I took a sip, Ricky chuckled.

"Hey, you remember the Thorns from First Lane?" I shook my head. "No, I don't remember them."

Ricky leaned back in his chair, a thoughtful look on his face. "Well, let me fill you in. When Caesar was two, he got caught in a house fire. His legs were so badly burned that they had to amputate his right one. Now he walks with a peg leg."

I raised an eyebrow, surprised. "How's he gonna play basketball on one leg?"

Ricky shrugged. "I don't know. I've never seen him play sports. But he's comin' to play with us today, so I guess we'll find out."

I took a sip of orange juice, turning the idea over in my mind. "Man, that's tough. But if he's up for it, I guess we should give him a shot."

Ricky nodded. "Yeah, let's see what he's got. Maybe he's got some moves we don't know about."

We finished our sandwiches in silence, both of us deep in thought, wondering how Caesar would manage on the court. It was shaping up to be an interesting day.

CHAPTER 79

BALANCE AND GRIT ON ONE GOOD LEG

Not long after, I heard the familiar thump of a bouncing ball—only this one had a softer, hollow sound. Must've been that balloon basketball Peewee mentioned. I stepped out onto the porch, and there they were: Peewee at the mailbox, and next to him, Caesar.

Caesar was a short kid, and sure enough, he had a peg leg.

I'd never seen anyone with a peg leg before—let alone someone I was about to play basketball with.

Peewee called out, "Alvin, you know Caesar?"

I shook my head. "No, I don't."

Caesar spoke up, voice steady. "I live on First Lane. Y'all ready to play some ball?"

Peewee grinned, bouncing the ball. "It's me and Caesar against you and Ricky. We 'bout to take y'all to school."

I laughed, feeling the old competitive spark flare up. "You got it. Me and Ricky gonna beat y'all so bad, you'll wish you never came around here."

Ricky joined us on the porch, laughing as he heard my jab. "Let's do this."

I locked the door behind me, and we all headed up Ellsworth Street toward Route 22. It was a bit of a hike—even for me with two good legs—but Caesar kept pace, bouncing the ball, shuffling forward, hopping from his peg leg to his good one. I tried not to stare, but honestly, the kid was amazing.

The balloon basketball bounced lightly between us. And despite that peg leg, Caesar moved with surprising speed and rhythm. I could already tell—this game was gonna be one to remember.

As we reached the court, Caesar turned to us, eyes sparkling with excitement. "Y'all ready?" I nodded, a mix of curiosity and anticipation bubbling up. "Yeah, let's do this."

Peewee was already standing on the line. "Let's shoot from the free throw line to see who gets the ball first." He took his shot, but it missed—bouncing off the front of the rim.

Ricky grabbed the rebound and passed it to me. I stepped up to the line, the balloon basketball feeling strange in my hand. I took the shot, but the wind caught it, and it didn't even come close to the backboard.

Caesar laughed. "My turn." He hopped over to the line and let it fly. For a second, the wind stilled, and the ball arced beautifully toward the basket. But just before it reached the hoop, a gust picked up and carried it wide.

Ricky caught the ball and shook his head. "Don't blame the wind. Y'all just can't shoot." He stepped to the line, took a breath, and let it go. The shot wobbled through the air and swished straight through the net.

Ricky grinned. "Told y'all, none of you can shoot like me." Caesar shook his head, smiling. "Man, that was pure luck."

"Luck?" Ricky puffed out his chest. "That was all skill. We get the ball first."

Ricky and I laughed, but Peewee grabbed the ball and said, "Let's get this thing started." He tossed it to Ricky. "Check."

I patted Ricky on the back. "Let's beat them like we beat him and Clarence the other day."

After Ricky checked the ball with Peewee, he passed it to me, and the game began. Peewee was on me right away. "I ain't letting you score," he said, eyes locked on mine.

I tried to drive toward the basket, but the ball kept taking wobbly bounces off the uneven court, making it tough to control. Peewee lunged in, stole the ball, and headed for the hoop—but he couldn't keep control either. The ball bounced out of bounds.

"Damn basketball! I can't play a good game with that thing," Peewee said, frustration in his voice.

I nodded, trying to keep things light. "Let's just keep playing, man. It's still fun." But Peewee shook his head. "Nah, I quit."

Disappointment settled over Caesar, his excitement deflating. "Come on, Peewee. It's just a game."

Ricky looked let down, too. "Yeah, we were just getting started."

Peewee sighed, looking at all of us. "I know, but this ball is just too hard to handle. It ain't fun when you can't even dribble right."

I could see where he was coming from, but I didn't want the game to end on a sour note. "How about we try something else, then? Maybe a different game or just shoot some hoops for fun." Caesar perked up at the suggestion. "Yeah, we don't have to quit. Let's just mess around a bit." Peewee thought for a moment, then shrugged. "Alright, what about playing H.O.R.S.E.?" Everyone agreed.

"I'll go first," Peewee announced.

Caesar grinned, mischief in his eyes. "Why you gotta go first? Let's play Rock, Paper, Scissors." He started counting, "One, two, three," and just like that, Peewee threw out Rock while Caesar flashed Paper.

"Paper beats Rock. I win!" Caesar said, grabbing the ball.

With only one leg, he wasn't about to try a jump shot, but he could still pull off a layup or a set shot. A set shot meant holding the ball with both hands, bending the knees, pushing off the legs, and aiming for the basket.

He started dribbling toward the hoop. I stood there, amazed at Caesar's grit and competitive fire.

As he approached the basket, he worked his peg leg with real control, maneuvering with effort and focus. Then he leapt off his good leg and gently laid the ball up. The balloon basketball floated up, kissed the backboard, and dropped through the hoop.

"Nice shot, Caesar!" I said, genuinely impressed. Ricky clapped. "Yeah, good job, man!"

Grinning, Caesar handed over the ball. "Alright, Peewee. Match that."

Peewee took it, eyes locked on the hoop. "Alright, watch this," he said, full of confidence. He tried to mimic Caesar's shot, but the balloon ball caught a gust of wind, bounced off the backboard, and flew into the grass.

Frustrated, Peewee threw up his hands. "I'm through. This ball is impossible to control." He walked off the court, shaking his head. "If y'all still want to play, go ahead. I'm done." I turned to Ricky. "You still wanna play?"

He shook his head. "Nah, I'm hungry, and I keep thinkin' about that homemade applesauce you're gonna make."

Caesar nodded. "Yeah, I'm ready to go too."

We decided to call it a day. Peewee, still a bit frustrated, left his balloon ball lying in the grass as we all headed home.

The four of us strolled down the highway, our laughter and teasing floating into the warm evening air. Caesar, grinning, nudged Peewee. "Man, that ball was so janky, it couldn't bounce straight if it tried."

"For real, Peewee. Next time, let's get a ball that ain't like a beach ball," I said.

"Aw, cut me some slack, boys. It was the best I could do," he replied.

"It's all good, Peewee. We'll get a proper one next time—no more bummers on the court," I said with a laugh.

When we reached Ellsworth Street, Caesar said goodbye and headed home to Floyd Street, while Ricky, Peewee, and I made our way back to the house. The sun was casting long shadows across the dirt road, which had been treated with oil and asphalt emulsion to keep the dust down. The fumes from it stung my nose and throat.

CHAPTER 80

THE SUMMER I THOUGHT ABOUT STAYING

When we got to the house, Peewee said goodbye and took off. Dad was sitting on the porch next to Junior. He spotted us and called out with a mix of amusement and affection, "Here come those two."

A smile tugged at the corners of his mouth. "You boys look like you've been through the wringer."

We shuffled toward the porch, my limbs heavy with fatigue.

As we stepped through the screen door, Junior clapped me on the back, laughing—a rich, hearty sound that filled the space.

"What've you two been up to today?" he asked.

"Picking apples, then playing basketball with Peewee and Caesar," Ricky said, smiling despite the tiredness in his voice.

I added, "Peewee brought this worthless balloon basketball we could hardly play with." Junior chuckled and shook his head. "A balloon basketball? That sounds crazy."

"It was more like an exercise in frustration," I said, laughing. "Every time we tried to shoot, the ball just floated away."

"After all that, I know y'all must be tired," Junior said.

"Tired and hungry," I replied, just as my stomach growled. A delicious smell was drifting in from the kitchen.

From his seat, Dad lifted his head, a smile spreading across his face. "I cooked some okra and peas with neckbones," he announced, his voice full of pride, like a man who knew he had something good on the stove.

The thought of a home-cooked meal was a welcome relief after days of TV dinners. Ricky and I exchanged a look, our eyes lighting up at the idea of real food.

Junior leaned back in his chair. "You boys look like you could use a good meal," he said,

laughing. "Granddad's been worried y'all were gonna turn into frozen food at this rate."

Then he turned to me, grinning. "Haven't seen you since that drive-in episode. Remember? Me, you, and Johnnie?"

I laughed, shaking my head. "How could I forget? That was a night to remember."

Junior's grin widened. "I learned a valuable lesson that night—mental and physical. Never follow your brother's lead when it comes to breaking Granddad's rules."

"Oh man, that night was something else," I said, chuckling. "I really thought we were gonna get away with it."

The memory of that drive-in escapade flashed through my mind—sneaking out after Dad left for work definitely wasn't our smartest move.

Junior stood up, his compact frame now filled out from months of hard training. He was heading into his senior year as a first-team defensive cornerback. Tomorrow marked the start of two-a- day practices.

"Yeah, man, that's gonna be tough," I said.

Ricky jumped in with a smirk. "You ain't never played football—how would you know?"

I laughed. "You got me there, Ricky. But I know greatness when I see it, and Junior's got it written all over him."

We all burst into laughter as we stepped into the house, the warm smell of Dad's cooking—okra, neckbones, and rice—filling the air. It was the perfect end to a long, worn-out day.

I went to the bathroom to wash up. When I came into the kitchen, Dad was at the sink washing

dishes. He didn't look up, but his voice was gentle and firm. "Y'all get y'all some plates and sit down and eat."

Junior, Ricky, and I exchanged excited glances, then headed for the cabinet. I reached for a white plate with gold trim, the familiar clink of porcelain ringing out as mine bumped against

Junior's—then Ricky's—as we took our places. Ricky chuckled and nudged me.

"Yeah, don't go dropping your plate," he said sarcastically.

"Yeah, let's take them outside and throw them around like Frisbees," I joked. Junior turned to Dad. "How long you had these plates?"

"Since before you were born," Dad said, glancing back at us with a grin. "Yeah, I remember— Azalie and I got those plates as wedding gifts. She was so glad we got something nice for family dinners. She believed it was important to sit down together and share a meal, no matter how tough things got."

"Man, these plates been around since before we were born," I repeated, amazed. "Yeah—like fragile little time bombs waiting for us to mess up!" Junior added with a grin.

We moved to the table, the smell of Dad's okra, neckbones, and rice pulling us in. We filled our plates, steam rising in waves that made my stomach growl even louder.

Ricky eyed my heaping plate and said, "Hope you left enough for the rest of us!" I grinned. "Relax, Ricky. I'll leave enough so you can lick the serving spoon!"

"Every Sunday," Dad said, a wistful smile on his face, "Azalie would cook a big meal after church, and we'd all sit around the table, just like this. She'd laugh and talk, making sure everybody had enough to eat. Those were good times, even when things were hard."

Junior, always the practical one, asked, "But how'd you manage with three kids after Grandmamma died? That must've been rough."

Dad lowered his gaze to his hands. "It was. The hardest part was losing Azalie. But these plates... they remind me of her. Every time I set the table, I feel like she's right there with me, telling me to keep going."

Ricky's voice was soft. "And you did it, Granddad. You kept Dad, Uncle Amos, and Aunt Ruby Nelle all together."

Dad nodded, a glimmer of pride in his eyes. "I did what I had to do for my children."

It would've been the perfect moment to ask Dad those questions I'd been holding in—about him and Mom. But with Ricky and Junior there, I didn't want to embarrass him.

"These plates, they ain't just dishes. They're a piece of my history, a reminder of where we come from," Dad said.

With everyone seated at the table, Dad looked around and said, "Let us bow our heads." He cleared his throat and began, "Heavenly Father, as we gather around this table, grateful for the food before us and the love that binds us together, we humbly thank you for this moment. As we share in this bounty, may we remember the blessings that surround us. For the love that fills this room, for the lessons learned on the journey of life, and for the bond that transcends time, we offer our gratitude. Bless this meal. Nourish our souls, not to defile the body, O Lord, but to give us strength. Amen."

"This looks good, Granddad," Junior said, his tone appreciative as he took a bite. "Been waitin' all day for this."

As we ate, conversation flowed easily, touching on everything from school to Junior's football practice. The okra, neckbones, and rice were tender and flavorful, perfectly seasoned. It felt like a reward for all the hard work we'd put in that day.

"I like this, Granddad," Ricky said between bites. Dad nodded. "Glad y'all like it."

Junior, who'd been quiet since we sat down, finally spoke up. "Tomorrow's the first day of practice, and I'm ready. You and Ricky can come watch if you want."

"That's all right, Junior," Ricky chimed in before I could say anything. "I'd like to come and watch. It'll be great to see you in action."

"What time does it start?" I asked.

"The morning session starts at 9 a.m., and the afternoon one's at 4."

"I like the 4 o'clock session. It's summer; I don't like gettin' up that early," Ricky said.

Junior grinned and nodded. "Alright, I'm going to bed. Good night." He headed to his room.

After we'd finished dinner, I said, "For dessert, I'm gonna make some applesauce out of those apples we got from the Snodgrass yard."

"That sounds good," Ricky said. "What do you need me to do?"

I smiled. "Just the apples we picked, some sugar, boiling water, and cinnamon. You can help me peel and slice them if you want."

Dad leaned back in his chair and let out a tired sigh. "I'm goin' upstairs. Y'all make sure to clean up behind yourselves," he said, his voice heavy with the weariness of a long day. He took the last sip of iced tea from his cup, then stood up from the table, the day's newspaper folded under one arm. His back was bent from years of labor, but as he rose, I couldn't help but notice the strength still in his frame.

His work pants clung snugly to his strong, muscular build. He loosened his black suspenders now that he was settling in for the evening. For a man in his mid-sixties, his shoulders, biceps, and arms were still impressively defined—dark and weathered from years of toil. His fingers, long and calloused, looked like they held a thousand stories of their own.

He headed toward the stairs, and I watched him go up, each step slow but deliberate. After he disappeared from view, I heard his footsteps overhead, followed by the loud blare of country music spilling through the ceiling as he turned on the radio.

Ricky shot me a look, a smirk tugging at the corner of his mouth. "You think he ever gon' let us pick the music, since the whole house gotta hear it?"

I laughed and shook my head. "Not a chance. That man loves his country tunes. I just hope Junior can sleep through all that noise."

Ricky and I kept peeling and slicing apples.

"I hope this is gonna be worth my time," Ricky muttered, cutting through another apple with a sigh.

As the apples simmered on the stove, the sweet, spicy aroma filled the kitchen, blending with the lingering scent of dinner. Ricky hovered near the pot, pacing slightly, eager for dessert.

When the applesauce was finally ready, we didn't even wait for it to cool. The taste was just

right—sweet, tangy, and comforting. Way better than anything from the store. We cleared the table and washed the dishes, talking and laughing as we worked.

After we finished cleaning up, I grabbed a bottle of Coca-Cola and stepped out onto the screened porch. As I sat down and took a sip, my thoughts drifted to Boston—how things were there, and how different life might be if I stayed in Ohio for school.

That would mean being away from my sisters, Gladys and Gloria, and from Momma. But Momma was always working, and Gladys and Gloria had their own circle of friends. They never really had time for me. Here in Ohio, I had space—the open air, the quiet—and a freedom that Boston's crowded apartments never offered.

Aside from my friends on the Falcons, Boston felt small. Outside of church, there wasn't much for me besides Momma, and that only deepened how much I leaned on her. I loved being on the Falcons, sure, but most of the time I was just sitting on the bench—jersey and pants still crisp and clean, untouched by the game—watching from the sidelines, waiting for a chance that hardly ever came. The high schools were huge, the competition fierce. Deep down, I didn't think I was good enough to make the team.

I wasn't growing in Boston.

Still, I knew I'd miss it—miss playing, or at least *being* on the bench. The Falcons were the best YMCA league team in the city— sharp, connected, relentless on defense.

I popped the cap off the bottle and took a sip. The cool fizz cut through the warm evening air. In the yard, lightning bugs flickered, their tiny lights dancing across the dusk. It felt good sitting there on the porch, a refreshing change from swatting mosquitoes back home.

The screen door creaked open, and Ricky stepped out, holding his own bottle of Coke.

"Hey Alvin, what you doing?"

I lifted my head and gave him a small smile. "Just thinkin', Ricky. Tryna figure out how things might be if I went to school here instead of back in Boston."

Ricky took a seat next to me and nodded. "I don't think you'll ever leave Boston."

I didn't respond right away. I just took a sip of my Coke. "I feel comfortable here. I don't know what it is, but I'm gonna ask Dad if I can finish school here. Up there, Momma has my sisters, and they'll be okay. Besides, I'm just sitting on the bench for the Falcons anyway."

Ricky leaned back, thinking it over. "That's a big step, Alvin. You really think you'll be happier here?"

"I do," I said, feeling more certain as the words left my mouth. "I think I've got a shot at making the basketball team here. I don't want to play football; it's just not for me. Too bad there's no baseball team. I'd make that easy. It's different here, but it feels right."

Ricky drained the last of his Coke and stood up, stretching. "I'm going to bed."

I nodded, taking another sip. "I'm gonna sit out here a little longer. Need to clear my head some more."

"Alright," Ricky said as he stepped back inside. The screen door slammed shut behind him. Yeah, I think it's time for a change. It's scary, but it's also exciting.

The lightning bugs kept dancing in the yard, and for the first time in a long while, the world felt full of possibility.

CHAPTER 81

THE KITCHEN HELD US TOGETHER

On Tuesday, July 10, 1962, at 4:30 PM, Ricky and I made our way to Wintersville High School under the blazing sun, the temperature pushing 92 degrees. When we arrived, the locker room door was propped open, with a steady stream of players moving in and out. They were dressed in practice gear—shirts and pants clinging to sweat-drenched bodies, shoulder pads strapped tight, football cleats clacking against the tiled floor, and helmets gripped firmly in hand.

The air was thick with the pungent scent of sweat and the buzz of anticipation, even though practice hadn't started yet. Coach Kettlewell stood tall among his assistants, his presence commanding. He barked instructions like a drill sergeant, his voice cutting through the humid air, setting the tone for the grueling session ahead.

Ricky and I stood just outside the practice field, scanning the scene for Junior. It didn't take long to spot him, sweaty and serious and standing near Kenny Moore and Bobby Yetts. "Hey, Junior!" we called as we walked over, stopping near the locker room door. Junior raised his head, sweat dripping down his face. "What's up, y'all?"

"Man, it's too hot for all this activity," Ricky complained. "But we here to see you do your thing."

Junior wiped his brow with his forearm. "Yeah, Coach ain't playin' around. This gon' be a tough one."

We glanced at Kenny and Bobby, both looking just as eager and worn out as Junior. I looked at the three of them. "Y'all ready for this?"

Junior grinned, teeth flashing. "We've been ready. This is just the beginning."

He turned to Kenny and Bobby and gestured toward me. "Hey, this here's my father's brother, Alvin. He visitin' from Boston for the summer."

Bobby nodded. "Nice to meet you."

Kenny smiled. "Boston, huh? You bring us some of them Boston beans?" "Not this trip—maybe next time."

Coach Kettlewell's voice rang out across the field. "Alright, let's get to it! No slackin' today!" "We gotta go," Junior said. "Y'all gonna stay and watch?"

"We ain't goin' nowhere," Ricky said, leaning against the fence. "Show us what you got, Junior."

Junior nodded. "See y'all later." "See you around," Bobby added.

Kenny quipped, "I'm going to hold you to that promise about those Boston baked beans."

I laughed. "Deal! Just be ready for a surprise—those beans might come with a side of Boston attitude!"

They all ran back, laughing, to rejoin the rest of the team already on the field.

The sun beat down, turning the grass into a shimmering sea of green. Coach Kettlewell—a tall man with a booming voice and a permanent scowl—stood in the center of the chaos, his whistle hanging from his neck like a badge of authority. His assistants flanked him, ready to back every command.

"Alright, listen up!" Coach Kettlewell's voice sliced through the hum of chatter. "We're starting with suicides. I want to see hustle out there!"

The players groaned but lined up without complaint. The drill was brutal—sprint to the 10-yard line, back to the start, then the 20,

30, all the way to the 50. Junior took the lead, his face locked in determination.

"Go!" Coach Kettlewell blew the whistle, and the players shot off like bullets, cleats biting into the turf.

Ricky and I watched from the sidelines, wincing at the intensity. "Man, they ain't kiddin' around," Ricky muttered.

Junior pushed himself hard, legs pumping like pistons. Sweat streamed down his face, but he didn't let up. He hit the 50-yard line, turned, and sprinted back, every muscle straining.

Next came the Oklahoma drill. Two players squared off in a narrow corridor, one trying to block the other. Coach Kettlewell paired Junior with Allen Jack, a stocky kid built low to the ground.

"Ready... Go!"

The boys collided with a thud that echoed across the field.

Junior held firm, muscles flexed against Allen Jack's weight. The struggle was fierce, both giving everything they had. Then Junior drove forward, pushing Allen out of the corridor.

"Nice job, Harris," Coach Kettlewell said, his expression still stern.

The drills continued—tackling dummies, passing routes, agility ladders. Each one pushed the players to their limits, their bodies moving like well-oiled machines under Coach Kettlewell's watchful eye.

During a water break, we joined Junior and the rest of the team at the fountains. Junior's chest was heaving.

"Y'all enjoyin' the show?" he asked with a tired grin.

"Man, you look like you been through a war. But yeah, you're lookin' good," I said.

Junior took a long drink and wiped his mouth. "This is nothin'. Wait 'til the season starts."

A few assistant coaches walked by, handing out clear plastic bags filled with thin orange and white pills. Curious, I grabbed a handful of both, wondering what they tasted like.

I popped an orange one into my mouth. It was sweet—like a burst of orange juice. "Hey, these ain't bad," I said to Ricky, who stood beside me.

Ricky raised an eyebrow. "Lemme try one." I handed him an orange pill, and he nodded in approval as he chewed. "Not bad at all. Like candy."

I tried a white one next. The moment it hit my tongue, I grimaced. "Ugh, this one's pure salt!" I spat it out quickly, the bitter taste clinging to my mouth.

Ricky laughed at my reaction. "Man, it's that bad?"

I nodded, tossing the rest of the white pills in the trash. "Yeah, I don't recommend those. Stick to the orange ones."

Junior, standing nearby, said, "The orange ones are energy boosters. The white ones help replace the salt we lose from sweating—but yeah, they taste like straight-up salt."

Coach Kettlewell's whistle blew again, calling everyone back to the field. Junior gave us a quick nod, then jogged off to rejoin his teammates.

As he dove back into the action, I felt a surge of pride. This was serious work, but Junior was more than ready for it.

We stood there, watching as the team lined up for the next drill. The sun climbed higher, the heat growing heavier, but those little bursts of orange sweetness made it all a little easier to bear.

As practice wore on, the players dug deeper, pushing themselves harder. The sun hung high in the sky, casting long shadows as the session neared its end. But Coach Kettlewell—relentless and determined—wasn't ready to let up. He blew his whistle and gathered the team for one final round.

"Alright, boys, we're ending today with some gassers and goal-line stands. I want to see maximum effort!"

The players groaned but moved into position. Gassers were brutal—sprinting across the width of the field and back, over and over, with barely any rest in between.

"Ready... go!" Coach Kettlewell's whistle pierced the air, and the players exploded into motion, using every ounce of energy they had left.

Junior led the pack, his legs churning as he sprinted from sideline to sideline. Sweat poured down his face, but he refused to slow down, pushing hard to stay ahead.

"Come on, Junior! You got this!" I shouted, caught up in the intensity of the moment.

Coach Kettlewell blew his whistle again. "Alright, bring it in!" The players stumbled into a huddle, breathing heavily and soaked with sweat, but they knew it wasn't over.

"We're finishing with goal-line stands," he said. "Defense on one side, offense on the other. I want to see some grit!"

Junior lined up with the defense, eyes locked on the offense. The first snap came—a run play. The offense charged, but the defense held, bodies crashing together in a fierce clash at the line.

The second play switched to a pass. Terry Scalise, the quarterback, dropped back and fired a quick throw to the running back. But Junior saw it coming—he lunged and brought the runner down just short of the goal line.

"Good job, Harris!" Coach Kettlewell called out, approval in his voice.

The final play came, and the offense gave it everything they had— but the defense stood firm, stopping them short once again. Coach Kettlewell blew his whistle one last time, signaling the end of practice.

"That's it for today! Good work, everyone," he said. "Hit the showers and be ready for more tomorrow morning at 9:00 a.m."

As the players headed toward the locker room, I watched Junior walk off the field, pride swelling in my chest. This summer was shaping up to be something special, and I was here to witness every moment of it.

CHAPTER 82

FRIDAY NIGHTS AND CHICKEN HEADS

August 4, 1962 I was having so much fun that summer—I wished it would never end. Slowly, I had made up my mind: the unfiltered happiness I had found in Wintersville didn't have to fade.

Junior leaned back, his voice full of nostalgia. "Man, there's nothing like those Friday nights, you know? The whole town shows up, and the air's thick with anticipation. You can smell the popcorn and hotdogs from a mile away."

I smiled, his excitement rubbing off on me. "Sounds like quite the experience."

Junior nodded, his face lighting up. "It is. And wait 'til you hear about Coach Gundling. That man is something else."

I raised an eyebrow, curious. "Oh yeah? What's he do that's so special?"

Junior chuckled. "Before every big game, he comes into the locker room to fire us up. And get this—he bites the head off a chicken."

I stared at him, stunned. "You're kidding."

"Nope," he said, shaking his head. "That's his thing. And it works. You should see the guys after that—they're ready to run through a brick wall."

This was Junior's final year of high school, and I wanted to see him compete. It would be the first time I had a close relative excelling at this level of sports.

Next week, registration opens for incoming freshmen at Wintersville High School. I'm going to tell Dad I want to stay. It's a decision I've been turning over in my mind for weeks.

I'll miss my mom, my sisters, and my teammates on the Falcons. My classmates Tommy and Jose are headed to different high schools, and I'll miss the fun we had back in Boston. But something about rural life here suits me. It matches my laid-back nature. Here, I can see a future—college, maybe even a way out of the poverty that shadows Boston.

I sat on the screen porch, surrounded by the sweet scent of honeysuckle and the steady chorus of crickets in the distance. The sun dipped below the hills, casting a warm orange glow over the rooftops and trees.

Now was the time.

I rose from my seat, the honeysuckle scent fading as I stepped into the living room. Dad sat quietly, sipping a bowl of iced tea. My heart thudded in my chest, but I knew I had to speak.

"Dad, can I have a word with you?" I tried to keep my voice steady.

He looked up from his tea, raising an eyebrow. "Sure, son. What's on your mind?"

I took a deep breath, gathering my thoughts. "I've been thinking a lot lately, and I've made a decision."

Dad set his iced tea down and leaned back in his chair, giving me his full attention. "Alright, let's hear it."

"I want to stay here in Wintersville and go to high school," I said, the words tumbling out faster than I meant them to.

Dad's expression shifted from curiosity to surprise. "You sure 'bout that? Wintersville ain't like Boston. It's slower, quieter."

I nodded, a mix of excitement and nerves churning in my chest. "I know, Dad. But I think that's what I need. I love it here—the peace, the space. And I've got a better shot at making the freshman basketball team, maybe even going to college if I stay."

Dad rubbed his chin, eyes studying me carefully. "It's a big decision. You sure you're ready to leave your mama and sisters? Your friends?"

I swallowed hard, Mom's warm smile flashing through my mind—her humming Mahalia Jackson songs while cooking. Sunday dinners were legendary. Collard greens and mac and cheese became something to count down to every week. Then there were my sisters, Gladys and Gloria. We had our share of squabbles, but our bond was strong. We fought and made up like nothing ever happened, always knowing we had each other's backs.

I thought about Tommy and Jose, the basketball games at Marcella Park, and the busy streets of Boston. "I'll miss them, no doubt. But I gotta think about my future. I can't let a divided family hold me back, Dad. I wanna make somethin' of myself."

Dad nodded slowly, a proud smile creeping across his face. "That's smart, thinkin' ahead. If this is what you want, I'll talk to your mama first."

I grinned, a weight lifted off my shoulders. We sat there in easy silence, the sounds of the summer evening drifting through the open windows. I knew it wouldn't be easy, but for the first time, I felt like the path ahead was clear. I was ready to take on Wintersville and whatever came with it.

CHAPTER 83

REGISTRATION DAY AND THE GOODBYE THAT FOLLOWED

August 15, 1962 I stood in line at Wintersville High School, a mix of excitement and nerves churning in my stomach. Today was registration day for the new school year. With college in my sights, I'd chosen my courses carefully—Spanish, Geometry, Biology, Chemistry, and Physics. It was going to be a tough year, but I felt ready.

As I filled out the registration forms, a voice broke through my thoughts.

"Hey, didn't we used to play together in first grade?"

A familiar face came into view. It took a second, but then it clicked.

"Billy? Is that you?"

Billy grinned. "Yeah, it's me! I can't believe it. We used to play kickball together!"

I laughed, memories rushing back. "And those bullies who stole our ball—remember how you tackled that one kid?"

Billy chuckled. "Yeah, and the principal scared the life out of us, said he'd expel us if we caused any more trouble."

We stood there for a moment, caught in the warmth of old memories. It felt good to reconnect.

"So, what classes are you taking?" Billy asked, genuinely interested.

"I'm on the college prep track," I said, listing my courses. "Spanish, Geometry, Biology, Chemistry, and Physics. What about you?"

Billy shook his head. "I'm not planning on college. I want to be an automotive mechanic, maybe own a gas station one day. I've been learning from my uncle, who runs the Shell station on Market Street in Steubenville."

His words hung in the air. I didn't ask if that was the same racist uncle who once threatened to burn down his house because I was there playing. I kept that memory to myself, though it sat heavy in the back of my mind.

"That sounds good, Billy," I said, choosing my words carefully. "I'm not exactly sure what I want to do yet, but I know I want to go to college and earn a degree."

Billy nodded. "Yeah, I get that. College is a big deal. My mom always says a degree opens doors. But me—I just love working with my hands. Engines, cars... that's where I feel at home."

We continued filling out our forms when a question came to mind.

"Hey, Billy, what happens after we register?"

He glanced up from his paperwork. "There's an assembly next, I think. But what they're gonna say I got no idea."

The line moved slowly, but eventually, it was my turn to hand in my registration paperwork. I double-checked everything, making sure the forms were filled out correctly, then handed them to the lady at the desk. She smiled, nodded, and placed them on the growing stack.

Behind me, Billy was talking with a group of his friends. He caught my eye and grinned.

"I'll see you when school starts next week," he said, giving me a thumbs-up.

"Okay, stay cool," I replied, watching him walk off, his laughter echoing through the busy hallway.

Feeling a little out of place now that Billy was gone, I scanned the gymnasium for a familiar face. That's when I spotted Bobby Evans from Third Lane. He noticed me and smiled, heading my way.

"Hey, man," Bobby said, his grin wide. "You going out for football this year?" I shook my head. "Nah, not football. I'm trying out for basketball."

Bobby's eyes lit up. "Me too! I heard Coach Patron's legit—he played with Jerry West at West Virginia."

My eyebrows shot up. "No kidding? Sounds like we're in good hands."

"Yeah," Bobby nodded. "I think it's gonna be a solid year. I've been practicing all summer. What position are you aiming for?"

"Probably shooting guard," I said. "Been working on my jump shot. You?"

"Forward," Bobby replied. "We should hit the court together sometime, get some runs in before tryouts."

I smiled, feeling more relaxed. "I've been playing with Peewee and Clarence. I'm looking forward to it."

We found seats together in the gym, talking hoops and the upcoming school year, until the principal stepped up to the microphone, tapping it a couple of times. The room gradually fell silent.

"Welcome, students," Mr. Anderson began, his voice strong and clear. "This marks the beginning of an important chapter in your lives. As the future class of 1966, you are embarking on a journey that will shape your futures and define your paths."

He spoke briefly, laying out the importance of the coming years, the opportunities ahead, and the expectations placed upon us. Then he introduced the assistant principal, Mr. Johnson, who stepped up to the podium with a broad smile.

"Good afternoon, everyone," Mr. Johnson said warmly. "I want to take a moment to welcome you all to Wintersville High School. You're now part of a tradition of excellence—a community that values hard work, dedication, and integrity."

He paused, scanning the room and making eye contact with several students, including me.

"You are the future class of 1966," he continued. "Each of you has the potential to do great things. High school will bring challenges and triumphs, and we're here to support you every step of the way."

The pep talk hit home. I felt pride rising in my chest. Mr. Johnson spoke about seizing opportunities, staying focused on our goals, and lifting each other up through the journey.

"Remember," he concluded, "the choices you make and the effort you give will shape not only your future, but the future of this community. Make these years count."

The assembly ended with a round of applause. I left the gym feeling both excited and determined. As I stepped into the warm August afternoon, I knew this was just the beginning— an important, transformative journey lay ahead.

When I got home from registering for school, my mind was still buzzing with thoughts of the year to come. I walked through the backyard, where Dad was filling Bull's bowl with dog food. The old hound wagged his tail eagerly, but Dad's expression was somber.

He looked up as I approached. "I talked to your mother," he said, voice steady but serious. "She wants you back in Boston to get ready for school."

My heart sank. It felt like a needle popping a balloon—everything I'd built up, gone in an instant. I'd been looking forward to staying here, starting high school in Wintersville, being part of something real.

"Be ready to leave on Saturday," Dad added, his eyes carrying a mix of understanding and regret.

I nodded, trying to keep my disappointment hidden. "Okay, Dad," I said quietly, though the sadness crept into my voice.

Dad sighed and set the bag of dog food down. He walked over and placed a hand on my shoulder.

"I know this isn't what you wanted," he said, "but your mother thinks it's for the best. She wants you to have every opportunity, and she believes Boston can give you that."

"I understand," I replied, though it was hard to accept. "I just... I was really looking forward to being here with you and everyone."

Dad gave a small, sad smile. "I know, son. But sometimes we have to do things we don't like because they're good for us in the long run."

I nodded, trying to take comfort in his words. "I guess I should start packing, then." "Yeah," Dad said. "Don't worry, Wintersville will always be here. And so will I."

As I walked back into the house, my mind filled with images of Friday night football games at the stadium. I could see Junior making the winning play, the crowd exploding in cheers, and the pride and excitement that lit up the night. It was hard to let go of that vision—the deep sense of belonging I felt here in Wintersville.

But reality was settling in. I had to face the truth: I was going back to Boston, leaving behind the dreams and plans I'd made for this school year. My future was in Boston—with Momma, Gladys, and Gloria. I knew I had to embrace it.

The path ahead wouldn't be what I imagined, but it was still mine. I took a deep breath, bracing myself for the journey and for the opportunities waiting in the city I once called home.

CHAPTER 84

GROWING UP ON THE WAY
BACK TO BOSTON

August 16, 1962 The sun was just beginning to rise, casting a golden glow over the familiar neighborhood. I sat on the front porch, my thoughts heavy with the news I had received the day before. I watched as Peewee and Clarence came bouncing down the dusty road, engaged in a spirited round of playing the dozens. Their laughter and jabs echoed in the still morning air.

"Your mother so black, you can't see her face until she smiles!" Peewee exclaimed, barely able to contain his laughter.

Clarence shot back, "Oh yeah? Your mother so old, she owes Moses a dollar!"

The sun was just beginning to rise, casting a golden glow over the familiar neighborhood. I sat on the front porch, my thoughts heavy with the news I'd gotten the day before. Down the dusty road came Peewee and Clarence, bouncing along, locked in a loud, playful round of the dozens. Their laughter and insults echoed through the quiet morning air.

"Yo mama so black, you can't see her face till she smiles!" Peewee shouted, barely able to contain his laughter.

Clarence shot back, "Oh yeah? Yo mama so old, she owes Moses a dollar!"

I couldn't help but chuckle. Their back-and-forth was a welcome break from the weight I was carrying. As they got closer, Peewee spotted me and held the basketball high in the air.

"Alvin! I got a brand-new ball! Let's go play some ball!" he called out, full of energy. Clarence grinned. "Yeah, come on, Alvin. Let's see if you can still beat us."

I forced a smile but shook my head. "Ricky's not here, and I'm not in the mood to play today."

Peewee's smile faded, confusion crossing his face. "Why not? What's goin' on?" "My dad told me I'm going back to Boston."

Both of them fell silent. The words hung there a moment before sinking in. Clarence was the first to speak.

"Man, that's tough. When you gotta leave?"

"Saturday," I said, eyes dropping to the ground. "I really wanted to stay here, you know?" Peewee nodded, gently bouncing the ball. "Yeah, we get it. But hey—let's go play some ball." I appreciated the gesture. "Thanks, guys. Maybe tomorrow."

Clarence nodded. "Whenever you're ready."

They walked off, still dribbling the ball, heading quietly up Ellsworth Street and over to the basketball court. I watched them go, a mix of sadness and gratitude washing over me.

The reality of going back to Boston loomed large—but for now, I was thankful for the time I'd spent here.

2:00 P.M. (Same Day)

I was lying in my room, staring at the ceiling, trying to wrap my head around leaving. Suddenly, the door creaked open, and Junior walked in with a mischievous grin.

"Hey, come with me," he said like it had already been decided. "I'm goin' up to Kenny Moore's house to hang out with Bobby and Kenny."

I sat up, curiosity piqued. "Aight, lemme grab my shoes." I followed him without hesitation, stepping right out the door behind him.

We made our way up to Kenny's house, the air filled with the sounds of summer—crickets chirping, kids laughing in the distance. As we approached, I saw Bobby sitting outside, shooting the breeze. Kenny's family owned Moore's Inn, up at the top of First Lane—a neighborhood bar where folks from Silver Stream Knolls liked to hang out. It's also where my brother Amos and his wife Bernice went to drink and dance.

Junior and I plopped down on the rail, while Kenny and Bobby stayed seated on the steps. Kenny glanced my way and started teasing Junior.

"Look at you, bringin' your young uncle along," Kenny chuckled, giving Junior a playful shove.

Kenny was a tough guy—a running back on the team with Junior. He had a rep for not taking any mess on the field.

He leaned back, smirking. "Man, when I get tackled hard, I lay there and kick out with my cleats. Anybody close gon' get cut up real good," he said, eyes shining with mischief.

Bobby, the quiet one, chuckled and shook his head. "You wild, Kenny." He'd had an accident as a kid and lost an eye. He mostly kept to himself, but his laugh was warm and real.

"And check this out," Kenny said, puffing up his chest. "I got me a leather coat with 'LBJ' on it.

Stands for Lyndon Baines Johnson—and the cattle ranch of the vice president himself." Junior snorted. "Man, you and that coat. Ain't nobody impressed." But he was grinning.

Even though the thought of leaving tugged at me, I found comfort in that moment—with Junior's teammates, surrounded by the easy banter and quiet joy of true friendship. Saturday, August 18, 1962, Sadly, the day had finally come. My bag sat by the front door—a quiet reminder that my time in Wintersville was coming to an end. I stepped out onto the back porch, taking in the familiar sights one last time. Bull was tied up, happily munching from his bowl. Mr. Curley sat outside his shack, puffing on one of his rolled-up cigarettes, the smoke curling lazily into the morning air. The smell of the oil-stained, dusty road on Ellsworth Street filled my nose, bringing a flood of memories.

I glanced over at Mr. Curley's shack, remembering all the times I'd seen him sitting there, always with a cigarette, always watching the world go by.

"Morning, Mr. Curley," I called out.

He tipped his hat in my direction and took a long drag. "Mornin', young man. Today's the day, huh?"

"Yeah," I said, my voice heavy. "I'm headed back to Boston." "Well, you take care now," he replied, his voice gruff but kind.

I nodded, grateful. My eyes drifted to the road, recalling the time Peewee, Ricky, and I stole apples from Mr. Snodgrass's orchard and got chased by his dogs. The rush of running, the laughter as we barely cleared the fence—it was a memory I'd carry with me.

Junior stepped out of the house. "Bus #22 should be getting to Steubenville soon," he said.

I nodded, a lump forming in my throat. "Yeah. I already said good-bye to Daddy. He's still in bed, catching up on sleep after working all night."

I took a deep breath and glanced back at the house one last time. We walked in silence up Ellsworth Street toward the bus stop, the weight of my departure heavy on my mind. The familiar sights of Wintersville blurred around us, memories of the summer flickering through my thoughts.

As we reached the stop, Junior broke the silence. "It's gonna be different without you here, Alvin."

I smiled faintly. "I'll miss it too. But I'll be back—the summers here are too good to pass up.

Good luck with your senior year. I hope you get that scholarship and make it to college."

Junior gave me a firm pat on the back, his eyes softening. "Thanks, Alvin. I'll do my best. You take care of yourself in Boston, alright? Don't forget us."

I climbed onto the bus and found a seat by the window. As it pulled away, I glanced back and saw Junior standing there, his expression resolute. He gave a quick wave before the distance settled between us. I waved back, knowing this wasn't goodbye—just see you later.

The memories of summer—the fun, the laughter, the little adventures—stayed with me, making the thought of returning to Boston a little easier to bear.

At the Steubenville bus station, I stood clutching my bag in one hand and my ticket to Cleveland in the other. Dad had given me ten dollars before I left, calling it "spending money for the trip back to Boston." As the Greyhound pulled in, I found myself wondering where *home* really was—here in Ohio with Dad, or in Boston with Mom, Gladys, and Gloria.

The bus doors hissed open. I took a deep breath and stepped on, a quiet sense of finality settling over me. I picked a window seat, hoping the changing scenery would distract me from the storm of thoughts swirling in my head. The engine rumbled to life, and soon we were rolling out.

I stared out at the fading streets of Steubenville, my mind already drifting toward the school year ahead. Boston's high schools loomed in my imagination like unknown cities. Would I follow my buddy Tommy to English High, the all-boys school? Or try one of the co-ed ones—Hyde Park, Jamaica Plain, Dorchester, maybe Roslindale?

Tommy was my best friend, and sticking with him would make the transition easier. But the idea of an all-boys school felt stifling. The co-ed schools pulled at me more, with the possibility of new friendships, and yeah, girls. I pictured the hallways, the faces, the classrooms. Each option tugged at me in a different way.

"Where do I really belong?" In Ohio with Dad, my nieces and nephews; it was simple, familiar. But Boston with Momma was vibrant, full of energy, and possibilities. As the bus sped toward Cleveland, the weight of that question pressed down on me. This wasn't just a trip between two cities; it was a journey to figure out where I truly fit in the world.

I leaned back in my seat and closed my eyes. The rhythmic hum of the bus was almost soothing. Whatever choice I made would shape the next chapter of my life. For now, I was caught between two worlds—a passenger heading toward an uncertain future.

Outside, the landscape blurred into a dark canvas as my heavy eyelids gave in. The hum of the engine became a lullaby, broken only by the slurred voices of two passengers behind me. Their drunken banter faded into the background, blending into the night's quiet symphony.

I dreamed of the summer, playing ball with Clarence, Peewee, and Caesar. Bits and pieces of conversations with Ricky and Junior floated through my mind. The steady rhythm of the ride ran through my dreams, tethering me to the moment. When I opened my eyes, the first light of dawn was breaking, and the Cleveland skyline loomed in the distance.

"We're about ten miles out," the driver called from his seat, snapping me fully awake. I rubbed my eyes, trying to shake off sleep. The skyline, with its tall buildings and flickers of morning light, looked like a gateway to whatever came next.

As the bus pulled into the Cleveland station, I gathered my things and prepared to get off. The terminal buzzed with early-morning energy, travelers hurrying to make connections, the air thick with the scent of coffee and diesel.

I stepped off the bus, stretched my legs, and looked around. The Cleveland station was a place between places—a blend of motion and stillness, a stop for people all moving toward something.

"Next bus to New York, departing in 20 minutes," came a voice over the PA. I checked my ticket and made my way to the gate. The waiting area was crowded with a mix of weary travelers and alert commuters, each wrapped in their own thoughts.

Outside, a couple of food vendors were set up, selling hot dogs. I hadn't eaten since breakfast. I bought a hot dog, a bag of chips, and a Coke.

I found a seat and started eating. An older man walked down the aisle, sipping coffee from a paper cup, and asked if anyone was sitting next to me.

"No one's there," I said.

He sat down and glanced over. "Where you headed, kid?" he asked, his voice gruff and a little unfriendly.

I looked him in the eye before answering. "Boston." He let out a short chuckle. "How old are you?"

It was starting to feel off. "Fourteen," I replied, guarded.

Then his tone shifted—low, almost sinister. "You wanna hang out when we get to New York? I know some girls there."

"No." My voice sharpened with anger and fear. "Leave me alone, or I'll tell the bus driver." He raised his hands slightly, nodding. "No need to do that. I was just making conversation."

He stood and moved on to another seat. I turned toward the window, trying to shake the uneasy feeling that had settled deep in my chest. The encounter brought back a memory from last year, something I'd pushed to the back of my mind.

I was walking home from school in Boston, heading past the Ruggles Street projects, when I saw a white man standing on the porch of a three-story building. He wore a brown suit with a white shirt and tie, the top button undone and the tie loosened.

"Hey, young man," he called out. "You wanna make some money?" "I sure would!" I said, not even thinking of asking how.

He stepped down from the porch and motioned toward a black four-door Lincoln parked nearby.

"Here's my car. Get in."

I walked over, curiosity mixing with excitement. He stood by the driver's side, door open, eyes locked on me. There was something in his stare that made my stomach turn. I opened the passenger door and looked inside. A rope lay on the floorboard.

A chill ran through me. I looked up—he was watching me closely, his face calm, but something about it felt off.

A voice inside me screamed: *Don't get in that car.*

I slammed the door shut, heart pounding. "I changed my mind," I said, my voice shaky but firm. His demeanor shifted to something casual, almost nonchalant. "Don't tell the police," he said, as if we shared some unspoken agreement—as if we were allies, even though we weren't.

I nodded silently. He got into his car and drove off without another word.

I stood there, my mind racing. The weight of what had just happened began to settle over me, a knot of fear tightening in my stomach. I took a deep breath, trying to steady myself. Around me, the street buzzed with normalcy, as if nothing had happened. But I knew better. I had narrowly escaped something terrible.

These encounters—with the man on the porch, and now the one on the bus—made me wary. I knew now more than ever that I had to stay alert. I had to trust that inner voice that had already saved me more than once.

The steady hum of the bus engine and the rhythm of the road offered a strange kind of comfort. It became an escape from the fear, from the confusion, from both the past and the moment I'd just endured. With each passing mile, I felt a little distance grow between me and those memories. My thoughts drifted back to Boston.

The rising sun spread a golden light across the landscape, casting long shadows and warming the sky. I took a breath and reminded myself—every journey comes with danger, but also with lessons. The skyline ahead wasn't just buildings and streets; it was the promise of something new.

The bus rolled on, the scenery shifting from open fields to scattered homes and suburban stretches. As we moved closer to the city, I sat quietly, sorting through my thoughts. Boston was a place of possibilities. A place to start over. A place where, as a new freshman, I might finally see what the future had in store.

CHAPTER 85

SUNDAY MORNING AT 58 ANNUNCIATION ROAD

The bus pulled into Boston's Greyhound station at 700 Atlantic Avenue. This time, unlike my last trip with Johnnie, Momma wasn't waiting. I had $6.45 left from the $10 Dad had given me—just enough for a cab ride home.

I stepped out of the station into air thick with exhaust from Greyhound and Trailways buses. The sun was rising over the city as I scanned the street for a taxi. I spotted a few and waved at the nearest. The driver eased to a stop.

"Where to?" His tone was flat. "58 Annunciation Road."

His face tightened. "I don't take passengers there. Get another cab." He drove off.

I tried again, but as soon as the next driver saw me, he shook his head and pulled away.

By then, I was tired and frustrated. My bag felt heavier with each step. I turned onto Dewey Street and walked a few blocks before spotting another cab. I flagged it down. The driver—a heavyset white man in a Red Sox cap with graying hair—slowed and stopped. I opened the door, slid my bag into the back seat, and got in.

"Where to?" he asked.

"58 Annunciation Road," I said.

He glanced at me twice, then asked, half-joking, "You're not going to rob me, are you?" I shook my head, worn out. "No, sir. Just need to get home."

He said, "Most cabbies didn't take fares to the projects, Roxbury, or some parts of Dorchester. They were scared of getting robbed."

I replied, "I'm not into robbing anyone. Don't be scared of me, and I won't be scared of you."

He nodded, dropped the flag bar on the meter, and pulled into traffic. We sped through the busy streets of Boston toward Mission Hill. The meter started at 50 cents and ticked up by 10 cents every minute. I began to wonder if I'd have enough money by the time we got there.

Trying to lighten the mood, I asked, "How about those Red Sox?" He glanced at me in the rearview mirror. "You a Red Sox fan?"

"Sure, I sure am."

He smiled and started talking. "There's this rookie, Tony Conigliaro from Swampscott—he hit two home runs in yesterday's win over the Yankees."

"Really? I've been in Ohio all summer and haven't been able to follow them," I said, staring out the window.

The driver went on, "They're in last place. We've got no pitching after Monbouquette and Earl Wilson."

I remembered Earl Wilson, the first Black starting pitcher for the Red Sox. He wasn't even in the rotation anymore.

"Yeah," the cab driver added, "Wilson threw a no-hitter a couple of months ago. He also hit a home run in that game—one of the few pitchers to do both in a single outing."

As the conversation flowed, the ticking meter reminded me of every passing second—and every cent.

The driver's voice faded into the background as I focused on the rising fare. It had reached $4.90 by the time the orange buildings of the Mission Hill projects came into view. From Tremont Street, he turned right onto Parker, passed under the railroad tracks, then took a left onto Annunciation Road.

He pulled up to my door, stopped the car, and dropped the little flag on the meter. The final fare was $5.20. I handed him a one-dollar bill and a five.

"I enjoyed the conversation—keep the change," I said, stepping out of the cab with my suitcase. "Thank you," he replied. "I've never had a conversation with a Black kid who was into baseball." "Yeah, I love watching and listening to the Red Sox. Hey, do you know what time it is?"

"It's 11:30. Take care, kid," the driver said.

"Thank you, sir," I replied, closing the door as he drove off.

I turned and looked up at the tall, orange, seven-story building looming above me. The smokestack next door puffed out a steady stream of smoke, making the place feel even more ominous. I climbed the concrete steps and opened the heavy green metal door to my building. After all the trouble it took just to catch a cab, I felt a strange mix of relief and comfort being back—back where Momma wanted me to be. This place, with all its flaws, was home. As bleak as it looked, it was where I belonged.

The smell of Pine-Sol tickled my senses as I entered the elevator and pressed the button for the third floor. Just as I did, it hit me—I didn't have a key. I hoped someone was home to let me in.

When the elevator reached my floor, I got out and knocked on the door. No answer. No one was home. I remembered the driver telling me it was 11:30 a.m. on a Sunday, and everyone was likely at church. Frustration set in as I realized I was in for a three-hour wait—until 2:30—for my family to return. I settled onto my suitcase.

Today, I find myself reminiscing about that moment. I had no transistor radio to keep me company, just the ambient sounds of the occasional creaking elevator, the slamming of the heavy green entrance doors, and children playing in the street below. In that quiet, reflective space, I think back to when I decided to attend English High School, an all-boys institution, instead of a co-ed school.

Looking back, I regret that choice. I believe attending a co-ed school would have better prepared me for interacting with women and helped me develop a stronger ability to relate to the opposite sex. Even now, it's hard trying to understand women without having had those early interactions.

I sat on my suitcase, moving it closer to the window so I could look out at the street below.

As time passed, I rested my elbows on the windowsill and watched the girls playing double Dutch. Two of them held long jump ropes, facing each other about six or seven feet apart, turning the ropes in opposite directions. Another girl jumped in, her timing flawless as she moved in sync with the ropes. Their coordination was impressive. The ropes slapped the pavement in a fast, steady rhythm as the girls chanted a rhyme: "Cinderella, dressed in yellow Went upstairs to kiss her fellow, Made a mistake and kissed a snake, How many doctors will it take?"

Another girl leapt in, matching the rhythm perfectly, adding a dynamic and social energy to the game.

I watched the girls playing double Dutch—their laughter, rhythmic chants, and the slap of ropes hitting pavement filled the air with a soothing, steady rhythm. It was entertaining, and I couldn't help but smile at their joy.

As I sat there, my mind drifted to my plans. The Red Sox were playing at Fenway at two o'clock.

I had just enough money to buy batteries for my radio. I would've gone to the store, but I couldn't leave my suitcase unattended in the hallway.

With no idea what time it was, I just sat there, waiting anxiously for my family to get home.

CHAPTER 86

THE CAB, THE HUG, AND THE TRUTH I COULDN'T HIDE

As I looked out the window, I noticed the chanting had stopped. The girls had finished playing and disappeared. The street had gone quiet. After the game, I planned to head to Marcella Park. The thought of hitting the court and shooting hoops sounded perfect after a long, idle day.

I must've drifted off because I was jolted awake by the sound of Momma's voice below. She was thanking Mrs. Owens and her grandkids for the ride as she and my sisters got out of the car. My heart lifted—I was so happy to see them after two months in Ohio.

I stood and leaned out the window.

"Hello y'all, I'm back!"

"There's my baby boy!" Momma said, looking up with a smile.

"Oh gee, things were great, and now here he comes," Gladys whined. Gloria giggled at Gladys's comment but said nothing to me.

"Yeah, Gladys, I'm back—and ready to beat you in a game of checkers," I chuckled.

Momma and my sisters grabbed their things from the car and headed inside. I picked up my suitcase and moved it closer to the door. I heard the elevator doors open downstairs. When they reached the floor, the elevator opened, and Momma rushed toward me, pulling me into a bear hug.

"I'm glad you're back," she said softly.

"I'm glad to be back," I replied, tears welling in my eyes.

As I stood there, guilt swept over me. How could I have thought about staying in Ohio while Momma and my sisters were struggling here in Boston?

Momma and my sisters gathered their things from the car and headed upstairs. I picked up my suitcase and moved it close to the door. I heard the elevator arrive, and when the doors opened, Momma rushed forward and pulled me into a bear hug.

Gladys pushed past us, rolling her eyes but smiling slightly. "C'mon, Momma, let him breathe."

Momma finally let go and wiped a tear from her eye. "Well, come on, let's get inside. We've got a lot to catch up on."

Gloria, carrying her Bible, said, "You missed us, huh?"

I chuckled. "Yeah, I missed y'all. Patricia 'nem says hello."

Gloria's face lit up. "I never met them, but me and 'Tricia been writin' each other since last year. She owe me a letter! I wrote her before the summer, and she ain't answered me back."

I laughed. "Well, you know how things can be sometimes."

Momma turned to the door, her expression thoughtful. "How's Amos and Newton?"

"While I was there, I only saw Amos once—when Ricky took me by the service station he was workin' at. I saw Newton more. He came to Wintersville when I first got there and took me to Weirton to visit with his children."

Concern etched across Momma's face. "And where was your Dad?"

I stumbled for a second, hearing a question that seemed to come outta nowhere. I didn't know how to answer. I stood there, recalling those two lonely nights, not knowing where my Dad had gone when he told me he was just goin' for a loaf of bread.

"I... I don't know, Momma. He said he was gettin' bread, but then he just... disappeared. I didn't see him until a few days later."

Momma's face tightened, a mix of anger and sadness. She sighed deeply, shakin' her head. "I figured as much. That man…" She trailed off, not finishin' her sentence, but the hurt was clear.

Gloria and Gladys exchanged a look as the hallway fell into an awkward silence. I shifted my feet, feelin' the weight of the moment.

Momma finally broke the silence. "Well, get settled. We got plenty to catch up on."

We stepped inside the apartment, and the familiar smell hit me like a wave of comfort. Gladys flopped onto the couch, and Gloria headed straight for the kitchen, probably lookin' for a snack. Momma gave me a look that said we weren't done with this conversation—but for now, I was home, and that was all that mattered.

As I stepped inside the apartment—neat, orderly, and filled with the familiar scent of a clean house and the aroma of Sunday dinner—it hit me like a wave of comfort. Gladys flopped onto the couch, and Gloria headed straight for the kitchen, probably looking for a snack.

"Boy, you look like you got taller," Momma said, eyeing me up and down. "Been eatin' good in Ohio, huh?"

"I don't know all about that. But I do know one thing—I got my fill of TV dinners. Ain't nothin' like your cookin', Momma."

She smiled, but there was a hint of something else in her eyes. "Well, you here now. That's all that matter."

I nodded, feeling a lump rise in my throat as I made my way to my bedroom, wondering what other questions Momma might have on her mind.

CHAPTER 87

MOMMA'S REFLEXES AND MY FOOLISH MOUTH

Winter 1962, in the living room, Momma sat in her rocker—the one that creaked every time she leaned in. I curled up on the couch while Gladys and Gloria sat on the floor, faces open and eager, hungry for something just beyond the silence.

Momma called us in to talk about dreams. Gladys sat up straight and said she wanted to be the first female president. She sounded like she'd already written her acceptance speech. Gloria followed—calm and certain—saying she wanted to be a doctor.

Then I spoke up. Told them I wanted to be a pimp.

I leaned back like I'd just said something slick, something cool. The room froze.

Before the last syllable of "pimp" even left my mouth, Momma's hand sliced through the air like a heat-seeking missile. I don't know how I ducked in time—maybe divine intervention, or just the reflexes of a boy who'd dodged enough flying slippers to sense danger coming. Her palm missed my cheek by maybe a whisper, but the whoosh of it passing left my ears ringing. The whole room shifted. You could feel it, like the temperature dropped ten degrees.

A few days earlier, I'd been hanging around Marcella Park. Man pulled up in a long, low car— Buick Electra 225, maybe a Cadillac. He stepped out like he owned the block. Sharpskin suit, gold chains and bracelets, confidence dripping off him. A woman leaned in close, laughing at every word. Tommy pointed at the Electra and whistled. Jose shook his head, calling it shady. I kept staring. Those men moved like the rules didn't apply to them.

Gladys looked at me like I'd just strangled her dreams with my bare hands. Her mouth hung open, eyebrows locked in disbelief. Gloria didn't say a word. Her eyes dropped to the floor like they'd just witnessed something too ugly to process. She started blinking slowly, like she was trying to erase the whole moment from memory.

I sat up, tried to explain—talked about the shiny car, the smooth clothes. "He gets respect," I said.

Momma let out a sound—half laugh, half growl—like she couldn't believe what she was hearing. "Respect?" she dragged the word out like it tasted sour. "Boy, you done lost your entire mind."

Then the lecture came—sharp, no pauses, no breaths between sentences. At that point, I was just grateful I still had all my front teeth.

Gladys finally shook her head. "Well, he's definitely not working on my campaign."

That cracked the ice. Gloria giggled behind her hand, and even Momma's lips twitched, like they wanted to forgive me—but weren't quite ready.

And me? I just sat there, humbled, smirking on the inside, knowing I'd dodged both a slap and a soul-check in one sitting.

Momma's face tightened—not from anger, but something deeper.

Back in the living room, Momma's words lingered. The weight of what I'd said finally hit. I dropped my eyes, and that little smirk faded fast.

Gladys broke the silence with a jab—said I definitely wouldn't be joining her campaign. The edge in the room softened. A little laughter slipped out. Even Momma cracked a smile, though the disappointment didn't leave her eyes. She reminded me how much words mattered in a home where love was our main currency. Her voice cut deeper than any slap ever could.

That moment stuck with me longer than I expected. I started thinking more about the things I said—and even more about the things I didn't yet understand. Somehow, that curiosity nudged me toward something new: reading.

CHAPTER 88

CATCHER, MANCHILD, AND THE DEUCE AND A QUARTER

November 1962 At first, I stuck to *Sports Illustrated*—stats, Red Sox stories, and write-ups on Russell, Cousy, and the rest of the Celtics crew. That was my lane.

One afternoon, I wandered into a dusty little bookstore. The place looked more like a fire hazard than a business—wall-to-wall with skinny paperback books, every single one missing its cover like someone had tried to hide the evidence.

I picked one up, just flipping through out of curiosity. That's when I realized… this wasn't about sports. These pages weren't talking jump shots or box scores. They were talking about bodies— and not in the basketball sense.

My eyes got wide, and my brain hit a growth spurt I wasn't ready for. I must've looked like a kid who opened his lunchbox and found a firecracker instead of a sandwich. I didn't know whether to laugh, run, or ask for a bookmark.

They didn't say much about baseball, but somehow, I couldn't put them down.

I left that bookstore feeling like I needed a glass of water and maybe a prayer from Elder Young. My education had taken a sharp left turn, and I wasn't sure if I'd just discovered literature… or committed a sin. Either way, the bug had bitten me.

A few weeks later, trying to keep things respectable, I walked into the library across from Timilty, looking for a real book on sports. I figured I'd get back on track—read something wholesome, maybe with a box score or two. That's when I picked up *The Catcher in the Rye* by J.D. Salinger, thinking it was about baseball.

It turned out it was about a teenage boy who was lost in a world far from mine. The book opened up things I hadn't read about—pimping, working girls, all kinds of stuff you don't expect to find in a school library. Life in those pages felt like it came from another planet, but something about it stuck.

When I returned it, the librarian—a Black man—greeted me with a warm smile and asked, "Did you like it?"

I nodded, my face heating up like I'd just run laps in a winter coat. "Yeah… it was, uh… interesting." I hoped my voice sounded cooler than it felt.

He kept smiling—one of those knowing smiles, like he already knew which part had caught me off guard, like he'd seen that same look on a few young faces before.

He told me that if I liked *Catcher in the Rye*, I'd love *Manchild in the Promised Land* by Claude Brown. That book was raw—drugs, crime, pimps—laid out on the page. It mirrored what I'd seen at Marcella Park: the men in flashy cars, the smooth talk, the deuce and a quarter. That lifestyle started to settle in my mind.

CHAPTER 89

THE DAY PRESIDENT KENNEDY DIED

November 22, 1963. The sun shone brightly on that brisk Friday morning as I made my way to Boston English High's Sophomore Annexe at Edison Jr. High School. The sophomore students occupied the third floor of the building, and the day held the promise of normalcy and routine. I had tried out for the basketball team, but the competition was fierce—some of the best players in the city were gunning for a spot. Instead, I found my stride in cross-country track and was gearing up for practice after school at Franklin Park.

As the clock ticked past 1:30 p.m., I sat in Mr. Thompson's history class, jotting down notes on the American Revolution. Suddenly, the intercom crackled to life, and a message from the office interrupted the lesson. The principal's voice, usually calm and composed, carried an unusual weight.

"Attention, students," he began, his tone somber. "Please gather your belongings and proceed to the courtyard immediately."

A murmur of confusion rippled through the classroom. I exchanged puzzled looks with my classmates, wondering what was going on. There was no fire alarm, no sign of a drill. I packed my books, my mind racing with questions, and made my way down the stairs to the courtyard.

Outside, we assembled in neat lines, the cold air nipping at my face. The principal stood at the front door of the school, his expression grave. The usual chatter of students was replaced by a tense silence.

"Students," he said, his voice heavy with emotion, "I have some sad news to share with you. President John F. Kennedy was shot today in Dallas, Texas. School is dismissed for the day. Please go home safely."

The words hung in the air, surreal in their impact. I stood there in disbelief, my mind struggling to process the news. President Kennedy—shot? It felt like a punch to the gut.

Next to me, my friend Tony sat equally stunned. "Did he say the President was shot?" he whispered, barely audible.

I nodded, still trying to grasp the enormity of the moment. "Yeah, that's what he said."

We stood there, the weight of the announcement settling over us. The courtyard—usually alive with laughter and movement—had fallen into a heavy, stunned silence. Students slowly began to disperse. I slung my duffle bag over my shoulder, my thoughts spinning in a whirlwind of confusion and fear.

As I got on the train to Dudley Station with Tony, we spoke in hushed tones, trying to make sense of what had happened.

"I can't believe it," Tony said, shaking his head. "Kennedy was… he was our hope, you know?" "Yeah," I replied, my voice low and heavy. "He was supposed to lead us to a better future."

When I finally got home, the usually comforting sounds of the house felt strange—muted, distant. I turned on the TV, and the news anchor's voice filled the room, carrying the same shock and sorrow we all felt.

"We have just received word that President John F. Kennedy has died from his injuries," Walter Cronkite announced, his voice breaking. His raw emotion on CBS became one of the most iconic moments in broadcast journalism history.

It was a dark day for our country. A lump rose in my throat. The reality hit hard. Our President was gone—and with him, a piece of the nation's spirit. The world felt different now, forever changed by a single, tragic moment.

When Momma came home, she set her purse on the kitchen table, her face heavy with more than just the cold from outside. Her eyes shifted to me and Gladys, and her voice carried a weight I hadn't heard before.

"Y'all heard the news 'bout the President?" she asked, unbuttoning her coat.

I nodded, still trying to process it. "Yeah, they let us outta school early. Everybody was real quiet—like they ain't know what to say."

Gladys was on the phone, twisting the cord around her fingers, talking fast. "Girl, I know. It don't even seem real. He was just on TV." She paused, listening, then shook her head. "Yeah, they say he ain't make it. Lord have mercy."

Momma exhaled, pressing her lips together before speaking again. "Gloria, come to the living room," she called, her voice reaching down the hall to Gloria, who was reading in her room. "Y'all come here while I say a prayer for the Kennedy family."

She pulled out a chair and sat down, folding her hands together. Her voice was steady, but the sadness in her eyes was clear. I bowed my head as she began, her words soft but sure.

"Father God, we ask you to comfort the Kennedy family in this time of sorrow. Give this country peace, Lord, 'cause we need it now more than ever. Amen."

For a moment, the house was quiet, except for the soft hum of the refrigerator. Even Gladys had set the phone down and sat still. Outside, life went on—cars passed, people walked—but inside, it felt like time had paused.

CHAPTER 90

WINTERSVILLE DIDN'T ASK ME TO SORT WHITES

The next day was Saturday, and it was laundry day. I accompanied Momma to the laundry house with four large bags of our dirty clothes. Only three of the bags fit into the laundry cart, so I had to carry the last one myself.

As we trudged along, my mind wandered back to June and July in Wintersville, where I had no responsibilities—just playing ball all day and chasing lightning bugs at night. What a summer that was.

When we got to the laundry house, the place was packed with other folks from the neighborhood. There were more than 30 washers and dryers, and they were all occupied. We had to wait, and it was the most boring chore I've ever had to do. The time dragged on.

"Lawd, this place is jumpin' today," Momma said, scanning the room for an open machine. "Why's it gotta be so busy, Momma?" I asked, sighing heavily.

"It's Saturday, baby. Everybody tryin' to get they clothes clean for the week," she said, sitting down on one of the hard plastic chairs.

I slumped into the chair next to her, the weight of boredom already settling in. "I wish we could just go back home. Ain't no fun sittin' here doin' nothin'."

Momma chuckled softly. "I know, sweetie. But we gotta get this done. Learnin' responsibility ain't always fun, but it's important."

I nodded, though the idea of responsibility did little to lift my spirits at the moment. The hum of the machines, the chatter of the people, and the clang of coins in the vending machines all blended into a dull symphony of monotony.

"Look, a machine just opened up," Momma said, standing up and grabbing the cart. "Let's go before someone else gets it."

"Come on, boy, help me load this machine," she said, nudging me, her voice full of urgency. I jumped up, eager for anything to break the boredom. We hustled over to the free washer. I grabbed one of the heavy bags, and we made our way to the machine. Momma started sorting the clothes, darks from the whites.

She began loading the washer with the first bag of clothes. "Remember, you always gotta separate 'em," she said, her hands moving quickly. "Don't wanna ruin the good clothes."

I nodded, helping her with the sorting. "Yes, ma'am," I said, staying focused.

The smell of detergent filled my nostrils as Momma poured the white *Tide* powder into the machine, the soap settling over the dirty clothes.

Momma dug into her purse and pulled out a dime and a quarter, sliding them into the tiny slots on top of the machine.

The machine clinked and whirred, filling with warm water. I watched as the water mixed with the detergent, creating sudsy bubbles that wrapped around our clothes. The washer began to spin, a rhythmic hum filling the air.

"See, that ain't so bad," Momma said, smiling at me. "Now we just gotta wait for it to finish, then we can load the next batch."

I leaned against the machine, feeling its vibrations through my back. The boredom started to lift a bit, replaced by the satisfaction of getting things done.

"See, baby? We gettin' it done. Before you know it, we'll be back home, and you can go back to daydreamin' about Wintersville."

I glanced around at the other folks. Some were talking, and others were just staring at their clothes, spinning around and around. The noise of the laundromat filled the air—the whirring of machines, the chatter of neighbors, kids playing while their parents constantly told them to be still, and the steady clinking of coins.

"This place is always so crowded," I said, feeling the boredom settling in again.

Momma chuckled. "Yeah, it is. But it's gotta be done. And you know what they say—many hands make light work."

We finished loading the machine. "Now, we wait," she said as she settled into one of the plastic chairs lined up against the wall.

I sat next to her, tapping my foot. "How long we gotta wait, Momma?"

"'Bout thirty minutes for the wash," she said, pulling out her Bible from her bag. "Then we gotta dry 'em."

I watched the machine start to spin, the clothes tumbling inside. "Hey, Momma, after a while... I'm gonna go outside to get some fresh air for a bit."

She looked up from her reading. "Alright, but stay close. And come back when I call, you hear?" "Yes, ma'am," I said, already jumping up. Anything to make the time pass faster.

"I'm going outside for some fresh air," I said to Momma. "Okay, but don't wander off."

As I stepped outside, the cool breeze hit my face. I leaned against the wall of the laundromat, thinking about JFK, the First Lady Jacqueline, and their two young children—Caroline and two- year-old JFK Jr.

I remembered seeing pictures of them in the newspaper, looking so happy and perfect. I used to wonder what it would be like to live a life so different from mine.

A couple of neighborhood kids were playing tag nearby, their laughter echoing through the air. I watched them for a bit, then started kicking a pebble around, trying to keep myself entertained.

The door to the laundromat opened, and I heard Momma's voice. "Boy, like I said, don't wander off too far now!"

"I'm right here, Momma!" I called out, making sure she could see me.

She gave a quick nod and went back inside. I took a deep breath and looked up at the sky, trying to imagine what it would be like to be Caroline or JFK Jr., with their big house and all the attention.

I was leaning against the old brick building when I saw a group of teenagers crossing the street, their eyes locked on me. One of them, wearing a doo rag that partially covered his conked hair, stepped up and stared me down.

"You from 'round here?" he asked, his voice sharp and suspicious.

A lump swelled in my throat, but I managed to say, "I live over on the Annunciation Road side. Just helpin' my momma do the laundry."

He glanced at his crew, then smirked. "We don't like y'all over there. You got any money?"

My heart pounded—a mix of fear and courage—but I planted my feet. "I ain't botherin' y'all, so leave me be."

One of the others spoke up, his voice low and cruel. "This dude's a square. I seen him walkin' to the store. He don't hang at the basketball court. All he does is go to the store and do laundry.

Let's jack him up."

I tried to calm things down. I swallowed hard. "I ain't got a dime."

Just then, another guy in khaki shorts and a T-shirt tugged on the doo rag kid's arm. "Come on, Nat, let's not bother him. I feel for him. Let's not beat him up with his momma inside. Besides, he looks poor—just like us. Let's go."

Nat hesitated, his face twisted with indecision. Finally, he shrugged, and they all walked away, leaving me breathing hard, relief washing over me.

I watched them go, the weight in my chest slowly easing.

That's how it was back then—every day was a dance between fear and survival, just trying to make it through without any trouble.

As they headed off, I leaned back against the building, feeling a bit more at ease. I glanced inside the laundromat and saw Momma reading her Bible. I knew I had a job to do—helping her however I could. And in that moment, I was just grateful I'd avoided any trouble.

I thought about how tough it was to navigate these streets—always having to prove yourself and stay out of the way.

When Momma finally called me back inside, I was a little out of breath but feeling a lot better. I headed into the laundromat, ready to help her with the laundry.

Momma was already busy, pulling the last few items out of the dryer, her hands moving quickly and sure. "Here, baby, grab this bag," she said, handing me one while she pushed the basket with the other three.

"Yes, ma'am," I replied, wrapping my hands around the heavy fabric. The bag was full and a bit awkward, but I could handle it.

We stepped out onto busy Parker Street and waited to cross as cars whizzed by. Finally, there was an opening, and with the bag in my arms, we rushed to the other side.

The walk to Annunciation Road wasn't far, but with the heavy bag, it felt like a journey. At least it wasn't cold.

The clock on the laundromat wall had said 1:30—I still had time to make it to the park to play some ball.

"You doin' okay, sweetie?" Momma asked, glancing at me from the corner of her eye. "Yes, ma'am," I said again, trying to sound strong. "Ain't nothin' to it."

We walked in silence for a while, just the sound of our footsteps and the occasional passing car. The neighborhood was quiet today. No kids were out—just tall buildings and empty sidewalks.

By the time we reached Annunciation Road, my arms were aching, but my heart felt light. We pushed open the green front door to our building, and the familiar smell of Mr. Clean greeted us as we stepped inside.

Momma pressed the elevator button, and when the door opened, we walked in. "Good job, baby," she said, taking the bag from me. "Let me put them away." "Yes, ma'am," I said, feeling proud.

CHAPTER 91

WHEN THE CHURCH BECAME OUR CLASSROOM

By December 1963, the civil rights movement was surging forward, and the world outside teetered between chaos and change. For us, a group of Black kids in Roxbury, the YMCA offered more than just a way to pass the time. It became a refuge. The friendships we built inside those walls carried a different kind of weight: a steady presence in a world that seemed to shift by the day.

During my ninth-grade year at James P. Timilty Junior High School, I took part in my first civil rights protest—a one-day boycott of Boston public schools known as the "Stay Out for Freedom" boycott. Organized to challenge segregation and the poor conditions faced by African-American students, the event drew many of us into something larger than ourselves.

St. Cyprian Church played a pivotal role that day. It had been transformed into a "Freedom School," one of several sites where students gathered instead of attending their usual classes. These makeshift schools served as alternative learning centers, offering lessons in African-American history, civil rights, and other subjects absent from the public school curriculum. The goal wasn't just to educate; it was to empower us and foster a sense of pride and community.

When I arrived at the church, the atmosphere was electric. The pews had been rearranged to create temporary classrooms, and the walls were lined with posters and banners honoring civil rights leaders and Black history. Groups of students, from elementary age to high schoolers, clustered in circles, engaged in animated discussions. The energy in the room was contagious; it felt like being part of something monumental.

I found myself near the front, joining a group that included some older students from Dorchester High. I hadn't met them before, but introductions were quick, and we fell into easy conversation. Something was exciting about being among high schoolers; they seemed to know so much more about the world, and I couldn't help but look up to them.

Mrs. Johnson, a local civil rights activist and our teacher for the day, stood at the front holding a book on African American history. Her presence was both commanding and warm, and she greeted us with a smile.

"Good morning, everyone. Welcome to our Freedom School. Today, we're going to learn about the incredible journey of our people and the fight for our rights. Now, can anyone tell me why we're here instead of at our regular schools?"

One of the high school students raised a hand. "Yes, Mrs. Johnson. We're protesting against segregation because we want equal education for everyone."

She nodded. "This boycott is our way of standing up and saying, 'We deserve better.' And today, we're going to talk about the heroes who paved the way for us."

Her words struck a chord. For the first time, I felt like I was part of something much bigger than myself—something historic.

"Let's start with Harriet Tubman. Who can tell me what she's known for?"

Lisa, one of the older students, raised her hand. Mrs. Johnson gestured for her to speak.

"Harriet Tubman helped enslaved people escape through the Underground Railroad," Lisa said. "She led them to freedom."

Mrs. Johnson smiled. "That's right, Lisa. She showed us the power of courage and determination. And like her, we're fighting for freedom in our own way today."

After Mrs. Johnson finished her lesson, the teachers rotated between groups, moving to different sections of the church. Mr. Thompson, a local historian, came over to where we sat. He adjusted his glasses and began to speak, his voice steady and commanding.

"The fight for civil rights isn't only happening down South," he said. "It's happening right here in Boston. By staying out of school today, you've made your voices heard. You're showing the city we won't accept injustice—not in education, not anywhere."

A student named David, whom I'd met earlier that morning, leaned forward, curiosity lighting up his face. "Mr. Thompson, how did you get involved in the civil rights movement?"

Mr. Thompson paused, his expression thoughtful. "Well, David, it started with small steps. I saw the injustices around me—people being treated like they were less than human. I couldn't stand by. I started attending meetings, educating myself, and speaking out. And now, I teach others, like we're doing here today. Every one of us has a role to play in making change."

His words settled over the group like a heavy but necessary truth. We sat quietly, letting it sink in.

Before long, another speaker stepped in front of our group. This time, it was Mrs. Green, the art teacher. She pointed to a large blank mural stretched across the wall. "Art is a powerful form of expression," she said, gesturing toward the mural. "This will tell our story—our pride, our struggles, and our fight for justice. Let's make it count."

She handed out paintbrushes and asked us to brainstorm ideas. David, now holding a brush, said, "We should show the March on Washington. And maybe one of those sit-ins at the lunch counters."

Mrs. Green smiled. "Great ideas, David. Those are powerful symbols of our fight for equality. Let's make sure we capture the spirit of those events."

Later that afternoon, all the groups gathered in the main hall of the church for the closing assembly. Energy pulsed through the room as Reverend Thomas stepped up to the podium. He adjusted the microphone, then looked out across the sea of young faces.

"Education," his voice rang out, "is a right, not a privilege. Today's effort proves you understand that. But this is only the beginning. Keep fighting. Keep learning. Never forget the power you hold to change the world."

Applause and cheers filled the room. Pride swept through the crowd—a shared sense of purpose uniting every student. That moment etched itself into memory, proof that rising, learning, and believing in something greater can shape the future.

As I left the church that afternoon, the conversations among my new friends buzzed with purpose. It was the beginning of understanding how we could make change, even as ninth graders.

The next day at school, tension hung thick in the air as we filed into Miss O'Hara's classroom.

She stood at the door, arms crossed, her stern expression daring us to explain ourselves. Her white blouse was crisp as always, but her demeanor made it clear: this wasn't a day for pleasantries.

Most of the class, entirely Black students, shuffled to their seats. A few glances were exchanged, but no one spoke.

Once the last student sat down, Miss O'Hara strode to the front of the room, her heels clicking against the floor like a metronome. She adjusted her glasses and scanned the room, her gaze lingering on those of us who had joined the boycott.

"I hope you all understand the consequences of your actions yesterday," she said, her voice calm but edged with frustration. "By staying out of school, you not only disrespected your teachers and the principal, but you also let down your peers and your education. Is this how you think change happens?"

The silence that followed stretched on—too long. It wasn't just quiet; it held weight. Her words lingered, taut and unfinished. No one moved. Then Richard shifted in his seat—not out of impatience, but with certainty—and raised his hand.

She looked at him for a moment, longer than usual, then gave a small nod.

His voice, when it came, wasn't loud, but it carried weight. "Miss O'Hara, we're not trying to stir up trouble. It's not about disrespect. It's about being seen. For a long time, people like us have been talked over and shut down. We're tired of waiting for someone to give us permission."

Miss O'Hara folded her arms again, her expression unreadable at first. "And you think walking out of school makes that point clear?"

Her voice had softened—just a bit. The sharpness was dulled by something quieter. Maybe curiosity. Maybe doubt.

Richard didn't answer right away. He glanced around the room, then back at her. Each word came slowly and deliberately. "Doesn't fix anything. But it says we care. That we're learning how to stand for something, not just in books. In real life."

Miss O'Hara sat down, just as slow and deliberate, as if resetting the tone. Her eyes drifted to the window, then back to her desk. A sigh slipped out—less frustration than resignation.

"Open your social studies books. Chapter Five. Answer the questions at the end." Her voice was flat, but not unkind. "Put your papers on my desk before gym."

No speeches. No scolding. Just the lesson, waiting. But the air had shifted, and everyone in the room felt it.

The room was quiet. Chairs scraped the floor as we pulled out our books and flipped to the assigned chapter. I glanced at Richard, who caught my eye and gave a faint smirk. We didn't need to say anything; the look said it all.

As I stared at the textbook, the words blurred together. My mind wasn't on chapter five or its questions—it was still at the church, replaying the powerful conversations and the sense of unity we'd shared the day before. I thought about how we'd stood together, how we'd made our voices heard.

The faint sound of pages turning filled the room, broken only by the occasional cough or shuffle. Miss O'Hara kept her head down, scribbling on a notepad. The tension had settled, but it was clear—something had changed, and it wasn't in the lesson.

The bell rang, signaling the end of class. As we gathered our things, I felt a strange mix of emotions: relief, pride, and even a little hope. Maybe we hadn't changed Miss O'Hara's mind, but we'd made her listen. And that, to me, was a victory.

CHAPTER 92

FROM SWEET TOOTH TO SMACKDOWN

The sun cast a fading orange glow across the tile floors of our living room. Gladys was slouched on the side of the couch, defiance etched across her face. She'd gone into my room earlier, taken some chocolates I'd been saving, and now sat there like she'd done nothing wrong.

I stood there, holding the near-empty box. "You're lying. Half the box is gone, and I didn't eat 'em!"

Gladys crossed her arms, her voice sharp. "I ain't take nothin'! Why would I need to sneak around for your little chocolates? What's the harm in sharing?"

"You think it's okay to take my stuff? What's the harm in asking, huh? It ain't even about the chocolates—it's about respect."

"Respect?" Gladys shot back, rolling her eyes. "You're actin' like I stole gold or somethin'. Maybe you should get over yourself for once. You make a big deal outta every little thing."

"It ain't little to me!" I said, standing up. "You think it's fine because it's not your stuff? That's the problem, Gladys. You don't care about nobody but yourself."

She sat up straighter, eyes narrowing. "Oh, I don't care about nobody? How about all the times I cleaned up after your messy self? Or when I loaned you my last few quarters for candy? You don't remember that, huh?"

I clenched my fists, anger rising with every word. "This ain't about you doin' me no favor, Gladys. This is about you goin' into my room and takin' what ain't yours. That's the line you crossed."

She stood now, closing the gap between us, her face hard with defiance. "You think you're better than me? Like you ain't ever taken nothin' that wasn't yours? You got some nerve, actin' like the victim."

"I ain't playin' at nothin'! I don't go diggin' through yo' stuff."

Her voice rose, sharp as a blade. "Yeah? Well, maybe I wouldn't have to if you shared once in a while. You hoard everything like you're some kind of king, but guess what? You ain't!"

Her eyes narrowed, the challenge clear. "Don't twist my words. I didn't take your precious chocolates. Maybe Momma did."

That was it. The way she brushed it off, like it didn't matter, pushed me over the edge. Without thinking, I grabbed what was left of the chocolates and hurled the box across the room. It hit her shoulder with a dull thud, the sound echoing in the tense silence that followed.

Gladys glared, her face twisted with fury. "Oh, so that's how it is?" She grabbed me by the shirt and shoved me back onto the couch. "You think you can throw stuff at me and get away with it?"

Her grip was tight. I struggled to push her off. "Get your hands off me!"

The front door creaked open, and we both froze. Momma stepped in, her face tired and worn, her eyes narrowing as she took in the scene.

"What in the world is wrong with y'all?" she snapped, slamming the door shut. "I could hear you all the way down the hall!"

Gladys crossed her arms, jaw tight. The chocolates on the floor mocked us both—a mess neither of us wanted to clean up.

Momma's lips pressed into a thin line as she shook her head. "I don't know what's gotten into you two. Fightin' like cats and dogs while I'm out here workin' myself to the bone. Y'all oughta be ashamed."

My eyes dropped to the floor, still seething but unable to meet her gaze. Gladys stared at the wall, her expression stiff and unreadable.

"Pick this mess up, and stay out of each other's way, you hear me?"

"Yes, ma'am," we both muttered, voices low and reluctant.

"Alvin, go to the store and get what we need for dinner. Ain't no time for this foolishness." "Okay, Momma," I said, scooping up the chocolate box and taking it back to my room before grabbing my coat. I glanced at Gladys, who leaned against the table, looking both annoyed and smug.

Momma's tone softened slightly as she scribbled a list. "Take this and come right back." "Yes, ma'am," I replied, still feeling the weight of the argument hanging in the air. Momma sighed and headed to her room, grumbling about how we were gonna drive her to an early grave.

I nodded and slipped out the door. Walking down the street, the tension still clung to me like a storm cloud. It wasn't just about the chocolates; it was about respect, trust, and everything in between. These little conflicts kept stacking up, and it felt like they were crushing whatever peace we had left.

As I left, I could feel Gladys's eyes burning into my back. I didn't care. Let her glare.

In the days that followed, Gladys and I made a conscious effort to mend our bond. We spent more time together, talking, joking, and finding shared interests to bridge the gap that had grown between us. One of those interests turned out to be checkers.

I had a checkerboard set I'd gotten for Christmas a few years back. It had been collecting dust, but I was excited to pull it out—I'd sharpened my skills at the Y, and I was eager to test them against Gladys. She agreed to play, though with her usual mix of reluctance and skepticism.

Sitting cross-legged on the living room floor, I grinned as I slid one of my black pieces across the board. "Your move, Gladys," I said, leaning back with confidence.

She narrowed her eyes, lips pressed into a thin line, and stared at the board. Her hand hovered over a red piece as she calculated. She slid it forward, hesitated with her finger still on it, then moved it back.

I nudged her, teasing. "C'mon now, you gotta make a move."

Her face flushed with irritation. She shot me a glare before finally moving the piece again—this time with a bit more resolve.

"Alright, alright," I said with a nod. "But watch this." I jumped two of her pieces with a dramatic flourish and grinned widely.

Gladys clenched her jaw, her frustration bubbling over. Without a word, she swept the remaining pieces off the board in one swift motion, scattering them across the room.

From her spot on the couch, Gloria burst into laughter. "Gladys, girl, don't take it so hard. It's only a game!"

Gladys shot her a glare, then turned to me. "I ain't playin' with him no more. He always sittin' there laughin' like he's the king of the world 'cause he's winnin'. That ain't sportsmanship."

I held up my hands in mock surrender, trying not to laugh. "Alright, alright. I'll ease up next time. You want a rematch?"

She huffed, arms crossed. "Nope. Go find somebody else to beat. I'm done."

Gloria shook her head, still smiling. "Y'all are somethin' else. Better luck next time, Gladys."

Despite her annoyance, Gladys wasn't truly mad—more like pretending so she could have the last word. And for a brief moment, the tension between us faded, replaced by the kind of sibling rivalry that almost felt like old times.

CHAPTER 93

TRYIN' TO BE GROWN WITH BABY SKIN

I found myself talking to myself the other day, lookin' back like I was talkin' to you, Momma.

"I'm like you, Momma," I said—meaning in the way I look, the way I cook. "I've adjusted the ingredients to fit my modern taste. I also remember you chasin' me out of the house, sayin' boys ain't got no business sittin' under their mother's skirts watchin' them cook. You wanted me outdoors."

You always believed boys needed to be tough to grow up manly. But there was some hypocrisy in that. I remember when I was about fifteen, you saw a razor blade on the bathroom sink and snapped, "Why's this razor blade out here?"

"I was shaving," I told you.

You gave me that sharp look and said, "Ain't no hair on your face. You wanna grow up too fast, and I'm not havin' it. Now get rid of that razor."

I can still see it as clear as day, Momma. You always had a way of keeping us in check, even when we thought we knew better. You wanted to make sure we didn't rush into things we weren't ready for. And I guess, in your own way, you were lookin' out for us—even if we didn't always understand it at the time.

CHAPTER 94

BACK WHEN BALL WAS LIFE AND MIMI LAUGHED

I went to my room, changed into my sneakers and basketball shorts, and headed to Marcella Park. I needed to take my mind off everything and just play.

When I got to the court, it was empty. So I decided to head over to Jose's father's store, near the corner of Marcella Street and Washington.

When I walked into the store, Jose was behind the counter. "Hey Jose, you think you can play some ball with me?" I asked.

He shook his head. "Man, I wish I could, but Pops ain't here. I gotta stay and watch the store."

Disappointment must've shown on my face, because he added, "Tell you what—you can take my ball and use it. I'll join you later when Pops gets back."

"Thanks, man. I appreciate it," I said, taking the ball from him.

I left the store, dribbling Jose's ball down the sidewalk, already feeling a little better. This was when I liked to practice my handles—working on my crossover, dribbling behind my back.

When I wasn't dribbling, I tried spinning the ball on my right index finger. I kept at it, but I just couldn't master it.

I dribbled past Tommy's house, slipped through the fence, and into the park. As I walked past an open field, I saw a group of kids playing touch football. I wanted to join them, but I didn't want to risk someone stealing Jose's ball.

At the court, the only ones there were three little kids—no older than six or seven—tossing balls at the basket, barely reaching the rim. I headed to the other hoop and started shooting. In my mind, I was Bob Cousy, dishing it to Sam Jones, who banked it in for the score.

It was getting late, and I was tired of waiting for Jose. I left the court and headed back to the store.

When I got there, Jose was still behind the counter, but this time he was talking to a cute girl from the neighborhood. I'd seen her in the store before, but never looking this good. I'd heard her name was Mimi Sadberry. They were laughing and joking about something.

"Hey, man! What's up?" Jose called out with a big grin. "Not much."

Mimi glanced at me and smiled.

"Mimi, this is my boy Alvin," Jose said. "You know Mimi?" "No, but I'd sure like to get to know her."

"Alvin's got mad skills on the court."

"Yeah, that's me," I said, feeling a rush of bravery.

Mimi laughed, her eyes twinkling. "I bet. You guys are always playin' basketball." "Yeah, tryin' to get better," I said, feeling more relaxed.

"Pops still ain't back," Jose said. "But hey, why don't you hang out for a bit? We were just talkin' 'bout this funny thing that happened in class today. I was tellin' Mimi how I almost tripped over my own feet tryin' to get to the blackboard."

I laughed, picturing the scene. "That sounds like something Jose would do."

We all laughed together, and for a moment, I forgot about the game. It felt good just to hang out and joke around.

"No, man, I'd love to, but I gotta get home before it gets dark," I said, glancing at Mimi. She was Cape Verdean, with short, curly black hair and a peanut-brown complexion. She wore a black polo shirt and crisp white shorts that showed off her smooth brown legs, and she had a nice booty, too.

"I've seen you before. Where's Simon and Theodore?" I joked, referencing the cartoon group. "Yeah, I get that a lot. But it's just me, no Simon or Theodore in sight."

"Well, you must be the star of the show, then."

She smiled. "I guess so! But I'll try not to let it go to my head." I thought I might have a chance. "Are you goin' with anyone?" "No," she said.

"Can I get your number?"

Mimi's expression shifted slightly, more serious now. "Not right now, Alvin. I've got a really sick grandma, and I can't have people callin' my house all the time. And besides, I think we should get to know each other better first."

I nodded. "I get it, Mimi. Family comes first. Maybe we can hang out sometime when things settle down for you."

"Maybe. I gotta go. I'm sure I'll see you around." "Okay, take care," I said.

She turned to Jose and grinned. "I'll see you, and stop being so clumsy." She waved and started to walk away.

Jose laughed and shook his head. "Yeah, yeah, I hear you, Mimi. Take care and give my best to your grandma."

Then he turned to me with a grin. "Don't worry, Alvin. She's fine, and she knows it. Everybody's tryin' to holla at her."

"I can see why. Thanks, Jose. I'll catch you later."

While walking home, I passed by Mr. Jenkins' radio store. In the window sat a shiny new phonograph record player, glistening under the store lights. My feet seemed to have a mind of their own, pulling me inside.

The door chimed as I stepped in, and Mr. Jenkins looked up from behind the counter.

"Afternoon, young man. What can I do for ya?"

I pointed at the phonograph in the window. "How much does that record player cost, Mr. Jenkins?"

He rubbed his chin, glancing at the machine with a twinkle in his eye. "That one there? It's twenty dollars."

I let out a low whistle, thinking about how much twenty dollars really was. "Twenty dollars, huh?" I muttered to myself.

Mr. Jenkins nodded. "Yep, but it's a good one. Plays forty-fives and thirty-two-inch records real smooth—makes the music sound like it's right in the room with ya."

I smiled, imagining the sounds of our favorite tunes filling the house. "When Gladys gets home, I'm gonna tell her all about it."

Mr. Jenkins chuckled. "Well, you do that. Maybe y'all can save up and get it one day. Music sure makes a home feel more alive."

I nodded, thanked him, and stepped back out onto the street. The thought of that phonograph stayed with me the whole way home, filling my mind with dreams of music and smiles.

CHAPTER 95

THAT BROOM WASN'T ABOUT ME

One day, Momma didn't like the way I swept the floor. She snatched the broom from my hands and started hitting me. After the first couple of blows to my arm, I had to protect myself. Before she could land another strike—this time aimed at my head—I grabbed the broom from her.

"Boy, what you think you doin'?" she cried, her eyes wide with shock. I could see the tears welling up, making them glisten in the dim light of our small kitchen.

With tears streaming down her face, Momma lunged at me, pounding my chest with her balled fists. "Why you gotta make it so hard? Why you gotta remind me of him?"

I dropped the broom and wrapped my arms around her, trying to hold her still, to calm the storm inside her. I would later learn that she had spoken with Ms. Livingston in Ohio, and found out Dad had fathered a child with one of his church members.

Momma broke free from my embrace and ran to her room, slamming the door behind her. It was closed, but I could still hear her crying. The tears weren't about what had just happened; they were for being alone in that room, with three kids to raise, while he was off living a new life. He had the chance to find happiness again—something Momma never had.

I stood in the hallway, my heart heavy with the weight of our shared sorrow. I knew her anger wasn't really meant for me. It was for the life we were left to endure.

As I walked away from her door, I vowed to be the strength she needed—the pillar she could lean on. For Momma, for my siblings, and for myself, I promised to find a way to ease the burden, to bring a little light into our dark days.

CHAPTER 96

WHAT WE GONNA DO WITHOUT MOMMA?

It was chilly on March 31, 1965, and I'd had a rough day in my junior year at Boston English. My math teacher, Mr. Malone, told me that if I didn't pass math this year, I'd have to attend summer school. I'd never been to summer school before, but I'd heard it was easy.

Still, I had a job lined up washing dishes at the Copley Restaurant, and I wanted to take advantage of the opportunity to make some money. It would help me support Momma. I was seventeen and could drop out, work, and get my GED later. Those thoughts occupied my mind as I approached our apartment building—an old brick structure with weathered steps leading to the entrance.

I walked up the three concrete steps with the metal railing down the middle, pulled the large metal handle, and opened the heavy door. Taking the stairs two at a time, I bounded up the three flights until I reached our apartment—#366—right next to the elevator.

I opened the door and noticed the couch cover needed straightening. Momma usually had the house tidy before I came home. The familiar scent of her cooking should've greeted me, but the air was thick and still. An eerie silence filled the apartment.

As I passed Momma's room, I saw her sitting in a chair by the window, the back of her right hand resting on her forehead. Her eyes were closed, as if she'd fallen asleep there, still in her nightgown, her body partly exposed.

"Momma," I called out, my voice edged with concern.

No response.

I stepped into the dimly lit living room, my heart beginning to race. It was too quiet. I passed her door, which was slightly ajar. "Momma, I'm home." Still no answer. I went into my room and dropped my duffel bag, but the silence weighed on me. She never failed to answer.

I returned to her door and pushed it open wider.

Fear gripped my chest as I stepped into her room, each step heavier than the last. I froze. Momma sat motionless in the chair, eyes still closed. Panic surged.

"Momma!" I cried out, walking slowly toward her. I reached out and touched her arm.

Her skin was cold. Lifeless.

Tears blurred my vision as I stumbled forward and fell to my knees beside the chair. I reached out with trembling hands to touch her cheek, praying for a response—a flicker of life—but she remained cold and unresponsive.

A wave of disbelief crashed over me, flooding me with sorrow. Momma was a modest and proud woman, so I took the blanket from her bed and gently covered her, honoring her dignity.

"How?" I whispered, my voice breaking. Memories flooded my mind—Momma's prayers, her singing throughout the house, her unwavering love carrying us through hard times. Now, only the haunting stillness of death remained.

My sister Gloria was babysitting next door. Before I went to her, I took a moment to gather my thoughts and calm myself. I rehearsed what to say, trying to find the right words for a conversation that felt impossible.

My heart pounded as I raced to the neighbor's apartment. Panic and fear propelled me faster. I knocked, and Gloria flung the door open, my breath coming in ragged gasps.

"Gloria!" I cried, urgency in my voice.

"What's wrong?" she asked, her voice tight with worry.

"It's Momma," I choked out. "I couldn't wake her up. Something's wrong."

She stared at me, stunned. "No… not Momma." She bolted past me, and I followed her back to our apartment.

She froze in the doorway of Momma's room, her eyes fixed on the still figure in the chair.

Slowly, she walked to Momma and touched her forehead. She recoiled instantly, snatching her hand away, and let out a blood-curdling scream. Covering her mouth, tears streamed down her face. She turned and ran next door to move the two children into the room she shared with our sister Gladys.

Still in a daze, I reached for the house phone. My fingers trembled as I dialed the operator, the world crumbling around me with each passing moment.

"Operator, what's your emergency?" The operator's calm, professional voice came through the line.

"I… I found my mom. She's not moving. I think she's… I think she's dead," I said, my voice shaking.

"Sir, I need you to stay calm. Can you tell me your name and address?"

"It's… It's Alvin Harris. We live at 58 Annunciation Road, Apartment 366," I said, struggling to stay composed.

"Thank you, Alvin. Help is on the way. I need you to stay with me. Can you check if your mom is breathing?"

I cried softly, my voice trembling. "I… I don't know. She's so cold."

"I understand, Alvin. Is she lying down or sitting up?"

"She's sitting in her chair. Her eyes are closed, and she's not responding."

"Okay, Alvin. Listen carefully. Can you gently tilt her head back and check if there's any air coming from her mouth or nose?"

I hesitated, then moved closer to Momma, gently tilting her head back. "No… no, I don't feel anything."

"Alright, young man. I'm sending a car to your location. They'll be there soon. I need you to stay on the line with me."

"Yes, I'll stay. Please hurry. I don't know what to do."

"You're doing great, Alvin. The officer is on their way. Stay calm and keep talking to me. Is there anyone else in the house with you?"

"Yes, my sister. Please... please tell them to hurry."

"Alvin, you're being brave. Keep holding on—help is almost there."
"Thank you... thank you," I said, my voice breaking.

"You're welcome, Alvin. Stay with me, okay?"

As I clung to the phone, every second felt like an eternity. The operator's calm voice was my only anchor. Then the sound of sirens pierced through the heavy silence that had settled over the apartment.

I stayed by the phone, clutching it like a lifeline, until finally, there was a knock at the door. A police officer stepped in—his presence commanding, yet compassionate.

He entered the dimly lit living room, surveying the space. I guided him to Momma's room. He looked at her still body in the chair, then slowly walked over.

"Is... is she dead?" I asked, my voice barely a whisper as I watched him, my heart racing.

The officer turned to me, his face solemn, eyes filled with quiet sympathy. He gave a slow nod.

"Yes, I'm afraid she is."

Grief surged through me, a crushing wave, but there was no time to process it. The officer turned back to the phone and calmly dialed another number, his voice steady as he began to speak.

"This is Officer Thompson. We have a deceased female at 58 Annunciation Road, Apartment 366. Please send an emergency vehicle to retrieve the body."

The officer approached me. "We'll take care of everything, son. I'm sorry for your loss."

I nodded, unable to find the words to respond. His presence offered a small comfort amid the overwhelming sorrow that had settled into every corner of the room.

He asked my sister and me to remain in our rooms.

As I waited for the folks with the stretcher to arrive, a profound sense of finality set in. Momma was truly gone.

When the coroner arrived, they went straight into her room. I couldn't bear to watch them remove her body, so I stayed in mine. I heard them lift her onto the stretcher, bumping into the walls as they carried her away.

Lying on my bed, I clung to memories of Momma—her laughter, the warmth of her singing, and the love that had always sustained us.

I picked up the phone and called Ruby Nelle, who lived in Cambridge. "Ruby, it's Alvin," I said, my voice breaking. "Momma's gone."

There was a heavy silence on the other end. "What do you mean she's gone?" "I said Momma passed away. She's gone."

"I can't believe it. I spoke with her last night. She told me she was fine."

Then I heard the sorrow in her voice through the phone. "Oh, Alvin... I'll be over as soon as Bobby gets home from work. How's Gloria?"

"She's okay," I said, trying to keep my composure.

Next, I called my brother Melvin. His wife, Mildred, answered.

"Alvin, are you and Gloria okay?"

"We're managing," I replied, my voice heavy with grief.

Melvin was at work, but Mildred said she'd catch the bus and come right over.

After hanging up, I returned to my room and lay back down, sorrow crashing over me in waves. Tears rolled down my cheeks as my thoughts stayed fixed on Momma. I couldn't help but wonder—what's going to happen to us now?

Although Momma had stopped going to Elder Young's church a couple of months ago and had started attending services led by a young preacher named Reverend Ike, I still felt closer to Elder Young. I picked up the phone one more time and called the church.

"Elder Young, it's Alvin. I have some bad news... Momma passed away."

"Oh, Lord, Sister Harris was such a great worker around the church. We're surely going to miss her around here," Elder Young said, his voice filled with compassion. "Alvin, are you, Gloria, and Gladys okay?"

"We're holding on," I said, my voice quivering. "But Gladys will be here soon."

"Have you eaten?" "No, not yet."

"I'll bring you all some food," he promised. "You take care of yourselves. We'll get through this together."

As I lay back down, the weight of the day pressed heavily on my chest. The house felt unbearably empty without Momma, and I clung to the sound of Elder Young's reassuring words, trying to find some semblance of comfort in the midst of my overwhelming grief.

Mildred was the first to arrive. She was always particular about how she dressed, but today I could tell she'd spared no time getting to us—she wore old sneakers and worn jeans.

Ruby and her husband, Bobby, arrived next. She appeared heartbroken, clinging tightly to Bobby. She said she had called and spoken with Dad. She told me he'd asked about us and said he would be up on Friday.

Gladys, who had graduated from Girls' High last year and worked at Sears Roebuck, arrived at approximately 5:00 p.m. I heard her turn the key in the lock and push the door open. I could see the confused look on her face as she stepped inside.

With a quizzical expression, she asked, "What's wrong?"

The house was bustling with people; members of the church gathered in clusters, murmuring in hushed tones. Confusion washed over

Gladys as she searched for Momma's familiar face amidst the crowd. Panic set in when she couldn't find her.

"Where's Momma?" Her voice shook with fear.

Ruby Nelle grabbed Gladys's arm and pulled her close. "Momma is gone."

Time seemed to stand still as the weight of her words sank in. Gladys felt a tidal wave of grief wash over her, threatening to consume her completely. She collapsed into the nearest chair, her mind reeling with disbelief.

Tears ran down her face as she pushed Ruby Nelle away, clutching her glasses in her hand. "Nah, Ruby Nelle, this can't be true. My birthday was yesterday." She went to her room and returned with the birthday card Momma had just given her.

Her mother, the rock of our family, was gone. As the shock began to ebb, Gladys went to the room she shared with Gloria. There, they embraced and cried in each other's arms.

"Gloria, what we gonna do without Momma?" Gladys sobbed, tears streaming down her face as she held her sister tightly.

"I don't know, Gladys. I'm scared," Gloria said, her voice trembling. "But we gotta be strong— for each other."

Fear and uncertainty gnawed at them, but they knew they had to hold on. Until then, and not since, I had never seen my sisters cry.

After a while, our small apartment was filled with family members offering their support. Uncle Willie B. and Aunt Sarah were among the first to arrive.

"Aunt Sarah, I can't believe Momma's gone," I said, my voice breaking.

"I know, baby. We all loved her," she said, hugging me tightly. "We gonna get through this together."

TJ, Eula Bess, and Johnnie came soon after. Bishop Young, Benny, Chick, and a young Reverend Ike followed to offer their condolences.

"Alvin, I'm so sorry. We all gonna be here for you."

"Thanks, TJ. It just doesn't feel real," I said, my voice shaking.

Eula Bess gently placed a hand on my shoulder. "Your Momma was a wonderful woman. We're all here for you."

Johnnie stood quietly, ever so resolute. He didn't say a word, but the tears in his eyes spoke volumes. In silence, he mourned.

Bishop Young, standing nearby, said softly, "Your family is our family. We'll be here for you."

Chick, her face somber, nodded. "The children are with my sitter. We haven't told them yet that their grandma is gone. Your Momma was loved by many. We're all here to support you."

Finally, Reverend Ike stepped forward. "Let's all gather for a moment of prayer," he said, his voice calm and soothing.

We formed a circle, holding hands as Reverend Ike began to pray.

"Dear Lord," he intoned, "we come to you today with heavy hearts. We ask for your comfort and strength in this time of sorrow. Wrap your loving arms around this family and give them the peace that surpasses all understanding. Help them to find solace in the memories of their beloved Sister Harris, and to feel her presence in their hearts always.

"Lord, we thank you for the time we had with Sister Harris—for the love she shared and the lives she touched. We ask that you guide this family through their grief and help them to lean on each other and on you. Bless them with the strength to carry on and the wisdom to remember that they are never alone.

"In Jesus' name, we pray. Amen."

"Amen," we all echoed, feeling a sense of unity and comfort in the shared moment of prayer.

As the prayers ended, my eyes scanned the faces of family and friends. The grief was heavy, but so was the love and the support. Even in our darkest moments, we were not alone.

Ruby, her face solemn, said, "I called Dad, Newton, Amos, and Barborah Nelle. They'll be driving up from Ohio." "Thanks, Ruby Nelle," I said.

Mildred added, "I also called Grandmomma. She's 80 now, so she can't make the trip, but Aunt Gladys and Aunt Eunice are coming from Georgia. Aunt Bernice and her husband are coming from Indiana. Momma's brothers—Uncle Richard from Ohio, Uncle Joe from New York, and Uncle Arbie from California—will be here too."

The apartment was crowded, but the presence of family brought comfort. Despite the sorrow, the warmth and support from everyone reminded us we weren't alone.

It all felt like a dream. I moved through the house in a fog, barely aware of my steps. People kept bringing in food, asking if we needed anything. I had never experienced so much attention. My sisters and I weren't little kids, but the care and sympathy surrounding us felt immense.

In the living room, I watched Aunt Sarah hold Gladys tightly, trying to soothe her.

"We gonna get through this, baby," she whispered. "Your Momma's watching over us now." Gladys nodded, tears still flowing. "I know, Aunt Sarah. I just can't believe she's gone." Benny approached quietly, respectfully. "If y'all need anything, just let me know."

"Thank you, Benny," I said, fighting back tears.

CHAPTER 97

FOR THE DIGNITY SHE DESERVED

The next day dawned heavy. I sat around the house with my sisters, the familiar surroundings offering little comfort in the face of such loss. The kitchen table was overflowing with food—in bags, in heavy pots—the smell filling every corner of the house. But I didn't want to eat.

As the afternoon sun filtered through the curtains, casting golden beams across the room, I decided to catch the bus and ride to the YMCA. Just the week before, I'd been cut by the Falcons. Coach Wimberly had asked me to turn in my jersey. They'd made room for Ron Texiera, one of the stars at Don Bosco High.

The YMCA had recently moved from near the Warren statue to its new building on the corner of Warren and Academy Homes Boulevard—now called Martin Luther King Boulevard.

With a quiet determination stirring in me, I made my way to the bus stop.

The ride was a blur. The rhythmic hum of the bus engine echoed my thoughts. I kept replaying my last conversation with Coach Wimberly, preparing myself for what I needed to say.

He was in the middle of directing a drill when he spotted me. His eyes widened in surprise. I walked toward him, heart pounding.

"Coach Wimberly, can I speak to you for a minute?" My voice was steady, despite the storm inside me.

He nodded, a furrow of concern forming across his brow, and motioned for me to follow. We stepped out of the gym and into the locker room. Alone, I took a deep breath and spoke.

"Coach, I gotta tell you something. My Momma passed away. I'll be going back to Ohio with my Dad."

He listened quietly, his expression softening from surprise to sympathy. Placing a hand on my shoulder, he said, "I'm sorry to hear about your mom, Alvin. We'll miss you around here. If there's anything I can do, just let me know."

"Thanks, Coach. I appreciate that."

As I stepped out of the building, the weight I'd been carrying felt just a little lighter.

When I got home, Dad was there with Newton and Amos. He'd kept a life insurance policy on Momma for a time like this. Without his foresight, things could have been much harder.

Dad lifted his head as I stepped into the apartment. "There goes my boy." In the weight of the moment, just hearing his voice brought a little light to the sorrow hanging in the air. Newton chimed in, "How you been holding up, Alvin? My kids send their regards." "Yeah, I know," I said, feeling the love and support wrapped around me like a blanket.

Amos, a chain smoker who never lit up in front of Dad—that was a strict no-no—looked edgy and nervous. "I'm sorry that Momma's gone," he said quietly.

I sat down, surrounded by the familiar warmth of home and family. Despite the sadness and uncertainty, I felt a flicker of hope. With them by my side, I knew we'd get through whatever came next together.

It was a gray, cloudy day when Dad handed me a $100 bill.

"Here," he said. "Take this and get whatever ya need. I'll grab me a dark pair of socks while you find yourself a suit and tie."

I held the money tightly, not fully grasping the weight of it—or everything it meant. But I knew exactly what I wanted. I'd been eyeing those ankle weights at the Army-Navy store down at Dudley Station.

With those, I could work on my jumping—get stronger, get higher. Maybe even dunk, like I'd always dreamed.

"Show me the way," Dad said, his voice low as he followed me down the stairs.

When we reached the front door, I pushed it open, and sunlight flooded in like waves crashing onto shore.

As the sun lit up the hallway, Dad said, "This day started all gray and cloudy, but now it has turned sunny and bright. Felt like the weather ain't know whether to be sad or hopeful."

We stepped out onto the landing and then down to the concrete sidewalk that led to Annunciation Road.

"Slow down, boy—you walkin' too fast. You ain't tryin' to catch one of those gals here in Boston, are ya?" I heard Dad say behind me.

"Slow down?" I shot back, grinning. "If I move any slower, those gals gonna think I'm lost!"

We both laughed. It felt good being with my dad. He could be such a funny guy.

We walked up to Ruggles Street and caught the bus to Dudley Station, then transferred to the elevated subway headed for downtown Boston.

It was 3:30 in the afternoon, and the train was crowded as usual.

"Dad, have you ever been on a subway train before?"

"Nah," he said. "You know the biggest cities I've been to are Wheeling and Pittsburgh, and they sure ain't got none there. Why are there so many people on here?"

"Guess everyone's got the same idea of getting somewhere quick," I replied.

Even though Dad had never set foot on a subway, he was no stranger to travel. His journeys took him all over the backroads of West Virginia, visiting small towns most people had never heard of. As the chairman of the Church of God in Christ's YPWW, Young People Willing Workers, Dad's responsibilities stretched far beyond our hometown. Whenever a church needed a visit, he'd call his friend Johnny. Johnny wasn't just a friend; he was Dad's driver, his co-pilot on countless trips across the state.

The train finally reached our stop: Washington Street. I glanced at Dad. "This is us. I don't want you getting lost in this crowd."

"Don't worry about me. I'm right behind you," he said.

We walked up Washington Street, past Jordan Marsh, another big department store, then stepped into Filene's.

"Hello, welcome to Filene's. How can I help you?" The clerk, a middle-aged woman with sparkling gray hair, greeted us warmly.

"I need a pair of dark socks. And my son needs a black suit and tie."

I stood beside him, my heart growing heavy. The words hit me like a brick. We weren't here for a celebration or a graduation. No, I needed that black suit and tie for something far more somber: for Momma's funeral. This was the suit I'd wear to say my final goodbye. Momma, the heart of our family, was gone.

"Follow me. The items you want are in the same department," the clerk said, guiding us toward the men's section.

A wave of sadness hit me, and for a moment, I felt like I might break down. But I pushed the feelings aside. I focused on the task at hand, even though its weight pressed on me with every step.

"Do you know your jacket size?" "No, I don't," I answered.

"Come over here," she said, motioning for me to step onto a small stool in front of three mirrors. She pulled out a measuring tape and ran it across my shoulders and chest. "Thirty-eight," she announced, then led me to a rack of black suits marked with sizes ranging from 28 to 40. She searched through the hangers and pulled out one in my size.

"Try this on, young man, and see how it fits," she said, handing me the jacket.

I slipped it on. It felt like a perfect fit.

She handed me the pants next. "Here. Go into the changing room, try these on, and come back to this stool."

I took the pants, went into the changing room, and returned as directed.

She measured my waist. "Twenty-six." Then my inseam. "Twenty-four."

"It'll take three days for tailoring," she said. "Your suit should be ready by noon on Friday." "I got my socks, so ring us up," Dad said.

That day, standing next to him at the register as the cashier rang up the suit, everything started to sink in. Momma was gone. Forever. I could still see her face, hear her singing, taste her cooking. But those memories were already beginning to blur, slipping away faster than I could hold on.

She had passed so suddenly. One moment, she was the center of our world, and the next, I found her still. Lifeless. Since then, I'd been drifting through the days like a ghost, not fully present, not fully there. I hadn't processed it—not really. I couldn't.

Dad stayed quiet, but I knew he was hurting too. Yet in that silence, he had done something that spoke volumes. Long before Momma passed, he had made sure we'd be okay. He had taken out a life insurance policy—a small act of preparation, but one that meant everything now. Because of it, he was able to give Momma a proper farewell, the dignity she deserved. And it gave me and my sisters something solid to stand on, at a time when everything else felt like it was falling apart.

CHAPTER 98

FINAL LESSONS FROM MOMMA

The funeral came, and April's warmth felt almost cruel as we gathered in the church to say goodbye. Momma lay peacefully in her casket, her face calm and still. I wanted to reach out and touch her hand, but the fear of that cold, final truth held me back. As Elder L.C. Young delivered the eulogy, his words brought her back to life for just a moment. He spoke of the loving, resilient woman she was—the one who always made us feel like everything would be alright, even when it wasn't.

Her kindness, her devotion to me, Gladys, and Gloria, her unwavering smile—it all came through in his voice. For a brief second, it felt like she was still with us. But when the service ended and the tears came, reality hit hard. She was gone, and nothing could bring her back.

On the Greyhound bus heading to Ohio, I sat beside my sisters, the weight of it all pressing down on me. Life doesn't always give you what you want. Sometimes, it hands you burdens you're not ready for.

Still, as we left Boston behind, I thought about what Momma would have wanted. She wouldn't want me to drown in grief or give up on my dreams. She'd want me to keep pushing forward both in basketball and in life.

The ankle weights? I bought them. Not just to dunk a basketball, but as a reminder that carrying weight can make you stronger. And though the heaviness of losing her would never truly leave me, I knew

I had to keep moving forward—step by step, leap by leap—with her love and memory lifting me when I faltered.

As the bus rolled on, the landscape blurred into trees and small towns, but my mind stayed fixed on Momma. Her laughter, her strength, her voice—they traveled with me, whispering the same words she always had: *Keep going. No matter how heavy life feels, just keep going.*

I glanced over at my sisters—Gloria resting her head on Gladys's shoulder, both lost in their own thoughts. We were all carrying the same weight now, bound by grief and the shared memory of the woman who had been our rock. But as I sat there, I realized something—Momma had been preparing us for this all along. Her love, her lessons, her unshakable belief in us had become the foundation we would now stand on.

The road ahead was uncertain, but a strange sense of peace settled in. Life would never be the same without her, but we had each other. And we had her memory to guide us. I thought about the ankle weights again, tucked away in my bag. They weren't just for jumping anymore; they were a reminder that even with the weight of loss, I could still rise.

As the bus rumbled forward, I closed my eyes and pictured Momma's warm smile. No matter how heavy life became, she was always there in spirit, steady and sure. In the end, the pain and sorrow were like the ankle weights—hard to wear at first. But over time, they built my strength. And in that strength, I found the power to rise higher than I ever imagined.

AUTHOR BIO

As a 77-year-old three-time cancer survivor, I have navigated many paths in life. Upon my discharge from the military, I spent 18 years in numerous dead-end jobs in the business world. At the age of 40, I decided to go back to school, earning my undergraduate degree and teacher training in English. I then spent three rewarding years teaching English and drama at the high school level.

Realizing that the classroom wasn't my ultimate calling, I pursued a master's degree in Guidance and School Counseling. During this time, I received my first cancer diagnosis.

Although returning to the school system proved challenging, I discovered meaningful work as a Mental Health Counselor. I spent two years as an Intake Counselor at New Horizons Community Mental Health Center. In this role, I guided clients through initial assessments and connected them with vital resources. My journey took another turn when I received my second cancer diagnosis, leading me to step away from my professional role to focus on my health.

Despite these challenges, including a third diagnosis in 2020, I remain committed to sharing my experiences and insights. Through all of these experiences, I've learned lessons that go beyond any single job or challenge. I share these insights on my website, where I explore the intersections of history, resilience, and mental health. On Alvinandhisthoughts.com, you'll find reflections on Black history, current events, mental health, and politics.

www.ingramcontent.com/pod-product-compliance
Lightning Source LLC
Chambersburg PA
CBHW071705120626
46550CB00001B/114